GW01398880

The Gifted Caesar Sant: Rising Above The Odds

Copyright © 2024 by Dr. Lucas Sant

ISBN: 978-1-326-83980-2

PROLOGUE

My son Caesar Sant was born in 2008 in Providence, Rhode Island with sickle cell anemia, a hereditary blood disorder. From the age of four, he began having strokes, suffering three within two years. Despite this, Caesar was always smiling and practicing his violin. Music has been his lifeline since he started his musical journey at age two. He has graced stages throughout the United States, from the MGM Grand in Las Vegas to the Kennedy Center in Washington, DC. He even had the privilege of performing for the renowned violinist Mr. Itzhak Perlman at the tender age of seven.

In 2021, Caesar underwent a bone marrow transplant at the National Institutes of Health (NIH) which fully restored his health. Our family will forever remain indebted to the NIH and its Children's Inn where we spent several months recuperating from this transformative procedure. Caesar fondly referred to the Inn as "a piece of heaven." In the morning, he began his day with a declaration: "The Lord is God, and God is good." We are profoundly thankful for the global support we received, much of which from kind strangers. Caesar's recovery might have remained an elusive dream without this collective goodwill. Though his legs are still weakened by the power of the strokes he endured, Caesar's musical prowess on the violin continues to flourish.

He has embarked on the formidable task of reacquainting himself—almost from scratch—with the seven languages he began learning before the debilitating strokes: Greek, Hebrew, Chinese,

2

Latin, Russian, German, and French. He still loves these as much as he did as a child.

Caesar's story embodies resilience and provides comfort and inspiration to all who experience it. It holds universal appeal, as many can relate to having a family member or friend facing health challenges and never giving up on their dreams. His message of hope underscores the importance of perseverance and the relentless pursuit of one's goals, even when faced with overwhelming odds. This book will undoubtedly warm your heart and touch your soul.

Finally, this book offers a special treat for readers—access to Caesar's composition of **his first violin concerto** at the age of 14, composed in the aftermath of his profound journey. The pieces emerged unexpectedly, serving both as gratitude for his renewed health and as an additional incentive for readers to delve into his story. Caesar composed the concerto in D minor, which concludes in D major. This piece, spanning four movements, is aptly titled *"Caesar's Four Seasons."* The movements are as follows: 1st— "Aurorae" (Spring); 2nd— "Vida" (Summer); 3rd— "Health" (Autumn/Fall); and 4th— "Adagio/Love" (Winter). In addition, he composed two Sonatas, which he affectionately refers to as "Sonatinas" specifically for this book. These pieces encompass his concerto's initial and final movements, which he calls "Aurorae" and "Sonatadagium." These two compositions premiere alongside this book, accompanied by showpieces from iconic composers, including one of his favorites, J.S. Bach.

On his 15th birthday, Caesar premiered the first movement, "Aurorae," to an intimate gathering of family and friends. As of this writing Caesar has not yet completed the piano part of these movements. He is contemplating the future, exploring the possibility of developing a full orchestral version with the assistance of his violin teacher, perhaps when he is in a music conservatoire. If everything goes as hoped, he aspires to join a prestigious music conservatory, with the Curtis Institute of Music in Philadelphia being a top choice, in 2025.

While finalizing this book, I reviewed and cross-checked substantial material from Caesar's medical records, detailing events related to his intense emotional battles during the recovery of the entire family situation. Then, Aline gave me a very short clip of him from his National Geographic Documentary (https://bit.ly/4cf8sUW), which captures a turning point for Caesar, which emerged from deep within, when he was regrouping to take violin lessons. This occurred after the third stroke took away virtually everything. This clip of a few seconds showed Caesar finishing a fan violin *Étude* by Prof. Jakob Dont last month. I thought that assembling these two samples, roughly ten years apart, would best show the progress from where we used to be to the present: (https://bit.ly/3VDnJrN). We hope that this book delights you as much as it has us.

Thank you for embarking on this journey with us.

www.caesarviolin.com

TABLE OF CONTENTS

DISCLAIMER

The beauty of our U.S. Constitution is that under the banner of free speech—the First Amendment—anyone is entitled to express thoughts and opinions freely. Quite certainly, this is the highest gift of freedom our founding fathers gave us. Yet, with a sense of profound irony and the weight of obligation pressing upon me, I find it necessary to craft the following words as a shield against potential litigation.

While every effort has been made to depict events as accurately as possible, some names, places, and identifying details may have been changed or omitted to protect the privacy and confidentiality of individuals besides Caesar. Thus, the information provided in this book should not be considered as medical, legal, nor professional advice. Readers should always seek the counsel of qualified professionals for specific medical or legal concerns. The author and publisher expressly disclaim any responsibility for any liability, injury, loss, or risk that may be incurred as a direct or indirect consequence of the use and application of any content in this book.

Finally, this work derives from intellectual pursuits, deeply held beliefs, and a chronicle of my family's decade-long journey through relentless health adversities, which began when the now-teenaged Caesar was born with chronic sickle cell anemia. Although we paid a high price—Caesar had three strokes, and I had two in addition to a heart attack—the triumph came after Caesar underwent a successful bone marrow transplant in 2021, which gave him a new life, and our dreams materialized into reality. Working with Caesar has been the most sacred responsibility bestowed upon me by the Holy Providence.

There are some names of those who, at one time or another, helped Caesar throughout this saga. Many are not even aware of how much they contributed to lifting this child when he was nearly about to leave us. But with a little from some and a lot from others, they all played a pivotal role in changing our lives forever. For this, we owe a special debt of gratitude. Without them, we might not be here telling Caesar's story—the one we pray will inspire other families undergoing similar challenges.

ACKNOWLEDGMENTS

My deepest appreciation goes to the following people, even though words alone cannot express my gratitude: Dr. Sam Deadwyler, Dr. Jeff Weiner, Mr. & Dr. Leo & Debbie DeOliveira, Demetri Kangelaris (the priest of the Greek Orthodox Church), Mr. & Mrs. Lui Heather Vlachoske, Make-A-Wish America/NC, Mr. Alex Filadelfo, Master Caxias (Capoeira Abu Dhabi Caxias – the Brazilian's culture voice), Mrs. Tina Morgan & family, Mr. Athanasios Boutis, Dr. Rafaela Aguiar and her husband, Mr. & Mrs. Patrick & Barbara McCaffrey, Dr. Ivan Nascimento, Dr. Daniel Yasumasa Takahashi, Mr. & Mrs. Pathil family, in memoriam the late Mr. John Mohan, Mrs. Jaya Soma, Mrs. Williams Latangela, Dr. Günter Hoffman & family, Dr. Mark Xu, Mr. Gray Rolfing, Mr. & Mrs. Jesse & Jannette Suggs, Mrs. Betty Crite, Dr. Joshua Berka & family, Dr. Rachel Fresco, Dr. Shelton Charles, Mr. Ivan Wolfe, Mr. & Mrs. Edimir & Suzana Silva, Dr. Thomas A. Nakagawa, Mr. Garfield Ducan & family, Dr./Mrs. Ye-Ye & HongMei Zhou, Mrs. Amelia Weesner, Mr. Matvey Lapin, Mrs. Marjie Sharpe, Mr. Fabrice Dharamraj, Dr. Marcin Jozef Arendt, Mr. & Mrs. Christina & Pedro Maia, Mr. David Holter, Mr. Pinchas Zukerman, Mr. Itzhak Perlman, Mr. Maxim Vergerov, Christian Congregation Church, Sister Cleide Silva, Mr. Vanderlay M. Felix, Mrs. Lilian Collevatti-Viti, Mr. Fernando Cruz, Mr. Roberto Barreto, Mr. & Mrs. Edilane & Daniel Stibs, Mrs. Lia Correa & family, Mr. Clemerson C. do Carmo, Mr. Augusto & Azalette and family, Mr. John Calegari, Mr. & Mrs. Wagner & Daniela Quevedo, Mr. Antonio

F. de Oliveira, Mr. John Gatti and Mrs. Debbie (in memoriam), Mr. Marcos Figueiredo & family, Mr. Andre LM Costa, Mr. Daniel Gardeazabal (honoring his father, Captain Jorge), Mr. Servio L. Ferreira, Mrs. Diana L. Ferreira, Mr. Hunter & Daniel and family, Mrs. Desiree De Melo and family, Memphis Ballet, Mr. David Dietz, Mrs. Celia Dixon, Dr. Daniel P. McMahon, Levine Children's Hospital, The Sickle Cell Foundations & Communities, Le Bonheur Children's Hospital, St. Jude Hospital, Baptist Memorial Health Care, Dr. David K. Ragland, Dr. Leah L. Akinseye, Vanderbilt Children's Hospital in Nashville, TN, Dr. Emmanuel J. Volanaksi, Vanderbilt, Mrs. Linda Kay Faulkner, ATC Fitness & Friends, Mrs. Mattie YMCA, Mr. & Mrs. Gus Anderson & Augusta, The National Institutes of Health: Dr. John Tisdale, Mrs. Nona (Wynona Coles), Dr. Matthew Hsieh, Dr. Corina Gonzalez, Dr. John Ligon, Dr. Paul Scott, Dr. Lori Wiener, Children's INN at NIH, Dr. Francis Collins, Dr. Robert Masi, Mr. Chaplain Michael Zoosman, Mrs. Donna Heathcock, Mr. Josh Williams, B. Bookclaw: www.bookclaw.com. And to Magister, my teacher Prof. Caesar Timo-Iaria, who would have been 100 years old this week (June 25, 2024) he is remembered fondly, and to Maria-Anita Sant, my savvy daughter, for overall assistance. Finally, my endless gratitude to the beta readers who provided insights and thoughts that went beyond mere proofreading to elevate the text: Mr. Ron Madera, Mr. & Mrs. Patrick & Barbara McCaffrey, and Dr. Debbie DeOliveira. The book wouldn't have reached this final stage without the topnotch editorial work of Mrs. Christen Johnson, to whom we are deeply grateful.

SPECIAL DEDICATION

This book is dedicated in loving memory to my parents, Antônio Manoel dos Santos and Maria Anita dos Santos. Your spirits and love illuminate every page of this journey, forever guiding my way. I owe everything to you.

AUTHOR'S INTRODUCTION

The following month after Caesar's birth, we received an alert letter from the hospital stating that he was born with sickle cell anemia, a devastating blood disorder. It was an unusual introduction to parenthood and it proved to be a long-lasting challenge for us. Among the most significant looming health risks was the possibility of strokes in the near future, as well as other serious health issues for the young baby born under such dire predictions. As parents welcoming their first child—a joyous time for any family—that letter cast a shadow over our happiness. The news imposed a sentence of the extremely challenging days that would come all too soon. If you look through medical reports and scientific papers, you will see that, in general, these blood disorders tend to become more aggressive by the time the child reaches the age of four.

We had a few options to navigate in the face of all of this. We could either dwell on the negative aspects of the situation or choose to bring hope and positivity into our child's life. Either way, the path ahead would be hard. And the higher the expectations for positive outcomes, the greater the risk of pain for that child and all who care for him. Soon those risks materialized into reality. Caesar's birth brought countless changes and joys to our lives. He has been a happy child from the start, smiling regardless of the situation. Though it was nice to see him smile even when he was in pain, I never quite understood whether he was doing it to comfort those around him or for some other inner reason.

Fortunately we never dwelled on the lack of effective treatments or even robust mitigating measures for Caesar whose condition was apparent from the onset. Clearly our path was destined to be long and filled with hurdles. Yet the shifts and turns—albeit sometimes disheartening, especially when witnessing others with the same blood disorder confronting seemingly insurmountable challenges—did not deter us. I remain persuaded that solutions emerge from adversity, and with new insights, a spark of hope and faith illuminate the potential of fresh approaches, offering ample opportunities.

However, venturing into experimental treatments presents its own set of trials. In many ways it is akin to undergoing a trial of new medications. Looking ahead, the most sensible strategy seemed to require integrating a holistic approach along with conventional treatments, despite acknowledging that a holistic health approach lacks the efficacy to cure this genetic anemia inherited from his parents. The reader is invited to read at least a few of the selected scientific studies whose articles are cited throughout this book to grasp our journey and decisions. In fact it may provide you with new information or fresh knowledge and understanding. Ultimately, after a slew of adversities, Caesar received a successful bone marrow transplant in 2021. Since that pivotal moment he has enjoyed a complete recovery.

I committed to working exclusively with Caesar all day long since his last stroke in 2014, and as his father, I'm not the typical "strong" man, as society expects (I have no problem crying, for example).

Occasionally his mood deeply affects me, making me both happy and emotional. This emotion fed my hope that one day we would be out of that painful situation as we are now. The fact of the matter is that Caesar's cheerful spirit has had a major influence on his parents, sisters, and everyone around him. We did not allow his condition to catch us off guard and always sought and dreamed of the best outcome for him, putting our best efforts towards this goal. In the end, hope is indeed everything.

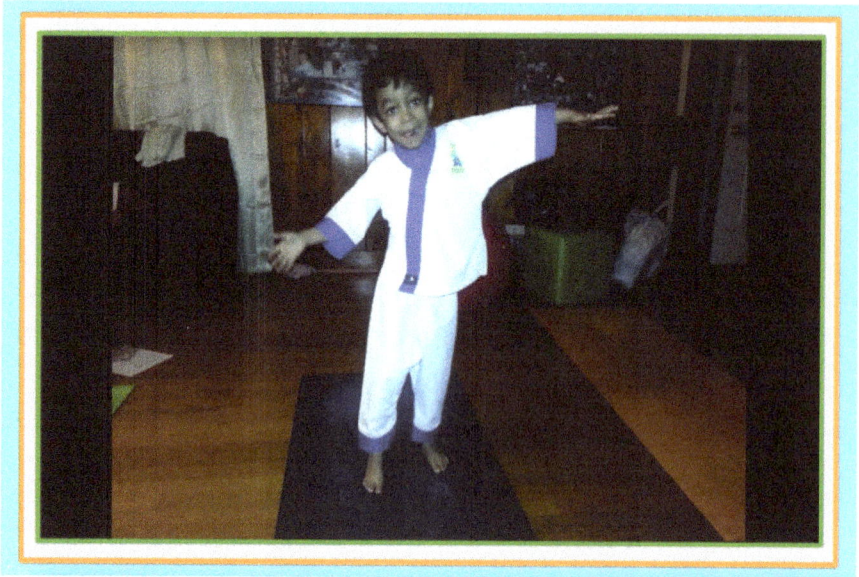

Fig. 1. *Caesar, at the age of three, having not yet experienced any severe sickness, at his house in North Carolina, just after removing his karate belt. A joyful moment from his childhood.*

PART I

(ILLNESSES' BURDEN, COSTS, AND EDUCATION)

SICKLE CELL ANEMIA: THE ROADBLOCK FOR MY SON

Oddly, sickle cell anemia—a blood disorder affecting millions worldwide, with one-third of them living in the U.S.—does not yet have an effective drug for treatment. If we could choose one fact that would distinguish this blood disorder among many, it is pain. The hallmark of this disorder is pain, both acute and chronic, impacting the patient about 38 percent [1] of the time—a harsh reality, especially because a child may start experiencing it as early as in the first year of life. For instance, on Caesar's first birthday, his hands appeared slightly swollen, indicating that blood circulation had started compromising.

"Life-threatening" is a strong term. When you hear this repeatedly about the illness with which your child was born, your body shakes with genuine fear. Furthermore, there is no cure for sickle cell, apart from bone marrow transplants. Gene therapy is also being explored today. Other than that, all you hear are palliative options that confirm the first word of this paragraph and just try to relieve the pain. This fact alone surprised me and demanded extra effort to comprehend why my son had no reasonable options. I hope every mother and father feels that anything besides the best care is unacceptable for their child. I truly believe that it is the highest law—sacred if you will—that parents have the primary responsibility to take care of and protect their child at all costs. Such belief moved me through all the decisions I made on this journey.

---

[1]*Hants, W, et al., 2016. "Sickle Cell Disease: A Review of Nonpharmacological Approaches for Pain"*. Journal of Pain and Symptom Management: https://bit.ly/3VJTrDE

Despite the challenges we faced with Caesar, hope never departed from us—the powerful secret weapon we relied on throughout this time. In practical terms, without it, we would have easily remained stuck in the hundreds (or thousands) of traps naturally set up by our boy's illness during these ten years. We had to use any hope and all means to survive, trusting that the following day something good would happen or someone would show up to bring relief—at least temporarily—rescuing us from this dungeon where we were under the gun, so to speak. Advances in research and treatment options are being made, and with continued support and advocacy, progress can be made toward finding a cure for sickle cell anemia. But it all depends on whether one can make it to the next day. Meanwhile, it is essential to provide the best care possible for those affected by this condition and to support families and caregivers in their journey. That includes the mind and spirit because none of this would work without a resilient and strong mind.

The above highlights the irony of medical advancements. There are treatments for life-threatening diseases such as HIV and cancer in the form of viral suppression, chemotherapy, and surgery, which can allow patients to live their lives close to normal. Sickle cell anemia causes excruciating pain and suffering, yet no standard drugs are available. One of the plausible nuances that resonate herein is the lack of scientific resources or a branch within medicine dedicated to this particular illness that contributes to this issue. As a result, sickle cell patients must rely on "efficient strategies" such as palliative options (blood transfusions, antibiotics, etc.) that quite often bring undesirable consequences. Thus, the absence of a devoted research branch for sickle cell anemia leaves unanswered questions about whether the benefit to the patient or the number of side effects should be prioritized in decision-making. Despite the challenges, research from other medicine branches, such as oncology, continues to bring innovations for sickle cell patients and produce palliative drugs. The positive developments come more noticeably from genetic development—or gene therapy—due to decades of research. This branch promises a real revolution to the sickle cell community in the years to come.

Furthermore, sickle cell research takes a deviant perspective on cancer, emphasizing the genetic pathology of sickle cell and its metabolic disorder. Starting a new scientific journey from there would be quite logical. Scientists, physicians, and nurses are eager to dedicate themselves fully to innovations in sickle cell research. The current medical institutions seem to lack creative ideas for feasible research and would require substantial funding from the most prestigious research institutions. These stark spectrums represent a reality that terrified me far more than my son's condition itself. Upon receiving the hospital letter that arrived so soon after he was born, we realized that we were being told there was nothing medically available for him. Again, the current establishment was showing failure from the start. Indeed, when it comes to your children, it's personal, and you cannot accept that there are no options. That was my number one frustration, mainly because I had been working in the medical field my whole life—about two decades of that were at prestigious universities in the United States. I could not accept such a discouraging reality. Unfortunately, ten years later, the overall current medical approach for treating this illness remains quite unchanged, and the gains have been very limited. However, with many scientific advances, some changes should happen. Thankfully, the pace of new technologies pouring into society will lead to great scientific innovations in the years to come, especially with recent genetic techniques.

Caesar's best friend—his 14-year-old sister, Maria-Anita—was born with the same anemia. She has been doing quite well so far despite not having a donor like Caesar had. Caesar's other best friend—his nine-year-old sister, Helen—was born entirely healthy, thanks to prior genetic counseling and intervention. She was a perfect match for Caesar and became his transplant donor. Consequently, we trust that this latest genetic technology will bring hope to Maria-Anita, culminating in a happy ending for her, akin to that of her brother.

I cannot stop repeating that hope is indeed everything, and without it we all become mere irrelevant pilgrims. The snare we were caught in is a reality for almost any family with a child born with chronic health conditions. What does one do when such a situation arises for their first newborn? Panic, desperation, discouragement, sadness, and even altercations come up. All those things must be replaced by hope—the first task we faced. In the meantime, when it happened, we were a family still quite naive and inexperienced in dealing with such challenges. This was the formation of a new world. "Jesus, God!" This strong exclamation would burst from my mouth like a desperate person very often when the pressure was overwhelming. The medical system offered nothing for my newborn son besides antibiotics and medical procedures that might cause additional health issues and long-term complications. We were unprepared. To be completely honest, I cannot imagine anyone being prepared for something like this. We had read that it could happen, but that's nothing compared to it becoming reality. Only hope guided us; we did not deny reality, but with the determination to do anything and everything, we committed to not let him falter and to come out on the other side no matter what.

Based on conversations with medical professionals, families with similar issues, and scientific reporters, we began working on potential challenges ahead since we needed to begin moving forward. The reality was clear: Every step would be uneven. Yet another voice in my mind reminded me of the value of sacrifice. Thus, at that point I realized that I had lost nothing in comparison to what I had left.

Our ultimate goal and personal challenge were to find a way to cure my son's blood disorder, or at least alleviate its symptoms. As an academic and father first, I had no peace with it and pictured all kinds of scenarios in my mind. Merely lamenting it would not help, so I tried to be positive and meditated with my heart, praying to God for strength to move on, which proved valuable. On a practical level, I took daily proactive measures. For instance, every day when I arrived at work, I secluded myself in my office for about two hours, searching for any approach that could benefit my son. My professional and personal dissatisfaction with this situation was profound. As a scientist with over two decades of experience in the medical field, I felt more than desolate, but I never lost hope throughout my life—my personal journey attests to it—even though I felt sick myself and nearly died on three occasions.

To add to the pain, I was not prepared for the full extent of this other side of the coin: being a patient myself or witnessing a loved one suffering, with little power to intervene, even though this knowledge was part of my academic training. Having academic information, I could understand some aspects of human biology more deeply than most. My decision to forgo becoming a medical doctor (MD) was driven by my frustration with the focus on finding cures rather than just working in science, which might have been more financially rewarding. Only later did I realize the unexpected benefit of my academic choice. As parents and guardians of a child with sickle cell anemia, we experienced firsthand the often-harsh ways society can treat minorities. Nonetheless, with the inconsistent standards and principles of various domains (e.g., science, medicine), we could not predict the decisions or discoveries that might emerge from one state or country, even if we tried—it's a dynamic world. What might not have been available yesterday could become a life-saving treatment tomorrow. This realization kept us on our toes, providing a constant source of hope and a reminder to persevere.

Then, there was faith again. Oh, how it sustains, especially when we feel trapped. Moreover, there is a natural and general societal expectation that families with sick children should provide the best available medical treatment—a reasonable expectation and a stark reality. The fact is, regardless of whether you like it or not, this "assumption" becomes irrelevant once everyone is absorbed with their own issues; you have to bear your own burden, period. You are essentially facing ostracism from the start. Indeed, facing reality helps, as it opens our minds to invest further in hope, work harder, and envision victory. This has been my prayer and mantra.

BURDEN, TREATMENT COSTS, AND CURE FOR SICKLE CELL

The impact of sickle cell anemia on a family is immeasurable. Caregivers often feel compelled to live life for the patient rather than for themselves. As parents, our love for our children regularly surpasses our love for ourselves. Thus, when they fall ill, our world shatters. It is paramount to remain steadfast as a caregiver and provide the best possible support and treatment—failing to do so could render our efforts fruitless. As Caesar's primary caregiver, my health deteriorated, leading to two strokes and a heart attack due to immense stress. Yet, with Caesar's successful bone marrow transplant at the National Institutes of Health (NIH) in 2021, my health rebounded to near-normal levels. We owe a deep debt of gratitude to the entire NIH team, who were truly a beacon of hope in our journey.

The financial burden of treating sickle cell is staggering, affecting not just the patients, but also their families and the broader community. From a financial perspective, Caesar's medical expenses averaged $40,000 monthly in 2020-2021, summing up to approximately $480,000 annually. Extrapolating this to the approximately 300,000 sickle cell patients in the U.S. alone, the annual cost reaches a staggering $144 billion[2,3]. Remarkably, after Caesar's bone marrow transplant, these expenses dwindled to nearly nothing, ushering in substantial savings for our family, insurers, communities, and the nation at large. Thus, prioritizing bone marrow transplants for all sickle cell patients could alleviate the colossal financial strain associated with the disorder. This effort would not just save lives, it would also be a boon to society and the nation, transcending our diverse, healthy philosophies and agendas. To put it simply, one does not need a Ph.D. in economics to recognize the merits of such an initiative; basic arithmetic is enough. What is more, a comprehensive meta-analysis would likely unveil billions in potential savings if all sickle cell patients in the U.S. (and in the world) could have access to successful transplants, thus lessening the financial load on the public coffers. Furthermore, when we consider the broader socio-economic ramifications, though difficult to pinpoint exactly, the societal benefits are immense. The intrinsic value of each saved life, regardless of racial or ethnic background, is irrefutable. We can universally agree that one cannot, and ought not, affix monetary value to a human life.

A fruitful first step would be to increase sickle cell funding for research institutes and universities by 100 times, as I have previously suggested. This should be followed by a clear timeline for achieving results, similar to what has been done for cancer research. Secondly, a percentage of these funds should be allocated

---

[2] *Kate M. Johnson, et al., 2023. "Lifetime medical costs attributable to sickle cell disease among nonelderly individuals with commercial insurance". Blood Adv:* https://bit.ly/3W8zSWX
[3] *Weatherford, Greg et al., 2021. "The true cost of sickle cell disease: $1.5 billion in lost productivity". VCU News:* https://bit.ly/4eQWfHE

to genetic therapies, as current research in this field shows promising results. The ultimate goal of this approach would be to liberate lives from the endless suffering—a considerable yoke—wrought by sickle cell anemia. Lastly, the eventual outcome of this approach would not only benefit those suffering from this genetic blood disorder, but it could also provide a financial return to society. This would allow the benefits of the outcome to be straightforwardly applied to other maladies in need of similar innovative treatments.

Overall, no one deserves to have their life hopelessly affected by any illness, especially if there are ways to treat it. Everyone dreams of having a healthy life if possible. Therefore, it is essential to focus on untangling sickle cell anemia from our society, just as we did with polio in the 20th century, when it was the most common terrifying childhood disease. The outbreak in Wythe County, Virginia, in the summer of 1959, illustrates how frightening the disease was in the U.S. and the world. Following the introduction of the remarkable polio vaccine in the 1950s—a collaborative global effort, the credit for which goes to the American doctor Jonas Salk—the number of cases plummeted dramatically. Nevertheless, the world was in panic, with multiplying outbreaks throughout the United States and elsewhere.

Polio holds personal significance for Caesar. His first long-term violin teacher, Mrs. HongMei Zhou, contracted polio as a child in China. Remarkably, she remains one of the few who ambulates unaided by canes or similar devices, albeit with a limp. Another poignant example is the iconic violinist, Mr. Itzhak Perlman, who contracted polio as a toddler in Israel. Despite relying on crutches since his youth, he has soared, not merely as a great and celebrated violinist, but also as an example of human resilience. Consequently, with the widespread availability of the polio vaccine from the 1950s onward, the World Health Organization reported 33, then 12, cases in 2020 and 2021 respectively. As of 2023, no cases have been reported yet. It doesn't take a prodigious intellect to surmise that polio claimed millions before the advent of this invaluable vaccination, correct? Quite certainly, had the polio vaccine been accessible during Mrs. Zhou's and Mr. Perlman's early years, it is doubtful this rampant virus would have struck them.

While sickle cell anemia is genetically inherited from the parents, it is neither infectious nor transmissible. Both Caesar's mother and I carry the gene trait, which is unexpressed and typically shows no symptoms. Almost every person has a trait of some genetic ailment; still, they might not exhibit symptoms or be conscious of its presence. Conversely, when a person is born with this trait in its expressed form, it indicates the individual was born with the disorder and will exhibit its symptoms. This concept mirrors the interplay of math in biology. For instance, both Caesar and Maria-Anita—the oldest of his two younger sisters—inherited the expressed gene for sickle cell anemia, which ranks as a foremost genetic ailment, with affected populations numbering in the millions worldwide. The hour has come for a determined individual to muster the courage to address this global health challenge.

Lastly, I wish to disclaim that, having surmounted the multitude of challenges we faced, we are entitled to be free from any potential political agenda. We intend to relay Caesar's journey and communicate candidly and honestly, unencumbered by biases swaying us in any specific direction. I assert that we have earned this right.

As this book is somewhat unconventional—different from the usual narrative—it demands an update while it is being written, as follows. This one has a frightening, sad beginning, an end with minimal complications and new lessons learned by the boy. For example, once he fell at home trying to do, in his own words, "normal things" like attempting to get into the bathtub and take a shower by himself. Mamma (his mother) and I were distracted for a moment, and we nearly found ourselves rushing to the hospital with Caesar due to this home accident. I believe from now on, we must be vigilant about such occurrences. As he grows stronger and gains more confidence, nearly two years after his successful bone marrow transplant, he will be eager to tackle things on his own. We should expect this.

Meanwhile, as of April 19, 2023, while I am drafting this text, the boy is 100 percent cured. We cannot afford leisure time among ourselves so far; all the same, through music and some amusing events or simply observing Caesar's new life unfolding, we rejoice momentarily. The stress from past traumas is indescribable. Moreover, we are immensely grateful that we no longer confront issues directly related to sickle cell, for after the success of his transplant, his health patterns shifted dramatically. For example, during Caesar's most recent check-up, his hemoglobin was measured at approximately 13.0 grams per deciliter (g/dL), meeting the criteria of a healthy individual. Prior to his bone marrow transplant, his hemoglobin levels were significantly lower, fluctuating between 5-7.0 g/dL, which was the norm for most of his life until 2021.

Here are some phrases from Caesar today when he was entering the office to practice his violin: "I do feel happy walking, Papa. Even if I limp while walking, it's better than not walking." He echoed the sentiment upon waking and heading to the restroom, reiterating, "It's so wonderful to walk, Papa." More often than not, I take on the responsibility of escorting he and his sisters to the bathroom, while Mamma is primarily tasked with preparing the weight-gain protein at night.

Although the aforementioned incident was surprising, it was made even more poignant by the fact that it occurred shortly after returning from a splendid swimming lesson with Mrs. Donna, a renowned teacher with over four decades of expertise. Engrossed in joyous conversation about his improved health, Aline and I were momentarily distracted. A sudden noise from the bathroom jolted us into action. Racing to the scene, we found Caesar narrowly saved from a nasty fall by a timely curtain grab. The minor injury to his legs caused him to regress momentarily to a mindset of illness. Such incidents rekindle behaviors reminiscent of his sick days. Only upon realizing that his injuries were minor did his anxiety diminish.

This aligns with what healthcare professionals have indicated: The emotional scars from Caesar's past health battles will take time to heal. The reality remains: Despite being free from sickle cell anemia, and while his legs are still in recovery, past traumas inhibit his trust in his body, particularly during stressful events. This mistrust becomes evident when he faces challenges that test his physical capabilities—all related to his legs. Yet bearing in mind his young age and considering that his current cells (the transplanted ones) are from his eight-year-old sister, Helen, it is important to consider the discrepancy between chronological events and biological ages, as it will have a significant impact on his new life's overall development. Furthermore, since it has been less than three years since these healthy cells began their transformative work, there is abundant hope and growing expectations for the years ahead. Our task remains clear: to persevere, maintain patience, and remain vigilant. I firmly believe that combining swimming (his instructor predicts competent swimming skills by the end of the semester) with gym activities, including yoga, will greatly benefit him. (He is not attending these other lessons yet). Specifically, swimming will bolster his legs' strength, balance, and proprioceptive skills, compromised by his past health issues, while gym exercises will further enhance his overall physical strength.

PRE-TRANSPLANT CHALLENGES: A HOLISTIC APPROACH

Regarding life's beginning and being alive, the primary goal is to live within the societal standards of longevity. Then, being happy—could the true purpose of life be summarized as simply being alive and happy?

Battles with any illnesses at the beginning of life, as in Caesar's case of being born with a chronic disorder where strokes are a potential part of the complication menu, you must devote yourself entirely to fighting for such a child—it is just not acceptable to have the child and accept things, like "It is what it is," a popular phrase everyone knows. It is what I would call the essence of resilience.

Regardless of the steps and directions the family chooses to take, there is no cure for sickle cell apart from the currently recognized bone marrow transplant, which carries about a 95 percent certainty of success. Thus, until one reaches this ultimate objective, all measures are considered part of the pre-transplant. Indeed, it is worth dreaming to achieve this goal. Seldom are there cases of a family having a child with such a congenital disorder and, around the same time, a transplant being accessible. Resources are always a concern; however, for a wealthy family, a transplant would be possible under similar conditions. But one issue that affects everyone on the same level is the experienced medical team and a hospital with the capability for readiness. In terms of medical requirements, it takes time to assemble, including patience, readiness, suitable protocols, and a donor, among other factors. In fact, there are no shortcuts in this process, and one cannot afford to overlook these aspects. This is why it is often referred to as a process: "I'm in the process of having a transplant..." or "He underwent the bone marrow transplant process."

In conclusion, it is inherent for families to aspire to the most favorable outcomes for their children—a notion beyond contention. Transitioning from aspiration to fruition requires the fulfillment of a narrative, with time acting as the separating agent. Thus, while we desire optimal results, we must maintain vigilance and exert unwavering effort, employing all accessible resources and exploring every alternative avenue—even attempting to turn what is unavailable into something possible—getting slightly set back by every single fault or eventual failure, to reach the marathon's end. It's not like sprinting for a 100, 200 or even 1500-meter race.

Indeed, using only the so-called traditional approach (e.g., medicine) very often is not enough or would not give the best result. One should wisely choose a broad approach to tune it, searching out of the box. Being innovative might suit this orchestra better once the music score is different from "normal," including exceptionally nuanced musicians (such as the deaf or blind). It has proven to be more suitable mainly because each person has an idiosyncrasy. What may work nicely for my brother, even if we were twins, may not be suitable for my body at all. Individualism is a concept widely accepted, although largely neglected by part of the healthcare community. Although humans are like machines, we are not robotics. Finally, for what we wish the most, the reality is that such a perfect recipe does not exist customized to my problem, my brother's, my sister's, or my child's. It takes a fair (sometimes unfair) amount of time to glue all those essential parts together. Your endurance will be put on the line and tested.

In conjunction with the standard medications given by physicians, periodic medical visits played a key role in higher-level clinical management. But not all of those things are meant to prevent painful crises or strokes, which can vary from person to person. For instance, while my son reacted adversely to some prescribed drugs, his sister, who was born with the same anemia, had the exact opposite reaction. Yes, that is a subset of sickle cell anemia's spectrum. Sickle cell anemia is the most common severe genetic disorder in the world, a blood disorder caused by a single mutation on chromosome 11 (humans normally have 46 chromosomes in each cell, divided into 23 pairs), which contains about 13,000 to 14,000 genes. A mutation in one of those genes, the HBB gene which encodes the β-globin protein, is associated with causing this genetic anemia and other genetic disorders; it's worth stressing that this same gene is already associated with at least 50 other genetic disorders[4]. The clinical spectrum of this anemia is wide. While its symptoms vary from person to person, the cellular pathophysiology is fairly similar for everyone with sickle cell anemia, and pain is the hallmark of it. Studies have shown that strokes are also common, though not as common as pain. In many ways, its association with metabolic dysfunction is the closest disruptor. Consequently, the entire body is affected, without exception, either due to a lack of enough blood or cells becoming stuck, compromising blood flow—thus, the main cause of pain. Considering blood transports not only oxygen but also nutrients, vitamins, and minerals—you name it—our blood cells need these fuels (e.g., oxygen, energy) every single minute for the purpose of functioning properly. Additionally, one of our blood's core roles is to remove and expel waste and toxins from our bloodstream, thereby cleansing the body.

In summary, people born with sickle cell anemia will experience multiple physiological challenges that can significantly alter their health and even jeopardize their life. This is the main reason there is no medication for sickle cell anemia besides a bone marrow transplant or gene therapy, which very likely will be widely available in the next decade (2035), not only for sickle cell anemia but for cancer and other illnesses—mainly degenerative ones.

As soon as we received the letter from the hospital stating that Caesar was born with this anemia, we began reading and learning

---

[4] *"Hemoglobin subunit beta" - Wikipedia. 2024 :* https://bit.ly/3zvqCU8

as much as possible. We asked, "What else can we do to support our son? Which approach would be soothing for him, either in conjunction with or without the standard medicine?" The only "bias," if you could call it that, has been to conceive the best health support for him. With all the frustration, I was concerned about having to face a reality without a comprehensive treatment or an approach that would help without hurting the body over time. I was fighting against hope. That it seemed fine to everyone else around as long as none of them had a child with it, made the whole thing frankly unbearable.

Regarding the difference between theoretical knowledge and real-life experience, nothing compares to the challenges life throws at us. Facing high-pressure situations, such as being at the center of a pressing issue, often provides more valuable insights than academic teachings. It's reminiscent of the old saying, "You don't truly know something until you've experienced it firsthand." Despite the immense stress that threatened my well-being on numerous occasions, the lessons learned from these experiences have been invaluable, even more so than any formal education.

Such reality brought all kinds of emotional torture to me, magnified by a real sense of powerlessness. You do not need to be exceedingly clever to conclude that the reason studies show people with sickle cell anemia have an average life span of 30 years is explicitly due to the downgraded treatments offered as a standard. I thought the scientific community was doing a good job in all the fields. Luckily, I have always been aware of medically logical and alternative approaches, though I had no experience using any in this case. Likewise, in addition to a substantial body of studies and anecdotes, there is a notable contrast between the number of close friends helped by innovative approaches and those who have departed this life—either for refusing the trials, not having alternatives available, or just not knowing about them. This world of poor medical innovations had been depicted clearly in my mind, and if we had some real chances, it would be relying on novel approaches. We went all the way through, giving it our all—not just with nice words, but genuinely with God. It is almost like a scientific experiment, trusting that it won't fail. Actually, Caesar's saga is quite similar to the story of five-year-old Lorenzo Odone, whose parents, Augusto and Michaela Odone, demonstrated remarkable and brave attitudes. They rolled up their sleeves, educated themselves, and devoted their lives to finding a cure for their child. Their undeniable influence extends not only to us, but also to anyone in a similar situation. These real stories transcend mere anecdotes, they set the tone and bless us all, serving future generations by proving that everything is possible when fueled by hope, love, and faith.

Then, starting from the beginning, the medical logic here was relatively straightforward: Considering this anemia affects the whole metabolic system, one possible way to support the body would be to start working on the biological, kinetic building blocks that sustain the body. Thus, it brings us back to the basics: proteins, vitamins, trace minerals, minerals, zinc, amino acids, chlorella-spirulina (just a few of a large list) and consuming extra water to keep the body super hydrated.

WATER, THE BASE OF LIFE

As humans, we are composed of approximately 37.2 trillion cells, not including nearly 100 trillion so-called non-human cells, such as the bacteria in our gut, which are responsible for about 80 percent of our immunological (physiological arm) system that keeps us alive. All of these cells die and are replaced throughout life, except for our brain (neuron) cells. To sustain this dynamic process, our body requires about 50-60 percent water, with roughly 60-65 percent of it located inside the cells (intracellular fluid), the body's largest compartment. About 35-40 percent of water is found in the extracellular fluid (outside the cells). Our blood's liquid component, plasma, constitutes about 55 percent of blood, of which 90-92 percent is water. It doesn't take a genius to realize that water is the most essential component of life, regardless of any debate about its significance—it's as clear as 2+2 always equaling 4. Consequently, life cannot exist without water. One of the primary reasons space missions search for new life is to determine if a planet has water.

Keeping the language simple without confusing citations or jargon that could complicate the discussion, I believe this subject will be of interest, especially to those who need it. Fundamentally, the reason we all need to eat is to provide energy to our cells. Similarly, just as we take a shower to clean our body, our cells clean their internal environment, eliminating water and unnecessary byproducts. Without sufficient water, cells may become toxic and might "refuse" to undergo apoptosis (a process that can contribute to cancer onset). A simple, well-hydrated body can maintain these processes, as noted in thousands of peer-reviewed articles accessible to the public (on PubMed or Google Scholar). Thus, to maintain a healthy life, we need to consume nutrients, which are transported by water to our cells, converting them into "food" (i.e., energy) to sustain life. Initially, food must be processed to absorb essential nutrients such as vitamins, minerals, carbohydrates, fats, proteins, and water, which enable the body to utilize them. This breakdown process starts in the mouth and continues through the stomach, duodenum, and intestines.

However, the byproducts of this process, along with consumption of unhealthy foods (processed, junk food, beverages), result in toxins, traces of pesticides, genetically modified foods, free radicals, and toxic metals—an extensive list that almost traps everyone without escape. Mitigating these should be our top priority. Water is the only natural means, through a physiological yet intricate process, to eliminate this metabolic waste and unrecognized foreign substances from the body. Additionally, water enhances nutrient absorption, supports cellular communication, and ensures the delivery of essential nutrients to our cells, which is vital for maintaining our health.

Now, if we disrupt this balance, we are likely to face significant health challenges such as cancer, diabetes, cardiovascular issues, and neurodegenerative disorders—the list goes on. The severity of our health issues is directly proportional to the extent of the imbalance related to water intake: staying well-hydrated! Regardless of the reason, if we neglect water, essential vitamins, proteins, and minerals, the body will eventually "send the bill" in the form of illness. Sometimes this takes one or even two decades, though early warning signs may occasionally appear. Nature's rules are rigorous and unyielding. However, if we are already managing conditions like genetic disorders (e.g., sickle cell disease) that currently have no cure except through transplant (bone marrow or genetic), the relationship between the body, water, and food becomes even more critical for health. It is particularly serious because one may quickly become ill or even face life-threatening complications, unlike a healthier individual who may only experience mild sickness. Simply put, prioritizing proper hydration and consuming whole foods are essential and wise actions for maintaining health.

Water is more than food. A body can sustain months without food, but with a lack of water, its cells become toxic enough to kill you. To further elaborate on the importance of drinking water and its roles in our body, especially for those with sickle cell disease and other illnesses, we should further explore its fundamentals. If we begin by acknowledging that our body is composed of about 60 percent water, a serious question arises: Why does the human body consist largely of water? To put it plainly, life—and all health processes—cannot exist without water. Water acts not just as a simple solvent to dilute substances in our body, regulate our temperature, and aid in hydrolyzing, but also plays a crucial role in complex biochemical processes. This includes breaking down chemical bonds of substances, which allows the body to eliminate, substitute, or incorporate nutrients. Our entire immune system, which serves as our secret weapon to protect us, does not function without water. This whole process occurs regardless of whether we are healthy or ill. Essentially, when we fall ill, in 99 percent of cases, it is because we have disrupted this vital process. In sickle cell disease, the situation is different because individuals are already born with an unhealthy condition, which is one extra reason to keep the body hydrated to overall dilute the unhealthy cells. But dehydration contributes significantly to many other health conditions. Lack of adequate hydration (about three liters of water daily) is a major factor behind our health problems. Therefore, a proper water intake regimen should be seriously considered, as nothing functions properly in a dehydrated body. For adults, this regimen of drinking water is about 30-40 milliliters per kilogram, or approximately 0.46-0.61 fluid ounces per pound. For those with sickle cell anemia, hydration goes beyond helping dilute unhealthy cells, preventing them from clumping together and thus maintaining hemodynamic stability as close to normal as possible. A common mistake people make—including myself until recently—is replacing water with beverages like tea or juice, which are no substitutes for water.

To provide a scientific illustration and solid proof of the benefits of drinking water (proper hydration), we should recognize the pioneering work of Dr. Fereydoon Batmanghelidj. Although early studies on water (specifically regarding blood plasma composition) date back to the mid-20th century, Dr. Batmanghelidj's research is considered foundational in providing clear scientific evidence that water not only enhances health but can also assist in managing a broad spectrum of diseases. However, for genetic conditions like sickle cell disease, while symptoms can be alleviated, they cannot be cured due to their genetic basis. Dr. Batmanghelidj was notably known for treating various ailments with salt water. His journey began as an immigrant from Iran; he attended high school in

Scotland and completed medical school in London, where he worked as a physician until he returned to Iran. During the 1979 Iranian Revolution, he was imprisoned for 31 months in Evin Prison due to political controversy.

In prison, Batmanghelidj observed many inmates suffering from conditions like peptic ulcers and asthma, among others. Due to a lack of medical supplies, he began treating them with just salt water. Initially, he noticed significant health improvements, leading to the discovery that chronic dehydration was a key factor in many of the inmates' health issues. Therefore, by hydrating the inmates, he cured them. As he documented these observations, he requested to extend his prison stay for a few more months to complete his studies. Upon his release, his findings led to numerous publications and best-selling books on dehydration and the healing power of water, particularly salt water, all demonstrating how he treated various diseases—truly fascinating material.

A decade ago, I purchased one of his books out of desperation due to my frequent illness. When we are unwell, we are less concerned with whether a treatment follows a strict "scientific protocol" or is endorsed by particular doctors; our primary focus is on getting better. This perspective aligns with the old saying, "An empty stomach is the best seasoning." However, we are often swayed by powerful propaganda and manipulation (not necessarily out of malice, but rather due to financial motives), and as a result, nature's role in healing is frequently overlooked. Mother Nature is often dismissed in favor of synthetic solutions, which is a significant oversight nowadays. Despite this, I had not fully appreciated the value of the book until recently, realizing that my declining health was partly due to inadequate hydration and replacing water with other beverages, thinking they would have the same benefit. Shamefully, I was not drinking two to seven liters of water daily as I was supposed to.

Recently, I delved into scientific literature on water, which opened my eyes to its importance. Among the influential names I came to know were Nobel Laureates Dr. Peter Agre, Dr. Mu Shik Jhon, Dr. Lair Ribeiro, and Dr. Gerald H. Pollack. These renowned doctors and authors have significantly shifted my understanding of water's power, improving my health dramatically without the need for medication. Remarkably, Dr. Peter Agre's discovery of aquaporins—water channels in cell membranes—earned him the Nobel Prize in Physiology or Medicine in 2003, which is the highest voice in Medicine for innovations. Aquaporins are crucial for regulating water flow in and out of cells, impacting essential functions like kidney operation and salivary secretion. This discovery supports Dr. Batmanghelidj's pioneering work on the physiological significance of water, reinforcing the foundational role of hydration in health and disease prevention.

Interestingly enough, Dr. Mu Shik Jhon, in his book "The Water Puzzle and the Hexagonal Key," summarizes 40 years of research about water literature, which perhaps establishes his name as a leading authority in the field. I quickly searched PubMed and found nearly 3,000 scientific publications on the water topic; a similar number was found on Google Scholar. Indeed, the confusion surrounding dehydration as a leading cause of disease was never due to a lack of "scientific evidence," as some health professionals claim, but rather a lack of knowledge. Additionally, there are no patents on water, which means there are fewer financial incentives associated with it. Water (and related fields like diets and nutritional science) is often overlooked or dismissed in academic settings, with its findings sometimes unfairly labeled as scams or "not backed by science," due to a mix of ignorance and, at times, pure malice. As a result, many health professionals primarily prescribe drugs, although we should remain open to exceptions, as there are always serious and renowned doctors—those who step outside established norms and think outside the box.

No drug can replace water effectively, especially not in the long term. Often, we treat our ailments with band-aids, addressing only the symptoms and not the root causes. Consequently, our bodies are frequently dehydrated, which can lead to potentially fatal outcomes. As previously noted, no bodily process functions properly without adequate hydration, which is why there is a recommended ratio of body weight to water intake needed for cellular functional operation—our organs because they are made of cells too. There are no shortcuts or magic solutions to compensate for a lack of water. Simply put, though not easy, tackling complex bodily function issues starts with water as the fundamental element required. When in doubt, one should read at least one unbiased article on the consequences of dehydration on our bodies and connect the dots logically.

The degree of dehydration, when combined with any health problem (such as sickle cell, cancer, diabetes, etc.), varies on a case-by-case basis as each ailment takes its toll differently. Himalayan salt or sole water (avoiding bright white refined salts, which are bleached and stripped of most minerals) is considered a beneficial approach due to its content of over 80 trace minerals like copper, potassium, magnesium, etc., which are vital for the body's needs. Although we are supposed to obtain these minerals from the food on our table, modern soils are often depleted (containing almost none of these essential minerals), leading our bodies to have a deficit that drinking water with Himalayan salt can help address. However, for those with a history of high blood pressure or heart issues, like me, sensitivity to salt must always be taken into account. I started cautiously with 1.4 grams of Himalayan salt in one liter of water, consuming several liters per day. Additionally, I add one gram of potassium citrate per liter. Remarkably, this regimen also aids digestion. It's important to remember to never attempt this without consulting your trusted healthcare professional. By following this approach, my previously uncontrolled blood pressure began to stabilize. Along with feeling better, it allowed me to resume jogging, something I hadn't done in years, particularly during the period of writing this book.

In conclusion, I don't believe that water itself "cures" anything in the strict sense. Similarly, as you will see in the subsequent topics about our holistic approach to managing sickle cell anemia, the goal was never to cure (or even replace the traditional medicine) sickle cell outright; to claim otherwise would be an ultimately naive approach. Instead, water facilitates the body's natural defense system, allowing it to handle the healing process itself or at least mitigate the impact of illnesses like sickle cell, though a person would not be free of having complications whatsoever. What many refer to as a cure for illness is not so much about the term used. Essentially, drinking enough water to stay well-hydrated poses no risk or potential side effects, which is a stark contrast to the risks associated with prescribed drugs. Moreover, it is well documented that without sufficient water, life cannot be sustained because water is the foundation of life. If a healthy person becomes ill, it is very likely due to dehydration or the consumption of modern wheat sub products (bread, pizzas, cookies, etc.) and processed foods, often a disastrous combination of both. A potential best approach would be to maintain a well-hydrated environment for the cells' mechanisms. The common misconception that I fell into is the belief that my drinking habits meant I was well-hydrated. Yes, I was drinking, but not enough: The adult body requires 2.7 to 3.7 liters of water daily. On a practical level, if our bodies are not sufficiently hydrated, existing health issues will worsen, or those without current health problems will start to develop them. Over time, the impact on the body becomes evident. Finally, it's not an overstatement to say that inadequate hydration is a primary factor in nearly all diseases, except genetic ones. Numerous studies support this, and similarly, processed foods are responsible for many modern diseases. Thus, the combination of both factors— dehydration and poor diet—acts as a detrimental force against our health. In summary, dehydration is, to a great extent, the villain of our health, and the power to alleviate or even remedy it is within our reach—by properly hydrating the body.

When it came to Caesar staying hydrated, there was one issue: Consuming more liquids leaves limited space for food in the stomach, thus resulting in an extra toll of weight loss. Altogether, the goals were always to support the immunological system that maintains the body, regardless of its health problems. Those cornerstone bases are responsible for arranging whatever it needs, aiming to balance life maintenances. Indeed, the body is pursuing all its functional goals to mimic the basic need to keep going (it is a real biochemical fight in a biological arena). Therefore, those supplements can fill this missing gap and be vital for such purposes.

Moreover, a special challenge in dealing with this anemia is the fact that the body is constantly being exposed to toxins. Ideally, it should be cleaned efficiently enough to handle the daily influx of toxins, which ultimately increases the level of body inflammation, a core issue in sickle cell anemia. That in itself is the real challenge for which there is no cure. We are grateful that, by navigating this daunting environment, we were able to prevent my son from dying, rescuing him multiple times from fatal deterioration. In certain instances, an illness can push you to the brink of death.

On the other hand, a system lacking a reliable approach offers a procedure (surgery) that would not make sense. In refusing several medical attempts at performing a questionable brain surgery to vascularize my son's brain, I always rebutted by arguing, how can you aim to vascularize the upper part of his brain (cortex) when the root of the problem is the production of defective blood from the marrow? Furthermore, such surgery poses a real risk of other kinds of strokes—without mentioning that any interventions in the brain offer no safe place to play around, no room for error; side effects of the brain are much different. They can impair a life forever. Once more, we were able to maneuver through these years avoiding all of this—yes, he had three strokes and faced sickness many times, but it was worth putting forth the immense sacrifice, partnered with hope and hard work.

It is worth stressing this point a bit further. Due to this approach, Caesar had remained a generally healthy boy until the age of four, experiencing only mild swelling and occasionally slight pain. The truth is that learning takes time; no matter how much information a person may have, applying it daily is an entirely different story. Besides, being able to repeat anything requires a will to untangle the natural doubt embedded in it. In this regard, my experience as a scientist has been instrumental. Much of our work revolves around the art of repetition, ensuring that both our experiments and findings can be replicated. However, feedback from colleagues often prompts us to revisit our methods, start afresh, or even change our approach entirely. The goal is always to produce results that other scientists can replicate. After dedicating decades to this kind of work, certain principles become ingrained in you. You learn to constantly question and appreciate the importance of repetition and the basics. Being critical of oneself is essential to improving future decisions, especially those that sometimes arise unexpectedly.

It takes time to learn the peculiar behavior of the physiological effort against daily toxicities to the body (especially since each body has its own rates, irregularities, and particularities). It takes time to learn all the quirks and eventually untangle some of them, considering the disorder's aggressiveness progressing over time. Especially as one of the main protective factors, fetal hemoglobin (HbF) produced during the fetal phase of 10 to 12 weeks of pregnancy, causes its level to shrink over time. This exposes the person to more symptoms—the older a baby becomes (e.g., toddler), the lower the level of HbF, thus increasing the chance of becoming sick.

The positive aspect above everything is that we never stop learning and every day we are evolving and making new adjustments that help tremendously—never being completely stuck, although maybe moving slightly slower to achieve our desires. In many ways, the seemingly precarious situation we lived under all this time was akin to a race to see who would gain the upper hand: the underlying spectrum filled with toxicities or innovative approaches. In the end, our labors are for those who come after us. Hence, as Caesar's first younger sister, Maria-Anita, was born with the same illness, she has taken full advantage of all the successful innovations we learned and applied to Caesar's care. Accordingly, she has been doing quite well—she was admitted to the hospital only once, at the tender age of seven months old with spleen sequestrations (this organ holds a large part of the body's blood), which is quite typical in sickle cell patients, though her brother never had it.

Nevertheless, it is unquestionably true that these approaches we adopted have helped tremendously, often aligning with the goals of the standard medical approach—and without carrying side effects. Yet they cannot cure anything. The challenge of managing every aspect of this natural, holistic initiative ranges from being daunting to dangerous. It demands familiarity with the innovative world in the health field and preparedness for potential mistakes. Should mistakes occur, many would criticize it, but if the same happens with mainstream methods, it's often overlooked because of regulatory approvals. Finally, numerous self-proclaimed doctors and experts are offering all kinds of alternative "miracle treatments"— they can easily exploit the desperation of families in such dire situations. In conclusion, I cannot recommend that anyone follow the approaches we used or any other that seems overly promising since the specific expression of disease for each person affected ranges so widely.

Sickle cell anemia is a chronic metabolic illness whose broad scope affects a person's entire body from head to toe. As a result, all vital organs, such as the heart, lungs, liver, and kidneys, function outside their normal ranges. The body utilizes its homeostatic balance (inner mechanisms) to keep life going, at least as much as possible. Over time, the body's struggle manifests in sickness, such as when the child experiences crises of pain or strokes. Hearing or listening to someone in pain is one thing, but witnessing the pain of a family member, especially a child, is an entirely different ordeal. The emotional and physical challenges we endured are just a glimpse of what we experienced because it is truly indescribable. The old saying, "Spending time in hell is bad, but when the person leaves, everything feels like heaven," resonates deeply with us. We may not have all that we desire or have achieved all of our goals, but we feel like we are journeying toward paradise. The word that best encapsulates our experience is "blessing."

Beyond the physical pain, there was also psychological torment. Caesar's health declined to a state that was so distressing it felt like my vision was dimming. However, my resolve remained unwavering and I always believed we would overcome this bleak situation. As an academic I'm no stranger to stress. Additionally, the loss of my mother when I was 12 and my father when I was two brought immense sorrow. Yet, witnessing my son's pain is beyond words. Any parent would likely feel the same. Seeing Caesar suffer pain throughout his entire body is heart-wrenching. Questions like "How can a child endure this?" and "Where is God in all of this?" inevitably arise. Nevertheless, one truth remained: My love for my son has never wavered since his birth.

When a pain crisis struck, it would typically last for about a week. Regardless of our efforts to alleviate it (since the root cause could only be addressed through a bone marrow transplant), we braced for this duration of suffering. Morphine, prescribed by the doctor, provided temporary relief but came with side effects and only lasted for roughly three hours. Anticipating the next dose and the onset of other complications was agonizing. The hope we clung to in these moments was invaluable. I faced my health challenges too, having endured strokes and a severe heart attack in 2018. Yet, a divine force seemed to sustain me, preserving my life and fortifying my determination. This unwavering spirit was evident in Caesar's eyes and smile. As a "pilot" (or driver), I felt an obligation to persevere, despite naysayers suggesting that Caesar's plight was some form of karma. Against all odds, we persevered and survived.

The turning point was in 2020 when COVID-19 hit, and the pandemic added further pressure on us. Caesar began to fall ill frequently and his health deteriorated rapidly. His spleen had enlarged to the size of a baseball due to monthly blood transfusions and the accumulation of broken-down cells, and his body was struggling to cope with the severity of the disorder.

Seeking advanced comprehensive care, we moved his care to another city, Nashville, where preparations for his transplant began to take shape. However, the harsh reality was that the entire world's healthcare system was crumbling rapidly. Doctors and nurses were not optimistic about short-term prospects, and even basic blood supplies were becoming scarce. A bone marrow transplant requires a large and frequent amount of blood to refresh and keep the body alive, as well as to eliminate the body's toxicities. Consequently, his transplant was postponed yet again. In 2021, the doctors attempted to resume the conversation, but Caesar's spleen had grown even larger and his iron overload had skyrocketed, given the monthly blood transfusions. They suggested surgically removing his spleen to proceed with the transplant but I declined their recommendation because removing a vital organ involved in the defense system and keeping him on antibiotics forever was something I profoundly disagreed with. So, we remained stuck with our decision.

I have no idea what to call the following but I refer to it as our persistence of hope. Amid a disconsolate air, I emailed a friend of mine who is a doctor and scientist at the National Institutes of Health (NIH), Dr. John Tisdale, asking if the agency had any updates that would be suitable for my son. To my surprise, I received a reply the same day from him saying that my request had been sent to the protocol program coordinator to inquire about such a possibility. It gave me a funny (in a good way) vision of how things would work at this time. Interestingly, although I am a faithful man raised as a Christian, it cannot be ignored that I am also a scientist. Therefore, events that we cannot illustrate or make clear—the illogical ones— do indeed sound funny to me when we feel them as real, unnatural events. Yet again, no external explanations can be given for them. I do think that those remarkable events were arranged by God. The following day, we received another email from Mrs. Nona asking for additional documentation, including my son's medical records and notes. Within a week, we received follow-up messages stating that Caesar had been accepted to have his bone marrow transplant at NIH, the best health institution in the world. It turned out that the vision of the transplant taking place became a reality.

This encompasses about six months for the first process, the so-called pre-transplant phase, during which the first screening exams and harvesting of stem cells from the donor, his youngest sister Helen, took place. The transplant's second part, including the transplant itself, took about four months. No surgical procedure was needed, and the transplant was just perfect. The boy even gained some weight during that critical time, which is not expected during such a tense period of chemo-radiotherapy and other drugs interacting with the body. He lost his long hair, but it was nothing. The pre- and post-transplant took place marvelously, and we were living in a hotel beside the hospital, a place like a piece of heaven called The Children's Inn at NIH. Therefore, we got used to saying, "NIH is good, but the Children's Inn makes it great." Due to the COVID-19 situation, only I was allowed to stay with him during this time.

Finally, after over ten years of waiting for this day, on December 23, 2021, father and son happily took a return flight from Ronald Reagan National Airport to Memphis, with my boy 100 percent cured. Furthermore, before the transplant, he was unable to properly digest almost anything; now he eats like a normal boy without any issues. Since then, he had to go back to the NIH for a quick routine check-up every six months. From 2023 onward, these check-up intervals will be held every year. With Caesar's favorite phrase that he has been repeating for quite a while, we conclude this introduction: "The Lord is God, and God is good."

PART II –

THE EDUCATION

CAESAR SANT'S EDUCATION

We knew that providing Caesar with a strong foundation in education would be key to his long-term success. Despite his health challenges, we wanted to give him every possible advantage in life. Contrary to the beliefs and opinions of many—including healthcare providers, literature, relatives, and friends—we never believed that his health issues would limit his future prospects. The curbs in his health indicated that the challenges ahead of us certainly would be greater than those expected for a child with normal health. We were certain that education would unlock his potential—believing that every child possesses innate brilliance—and that the most opportune period for this was during his early years. This stage is crucial in a person's life and we are determined to maximize its potential.

To ensure this, when he was two we enrolled Caesar in music lessons (violin twice a week), Kumon Math/Reading program (a Japanese method, one hour twice a week), Greek language lessons (once a week), and karate (once a week). Central to our approach was making each activity enjoyable, playful, and fun for Caesar, rewarding his positive behavior. As a modest family, our rewards were simple yet meaningful. For example, one of his favorite rewards was Chinese food, particularly chicken wings, which we would often treat him to after his Kumon lessons. I was tasked with work while transporting him to these activities daily after his mother got him ready for my arrival around 4:00 p.m. It was a rigorous routine, particularly after a full workday at my job, but we believed in its value for Caesar's bright future.

Aside from our spirituality and faith in God which kept us strong and gave us hope that we could prevail, no matter how long it took, we implemented a practical strategy focused on education from the beginning. We conducted our research by reading many scientific articles and consulting various medical professionals and experts in early childhood education. We sought every single resource to enhance his education. Many sources, including academic publications, stated that children with sickle cell anemia might experience cognitive development delays due to health complications. This can lead to learning difficulties later in life—and they could potentially lose out on some of life's best experiences. Many children with sickle cell anemia spend a lot of time on painkillers and are frequently hospitalized. By focusing on education from a young age, we aimed to mitigate these potential challenges.

My own early life experience helped me to believe that whatever foundation we could establish in the early years would serve us well in the future once the immediate challenges had subsided. Thankfully, this proved accurate in Caesar's case. Nothing is better than a good education, which holds the key to unlocking any door.

The educational strategy we developed was tailored to Caesar's needs and abilities. We never allowed pessimistic thoughts to dominate, suggesting it was impossible or that he could not achieve something. Instead we remained steadfast, believing in his limitless potential. We enrolled him in specialized educational programs—as mentioned above—and activities designed to enhance cognitive skills such as reading, writing, foreign language comprehension, and critical thinking. We also emphasized physical activity—he attended karate lessons twice a week—and socialization (interacting with our friends and their children, going to church, etc.), which are vital components of early childhood development. Music was a primary focus and he began violin lessons twice a week at age two. He had so much fun that he asked at the end of each lesson why he couldn't have a lesson on the following day, meaning every day?

THE ROLE OF SOCIAL ENVIRONMENT IN SHAPING INTELLIGENCE AND EMOTION

Our cognitive faculties, especially what we term "intelligence," are largely influenced by our environment and parental upbringing. Parents often emerge as the foundational pillars in a child's learning journey. I would not be here writing to you, nor would my life have changed, especially with all those events aiding Caesar, without the voluntary sacrifice of my parents, particularly my mother, Maria-Anita. She placed her life in the crucible to propel me toward the future. I would never be able to stand close enough to her feet, given such a giant gesture of love, except through my children. Thus, I can feel a fraction of it going back to the same grace with which it was received.

This potent parental influence is deeply rooted in the early lessons we imbibe. The significance of a nurturing environment combined with foundational social skills, which spark a child's creativity, can be underscored using examples of certain luminary figures. Through their stories, we can see the lasting impact of an enriched environment during these formative years, which is often realized only in hindsight. It is worthwhile when families prioritize such an environment, navigating through challenges as every household grapples with its unique set of hurdles. While some may find it insurmountable, others who triumph offer invaluable lessons. Amidst the natural discrepancies in opinions and characteristics, it is pivotal to respectively approach perspectives with regard. Even in the face of disagreements, nobody has to agree with anyone; we should all respect the differences of others.

A few famous people that come to mind perhaps would illustrate the point I am attempting to construct about the importance of a good education: Steve Jobs, Bill Gates, and Elon Musk. Only three are necessary, avoiding spare extensions. Their life stories might elicit varying opinions and passions, given the fact that these figures are global entrepreneurs with celebrity status since their pioneering contributions and the ubiquitous influence they wield cannot be contested. Thus, a deep dive into their early lives reveals that the genesis of their groundbreaking innovations can be traced back to their childhood, familial influences, and nascent years, resulting in tenacity to pursue their dreams. This part always intrigued me to think further and further about the relevance of environment in all facets of life.

For instance, Mr. Jobs, an adopted child, redefined the innovation landscape while Mr. Gates transitioned us from a rudimentary typewriter computer device to a versatile, friendly household tool we all have today (through the novelty interface graphics of Windows). It is easy to maneuver even by one who bears a disadvantaged curve of learning, who was helped by just using the mouse tool and intuitive interface—an advent that delves us into further reshaping human-machine interactions. One would be puzzled by the fact that until today, the majority of people were unable to use the computer without the mouse tool and an effortless interface. That would lead us to give credit to Mr. Douglas Engelbart's invention of the mouse in the mid-1960s. Recollecting my own tryst with technology in the 80s, I remember the awe surrounding computers like the CP 500 (akin to the American TRS-80 or Apple II), which are now museum relics. Likewise, Mr. Musk's tale is equally compelling. Hailing from a middle-class background, his relentless pursuit of knowledge and the solid educational foundation laid by his parents paved the way for his groundbreaking innovations in every endeavor he undertook. Yet, Mr. Jobs' story stands out distinctly—a child of a Syrian mother and a German-American father, adopted into a family chosen based on specific criteria set by his biological mother. Her insistence on an educated family for her son serves as a testament to the power of dreams and aspirations. These visionaries, stemming from modest backgrounds, with their minds nourished by dreams and resilience against imperial (mainstream) prevailing norms, certain traditions, and health and life adversities, created their visions, reminding us of the unparalleled influence of upbringing and environment in shaping futures. After all, breaking free from mediocrity while avoiding biases, prejudices, and baseless beliefs from others comes at a high cost; very often, we seek only the comforting side of things. Yet the reality is that both the soft and the rough are part of the same fabric, integral to the journey. Sporadically, we miss out on opportunities, but it's better to keep trying and dreaming big instead of feeling sorry for not trying or missing out.

In fact, I could easily cite at least a hundred remarkable individuals to illustrate the impact of foundational education set in early life. I firmly believe that education is the number one element of any family and society is supposed to pursue it relentlessly. Shaking this up a little, if we were even one-tenth as serious about education as we are about national security (not just in the U.S., but in every country), beginning at the early age of one, education would be the outstanding pinnacle. It promises profound enlightenment and benefits not only for the family, city, or country where an individual resides, but also for humanity as a whole. Looking at history, we learn that every family, individual, and even country has achieved success through various innovations, with education playing a pivotal role. The degree of innovation, intellectual or otherwise, varies from one historical context to another. Consequently, there is a vast array of fields open for exploration, into which anyone can venture.

The point I am trying to get across here is simple and practical: None of these remarkable figures would have been able to achieve so much without a good education in their early lives, which is the unique gift that their parents provided them during their childhood. Feeding a mind early will be for your own environment's sake. Furthermore, some noteworthy human beings were born with hideous illnesses, like Mr. Leonard Bernstein, a great musician with asthma so terrible that his mother thought he would not survive. Yet still, he managed to beat the odds. Evidently, an extra ubiquitous challenge presented herein is when a child has health issues, such as being born with sickle cell anemia, cancer, degenerative and autoimmune diseases (just to mention a few of a vast slew) because overnight the parents are tied up with the child's health rather than anything else in the world. It adds another weight upon them, with chances of success ranging proportionately to the fire of each dream. To nourish the hope of the individual day-by-day journey is vital for the lonely pilgrimage—long for some, not too much for others.

As parents, we have been actively involved in Caesar's education, providing support and guidance every step of the way. From the beginning, homeschooling was at the core of our educational approach, supplemented with private lessons. We encouraged him to ask questions, explore new ideas, and challenge himself, while also creating a safe and nurturing environment for him to learn and grow. Through our efforts, we have seen Caesar thrive academically and socially despite the challenges posed by his health condition.

Music emerged as Caesar's natural passion. He grasped concepts effortlessly and played with fervor from the age of a toddler even though he lacked the strength of a "normal" child. We believe that this investment in his education has been one of the most vital decisions, and we're heartened by the profound impact it has had on his life. However, his health has always been paramount. An optimal early education is the definitive route to achieving not only tangible dreams, but also effective solutions to overcoming challenges repeatedly. Yet, although the term "optimal" often seems more aspirational than achievable, it remains a key catalyst for innovation. If we aim for transformative change, we must be inventive in our decision-making. Conversely, when venturing into unknown territories, mistakes are inevitable.

Predicting even the immediate future is challenging given the tumultuous times we've experienced over the past decade. The tangible outcomes of Caesar's education have been enlightening and uplifting. Witnessing a child, not even three years old, beginning to read and tackling third-grade math is indescribable, especially when once told he might merely survive. Such milestones, along with countless others, have fueled our determination and hope.

To elaborate further, it might sound redundant to state that Caesar's education is instrumental in molding his character and future. After all, education shapes the trajectory and professional growth of every child. Would Alexander the Great have built his empire without the mentorship of Aristotle, bestowed upon him by his father, King Philip? It was education that propelled the young prince to kingship, not just his title. This perspective is always rooted in practicality, as an ideal education should not solely impart academic knowledge. It should instill practical skills and values that equip a child for real-world challenges. This includes fostering critical thinking, creativity, social skills, and problem-solving, helping them navigate life's intricacies, given that the emotional gearing—or evolution—a child takes at an early age to figure out the new world is barely touched. These were the tenets we had in mind when charting Caesar's educational journey a decade ago.

Waiting, analyzing as many do, learning from the elders, studying—20 years lapsed in my life, waiting for a time to move on, building my family so that a child could come from it in more than just the biological sense. It was a surreal gift, akin to rare gold, yet it had not begun to shine. It falls upon the parents to fully immerse themselves, utilizing every resource to refine and polish it. Parents should be aware from the start that the journey will require enduring sacrifices, relentless effort, and unwavering dedication—minimal expectations for a labor of nearly 20 years. An enchanting proverb states something close to this: "Twenty years of investment or a life of headaches." This captures everything I learned from the example of my parents.

Actually, we embraced a completely unorthodox approach to education that began before we even knew the gender of our child in his mother's womb. The music! Based on a plethora of evidence—historical, anecdotal, and scientific—we believe that it is the best method to invest in for guaranteeing success and attracting desirable support during the long, difficult battle predicted ahead of us due to this illness. Soon, the early sprouts were already starting, showing that such a way had been wise to pursue.

No one can win this type of struggle alone. Even if you are close to victory, setbacks can arise which threaten to undermine your progress. The frustrations were sometimes so scorching that we were nearly reconsidering what we were doing and questioning the purpose of our lives. However, my family has experienced tastes of victory, which always came in little fragments from small achievements such as being able to practice homeschooling, violin, musicology, math, and reading (Kumon)—the highlights—but also including a slight touch on science, psychology, religion, philosophy (thinking), sociology, anthropology, economics, history, karate, and languages. Most of the time this happened without the pain or typical difficulties that other families share, though it was not easy by any means. The disruptions of Caesar's health setbacks were horrible, but otherwise, the medical appointments were on point (unquestionable) and thoughtfully scheduled. In a span of two years, promising results sprouted from all of our investments.

The costs, over $1,000 monthly, made us trim down everything apart from food, medicines, and health support. We took the hard line to survive. Thus, it tested my salary limits and put a strain on us in the 2000s. These simple achievements have helped us overcome setbacks and move forward because it would be worse dying, giving up, sitting down at the crossroads, and looking down. On the contrary, being positive, always moving forward—our favorite motto: "Still, a person needs something to target the positivity on." But when things go wrong ("the going gets tough, and the tough gets going"), we tend to withdraw from all activities and think, "It's time to retreat into our shell," like lepers in the past or a dog licking its wounds, anticipating Providence. Nevertheless, upon reflection, we acknowledge our blessings compared to other families facing similar illnesses who find themselves completely immobilized by their circumstances. It dawned on us that we were not in hell, but rather on the other side—the blessed part. Through a process in which pain initially brought angst, it subsequently facilitated growth, fostered love and happiness, and is set to provide profound enlightenment for my entire family. At the same time, we receive confirmation of our blessings in various ways. One simple example is when we would glance at some other folks whose lives were healthy with good socio-economic stability, but even then, Caesar the toddler was having moments of show-off (with grace) that they perhaps even never dreamed of. Because we hoped to be healthy, and hope was the only thing left, we had to work to feed it daily! Yes, we are grateful for our health and the opportunities it affords us, even if they are small moments of pride many may never even dream of experiencing due to their inner limitations. Once again, I am not the best religious person, and at the same time, we must be humble and give all the glory alone to God.

A HINT: A QUESTION ABOUT SOCIAL SKILLS

While we were confident in our educational strategy for Caesar, there were concerns about his social skills, often stemming from the feedback we received from friends and acquaintances. Though I may not always agree with some views, it is beneficial to consider fresh perspectives, as they can illuminate areas for growth and understanding. I must confess that by listening to others, even if not on the same page, I have learned to open my eyes through my life. Caesar was undoubtedly sociable, and we continually encouraged his involvement in our discussions, especially during social events. Yet, we hadn't observed him fully engaging with his peers. Still, he was not four yet, so to observe this, I invited a fellow from Kumon school who also had two children to our home. The family is of Chinese descent, as the majority of families in that community are from foreign lineage and deeply care about their children's education. Their children, like ours, were part of the Kumon Math & Reading program. Our Brazilian customs teach us to greet guests with some food. So, I asked my wife to think about something for this occasion. She prepared cheese bread and fresh juice for our guests. Despite both children attending Kumon, the twice-a-week class format—where they either sat individually or in small groups with teachers—did not allow for much peer interaction. My kids, aged four and three, were in a unique class tailored for younger learners, accommodating children up to age five. Meanwhile, the parents, myself included, would wait outside, often engaging in discussions about our hopes and dreams for our children, especially after a tiring workday. Our guests' children were notably older, around nine or ten years of age. As we adults indulged in our meal and cultural exchanges, our children played harmoniously for over an hour, their interaction suggesting a deep-rooted friendship as if they were regular play pals. This experience, the inaugural of many more pleasant ones, cleared up several queries I had about Caesar's ability to socialize.

COGNITION & PERSPECTIVES

From a cognitive perspective, numerous scientific publications demonstrate that babies can learn from their environment even before being born, both in the uterus and the outside world. Music is a particularly effective tool to assess this phenomenon. Hence, I successfully persuaded Aline to commence listening to classical music early in her pregnancy. Despite not being initially fond of this genre, she embraced the experience and also grew to love classical music, even though neither of us played any instruments. (An interesting side note: I was a tenor during my younger years but had a short singing career due to a lack of talent). During her pregnancy, she listened to orchestral music all day, and the little baby, later named Caesar in honor of my professor (Magister Caesar Timo-laria, who passed away in 2005), was constantly exposed to these melodies.

We invested in a comprehensive collection of educational DVDs from the Baby Einstein series when Caesar was born. This series consisted of 32 DVDs, each showcasing serene images and gentle scenes set against a backdrop of soothing lullabies. The visual content featured picturesque gardens, quaint farms, and friendly animals, all harmoniously accompanied by beautiful compositions of classical music giants like Bach, Beethoven, and Mozart. "Heavily" is the right word to describe how those scenes have imprinted on my memory.

As someone with a background in academia, particularly in the fields of education and cognition, I experienced an immense sense of joy and hope watching my son become engrossed in the Baby Einstein DVDs. The innocent scenes, paired with the soothing music, created an atmosphere of pure bliss. It was a heartwarming sight: my precious son lying on the carpet, his head propped up in curiosity, as he played with his toys, attentively absorbing the enchanting combination of Bach's music and the idyllic visuals. Often, in my moments of wonder, I'd ask Mamma to pinch me.

Typically, Caesar would sit in his calming baby chair, happily swaying slightly to the gentle rhythm of the music. I believe that his exposure to the Baby Einstein DVDs played a significant role in his generally calm and content demeanor. In fact, Caesar rarely cried. Our neighbor even made this observation many times.

Rather than showing distress, Caesar regularly appeared to be constantly smiling and radiating happiness. The influence of the tranquil scenes and melodic music in his early life surely contributed to his overall sense of well-being. This sense of delight seemed to fortify his resilience as he faced his health challenges with a spirit of happiness for nearly ten years. The extent of the suffering he endured is difficult to articulate, but through it all, he never ceased to smile. In these inexplicable moments, we frequently find ourselves pausing to reflect, attributing the mysteries of life to a higher power—to God.

CAESAR'S INTRODUCTION TO MUSIC

Allow me to share details about Caesar's inaugural musical episode. This experience was instrumental in shaping an educational approach centered around music, math, science, history, culture, foreign languages, and sports. We often refer to this concept as MMCFL, though its variations can be represented as MM, ML, or MC. However, the name or abbreviation is less important than its essence and application. In 2008, the year Caesar was born, I was a scientist in Brown University's science department. As someone devoted to my work, my days typically started early and ended late. However, Caesar's arrival impacted my daily routine. Each day, I found myself eagerly waiting for the moment I could return home to see him, an emotion so profound that it defies description. It is perhaps a sentiment many new parents can resonate with. When Caesar was seven months old, we had introduced him to a basic caterpillar toy piano. Despite its modest design, the toy's keys produced distinct cricket-like sounds reminiscent of musical notes, especially those from Brahms' lullabies. This early musical interaction underscored the significance of music in Caesar's development and reinforced the belief that learning can start even before birth. One day, to our utter astonishment, we found a seven-month-old Caesar lying on his belly, his head raised, and arms

65

outstretched, expertly playing the very music he had been listening to earlier on his caterpillar toy piano. We exchanged amazed glances and my immediate reaction was one of awe and recognition: "Mamma, we have a long and exciting journey ahead of us and a tremendous responsibility to nurture and support this child. He is already displaying signs of exceptional natural talent, perhaps even verging on genius." From that day on, we continued with the same routine, ensuring that Caesar had ample opportunities to explore and develop his musical talent and other interests. I fondly referred to this joyous incident as Caesar's first playful and ludic training session that foreshadowed his extraordinary potential. This experience also served as a reminder of the importance of fostering a nurturing environment for young minds, as they may be harboring remarkable talents that could blossom with love, encouragement, and guidance.

Indeed, every child is born potentially as a genius, without exception. However, this potential depends on the child's environment, which can either nurture their talents like beautiful flowers or stifle them. Specifically, a rich and stimulating environment during the early years is the most powerful source of development for a child's mind.

A short special note is deserving herein: Ironically, during the final years of my Ph.D. studies, I conducted a study comparing animals born and raised in an enriched environment (group A) to those in a normal setting (group B). I even incorporated specialized food and an abundance of toys for the enriched environment group. We quickly observed stark differences between the two groups: animals from the enriched environment (group A) consistently outperformed their counterparts in a simple test known as "behavior operant." In contrast, animals from the standard environment (group B) generally exhibited low to average performance and lacked problem-solving curiosity. Even more striking, our analysis of their brains revealed significant micro-anatomic (brain cells wiring) differences. Unfortunately, due to my sudden move to the U.S., the study was not fully published, though some of its findings were later incorporated into a paper[5] that I published examining the relationship between the brain's theta rhythm and intelligence.

There is a worldwide body of academic publications offering numerous similar findings with rigorous controls that inspired me to apply such insights into my children's education. As life is full of twists and turns, and without any pretensions, I thought that one day such privileged (almost secret, someone would say) information would be used for my sake—because as a scientist our job is to provide answers that quite exclusively will help humanity—not us directly. Thus, it was a good fortune. Ultimately, this approach has proven to be valid and beneficial for my wife, myself, and everyone–including friends—we cherish in our lives.

Notwithstanding the above, some dismiss the idea of nurturing genius and instead focus on achieving standards and "normality" or see such a family's misfortune as a simple fate. Hence, they often engage in arguments or endeavor to dismiss nurturing, while also embracing the inevitability of accepting the odds, abandoning the distractions of endless blemishes and illogical points. And how

---

[5]Sant, Lucas et al., 2008. *"Baseline hippocampal theta oscillation speeds correlate with rate of operant task acquisition"*. Behav. Brain Res: https://bit.ly/4cO3VZs

about a child with sickle cell anemia, epilepsy, cancer, or physical limitations such as being born without legs, arms, or sight? The list could go on. Each situation is unique in that it is complex and private. It is virtually impossible to dig into any of these real situations that happen in society as a whole; with tested family closeness, no one can predict the problem's length or its outcome. Truly, who and how many will have to face potential catastrophe or triumph, nobody can predict. I must refrain from extending beyond sickle cell anemia, the condition that ensnared my family, though suffering is universal. Blood loss or excruciating pain are the same dilemmas for any person—the only differences being the person's name or their address. Therefore, we do hold a trace credit for saying something regarding this matter, but not extensively. The psychological trauma and financial consequences can be devastating for a family and it is difficult to discuss it without exposing personal experience. Moreover, there is no need to mention the financial downfall—approaching bankruptcy—that can be devastating, though it might be recoverable. A lost life is not.

A family's biggest asset of possessions is the children, so their Education (again with big "E") is supposed to be the number ONE priority for any family to strive for. That is indeed an extraordinary gift, and we must sacrifice for them. Anything else would be achievable (probability speaking) if the first big step, Education, is in place, especially if a rich environment is fostered early.

Fortunately, regardless of the degree of belief a person may have, nowadays parents have more tools at their disposable which are available to handle this matter. For instance, research has shown that, in general, there are intriguing biological laws that govern all human conditions. For example, if a person is missing one leg, the other will be stronger, even though such a person will likely require a prosthesis if they wish to walk or run better. Similarly, someone who is visually impaired, especially a child, will have much stronger auditory abilities than someone with normal vision, and vice versa. A natural compensation for every situation can be read throughout nature. However, the general limitations herein are, once again, largely determined by the environment, whether it is rich, poor, or "normal." The degree to which parents can endure self-torture and expose themselves to "mistreatment" is also a real sacrifice, a big factor, and this can be similar to what is experienced by people experiencing homelessness (at least inside us emotionally), if one decides to stay in this good fight!

Despite this, it is imperative to resist the temptation of shortcuts and explore innovative approaches. Managing this matter requires careful handling, exerting continuous effort, and maintaining high hopes daily to prevent an easy halt. Furthermore, we must maintain a positive and often unconventional outlook, steering away from restrictive thinking (out-of-the-box thinking is crucial), especially from those who act as advisors in a war but have never experienced the battlefield firsthand. They may be deemed experts in this or that, but real expertise comes from practical experience. Additionally, we should heed the wisdom of a well-known old saying: "There is a time for everything," and the optimal time for acquiring an ideal education is during our formative years when we are young. The reality is that in this dynamic world, there will always be a gap and unpredictability between events and our ability to comprehend them. No one can foresee the next turn of events or who will be affected. Our limitations in understanding the cutoffs and endpoints can make things seem chaotic, but it is merely a reflection of our own restrictions—our angle of vision. I do not know how to navigate these limitations; however, drawing lessons from the experiences of others who have done so has proven to be very instructive.

Regardless of everything, any health issue that may happen to you, me, or our families, whether we are poor or rich, brings a toll that usually exposes our limitations: It demonstrates that we assuredly do not know everything (we even know nothing quite often) and the fate of the outcome varies from person to person, family to family. I felt so powerless and disappointed, yet fortunately, I gave my all, relying on the hope that we would make it through. Simultaneously, we should remember that we are all human beings entitled to happiness, which is the most beautiful enlightenment we can experience as humans. It should be anchored without delay. Nobody was born to be forever stuck in sadness. (If I may offer one key piece of advice: never accept sadness as normal; always find a way to strive to seek happiness). Regardless of ethnicity or birthplace, health status, or any other factor, we all share the same destiny: to be happy—who would not enjoy being happy? However, there is actually a rather high price to pay for happiness, although there are many ways to achieve it.

PART III

HEALTH VS. SICKNESS

MOVING FROM RHODE ISLAND TO NORTH CAROLINA AND MEETING OUR MOST REMARKABLE CHALLENGES

When Caesar turned fifteen months old in 2009, our family reached a crucial juncture. My academic team was transitioning to the University of California, Los Angeles (UCLA). Nevertheless, I chose not to accompany them due to concerns that my salary would not be sufficient to cover the high living expenses on the West Coast. The stakes were significant, and while my children had their birthright in the U.S., their lineage, including mine, trace back to Brazil. A particular challenge stemmed from my special skills visa at that time, which defined my stay with a 30-day grace period post-contract. Failing to secure a subsequent job would relegate me to an undocumented status.

With unwavering determination for my family's stability, I embarked on a nationwide quest, delivering talks and interviews at various academic institutions in the hope of advancing my science career and securing a new job. This exhaustive endeavor culminated in an offer from Wake Forest University in Winston-Salem, North Carolina. This role preserved my legitimate residency and prevented me from entering undocumented status. As 2009 drew to a close, we prepared for our transition to Winston-Salem. Simultaneously, Caesar's mother was already awaiting the arrival of our next child, Maria-Anita. Intriguingly, North Carolina was the very state that had initially greeted me for my post-doctoral journey at Duke University's biology Department. This return to my "heart state" rekindled fervent sentiments. Our relocation manifested as a monumental—and arduously challenging—voyage. We embarked on a grueling 20-hour expedition in a mammoth 24-foot truck, our car in tow——a journey which we had never done before.

Mamma (who was approaching her delivery date) and young Caesar were my co-passengers, with Caesar's safety seat securely positioned between us. While the journey's length was a source of anxiety, my conviction of our eventual safe arrival was unyielding. Yet at the very outset in East Providence, the curve from our street presented a hiccup: Our towing vehicle brushed the sidewalk curb. Despite the faintness of the resultant sound, it was a strong reminder of the journey's natural unpredictability and the imperative to exercise utmost caution—evidently, the truck's value with my family in it seemed to overshadow the value of life itself, even more than my own.

As the early hours of the morning approached, around 2:00 in the morning, we were exhausted from a full day spent loading the truck. Our resolve to embrace our new chapter in North Carolina was unshaken. The open road had an invigorating effect on me, filling me with a sense of watchfulness, relaxation, and happiness. It was a unique, indescribable feeling that remains etched in my memory. Even though it has been a short span of years, it feels like distant history since every one of those events became pillars of my family's saga.

A brief reprieve from our journey arose after about an eight-hour road stretch. We stopped at a large gas station to replenish ourselves, grab some food, and also refuel the truck. I bought two hot dogs, assuming one for me and one for my wife would be enough, with Caesar taking bites from both. Yet, Caesar's eyes gazed at my hot dog, and he promptly grabbed it for himself. Left with no other choice, I returned to the gas station and purchased several hot dogs to quell our hunger. Once we had all eaten our fill, we continued our journey toward our new home (our El Dorado!) in Winston-Salem, filled with anticipation and excitement for the life that awaited us there. That place would embrace us for nearly a decade before we moved to Memphis, Tennessee in 2019.

Replanting our roots in the pleasant state of North Carolina, this tranquil town bore witness to profound milestones in our lives for roughly a decade, hosting the most remarkable events in my family. It's utterly impossible to report all of them. It was where I started to get sick—I suffered a hemorrhagic stroke a few months after I started my new professional chapter. It is a miracle that I was able to survive without needing brain surgery, along with the expected consequences. However, for the first time, I was put on a lifelong regimen of medication to control a very high blood pressure, which I had never had before 2010. Tight health regulation is in place for people who work in medical institutions, as was my case, therefore, those records speak for themselves. Briefly, my life flipped from that of a healthy person to one in survival mode. I say this without exaggeration because uncontrolled blood pressure is akin to a ticking time bomb—ranging between 240 over 130 (systolic vs. diastolic measurements) is, medically speaking, like a walking dead body. During that time, no medication would work. After 2021, with my son's successful bone marrow transplant that reestablished his health, all of my medications started performing accordingly. Yet, previously in 2018, a heart attack hit me like a truck hitting a bull, putting my heart in silence mode for about 30 minutes (not working or signaling), according to the physicians. As per their account, they had never seen anything like it. One week later, I was homebound.

In 2019, a year later, life served me another blow, when we were already living in Memphis, Tennessee. All of these were a result of mammoth stress levels from my son's illness. This specific topic will be the subject of another book I've been working on. Love is not cheap—indeed, it is costly—but its value is beyond any price tag. Practice is the key to it. A miracle is an extraordinary event that defies rational explanation or scientific understanding. It is something so otherworldly that we cannot find a reason to explain. Given my constraints, I cannot illustrate it better.

Still, turning back to the early years of 2010, 2011, 2012, something began to flicker in alarm. The worry was that every piece of information was suggesting time was running short for my family, especially for me. Caesar, during this period, was not showing many signs of illness. Instead, he was excelling in his special education in languages, math, science, martial arts (karate), and music— particularly the violin, which he took to remarkably in the years 2013 and 2014. Everyone was elated. For me, the predominant goal was to provide the best possible environment until he could get a bone marrow transplant, even though warning signs were already hinting (as predicted) that we might face significant obstacles. As mentioned earlier, over time—as the toddler ages—this blood disorder's aggressiveness intensifies. On the other hand, happiness was my lifeline—it is the best medicine essential for me to keep moving forward. Thus, while I was grateful for our progress, the pressing reality was always at our doorstep; I often felt like a soldier entering a perilous battle, uncertain of the outcome. That feeling became a constant shadow, foretelling the challenges on the horizon. Over time, this became a familiar sensation as I became attuned to the nuances of Caesar's health condition.

The blunt truth is that no matter the efforts, a person with sickle cell will endure pain, even when adhering to all medical guidelines recorded in the literature, serious anecdotes, and personal experience. At that juncture, our experience with sickle cell at the time was limited given it was our first child and we were acutely aware of the restricted medical options, such as administering antibiotics for infection prevention. I had an in-depth understanding of antibiotic research and their efficacy against bacterial infections. But even with the potential benefits of preventive antibiotics, the possible side effects were concerning. There is a latent bias in the treatment approaches for sickle cell, notably because a significant proportion of the patients are African-American and historically socially mistreated and racially discriminated. Thankfully a rising number of healthcare professionals were showing empathy and advocating for better care. Overuse of antibiotics can lead to bacterial resistance—a pressing issue worldwide—according to countless medical reviews. Moreover, antibiotics can disrupt the beneficial gut bacteria, which is of crucial importance for a robust immune response. Isn't this especially crucial for someone with sickle cell, whose immune defenses are already compromised? In essence, we felt stranded in the middle of nowhere—a sentiment only truly understood by parents with special needs children.

As we grappled with these realities, Caesar's health began to decline. Furthermore, by just looking into his eyes, I could see Caesar was expressing many things. Mainly, "What is going on with me, Papa?" And yet, a smile from him was enough to fill up my heart with all the love in the world—his smiles ultimately fed us with real hope to stay in the fight and to work even harder. Time was of the essence and we had to rapidly adapt and seek innovative solutions. Under this situation, it was like receiving a daily message saying, "It seems like our final chance."

If we could summarize everything in this book in one word, it would be HOPE, or perhaps INNOVATIONS—or both? Conceiving and possessing the courage to try out novelties and applying out-of-the-box thinking or new insights is the key for anyone wanting to enhance their chances of success. Overcoming every obstacle in the human experience is tied to this. However, there's a further significant vector to consider for those who decide to embark on this journey, although we do not recommend anyone trying it. The pitfalls are immense. Thus, understanding the risks and weighing their pros and cons is crucial, especially when facing a virtual dungeon of ostracism and loneliness at the top of the list.

Winston-Salem, located near Greensboro and, a bit further, Charlotte, exudes a sense of tranquility. Our home, somewhat secluded, bears witness in silence to our trials and tears. But humans, by nature, possess an inherent ability to adapt to solitude; it's a burden we learn to bear. We often find joy in the company of others, and while the presence of friends brings temporary relief, their departure leaves the challenges untouched.

Until this point, there had been numerous instances where our friends did not disappoint us, providing more than mere companionship and empathy. Friends like the DeOliveira family always honored these traditional dates with a birthday gift box that arrived one or two weeks early for the children. These gestures soothe the children's hearts as much as ours. In 2014, although I had ceased my role as a scientist, my former colleagues Dr. Deadwyler and Dr. Weiner continued their visits, serving as guardian angels, always providing exactly what we were missing. Mr. Suggs, a retired prodigious music teacher and the first to become Caesar's fan after his story was highlighted on the cover of the *Winston-Salem Journal* when he was just four years old, frequently spent time with us alongside his wife, Mrs. Jannette. They took my wife shopping and ensured she enjoyed fresh air outside the confines of our home. Teacher Zhou (Mrs. Hongmei Zhou), Caesar's dedicated violin teacher and a cherished friend, along with her family (especially her father Ye-Ye), consistently demonstrated their kindness toward us. They even made our last day in Winston-Salem memorable, treating the kids to their favorite meals as a farewell gesture to the city we had grown fond of.

Amid these heartwarming experiences, one incident stands out. Caesar suffered one of his worst pain crises, which seemed to appear suddenly after a routine pediatric visit. Initially diagnosed as a simple allergy accompanied by a dry cough, we became concerned, and I took him back to his doctor. After they conducted tests and sent us home with a reassuring diagnosis, we later received a letter revealing the true ailment: SARS-CoV-2, the virus that preceded COVID-19. He almost died; his appearance was skin and bone only. We reached a pinnacle of stress with his cough when the doctors said they, nor our last resources, were able to do anything. After catching each other's eyes, Mamma and I knew what might come next, so we knelt down and simply prayed. Following a hot water bath with eucalyptus, which we have done since the crisis's beginning, he went to sleep, and the following day, he woke up with no cough.

That first night of recovery we had a surprise visit on the other side of the river. However, a late-night knock typically brings apprehension—who might it be? We asked ourselves this quietly but at this point we had become somewhat immune to fear and answered the door. In fact, it was our friend Shelton bearing a letter from a family unknown to us, along with a donation exceeding $1,000. This benevolent family from Ohio, as far as I recall, had been touched by Caesar's story. Honoring their own child, they chose to offer us their savings. Knowing Shelton, they trusted him to deliver their gift. This act of kindness came just when we were about to run out of food. Indeed, it felt like a miraculous intervention. I firmly believe that such events may not come by mere coincidence, with the last one particularly resonating with me. I ascribe these events to what I deem as Divine Providence, or in other words, God.

These moments, vividly etched in my memory, involve friends who many might expect to drift away as time passes. Yet they remained steadfast, supporting us during our most challenging periods, whether spontaneously or intentionally. Without their unwavering presence and assistance I might not have had the strength or inspiration to pen this book. Beyond that, their support was invaluable in helping us navigate the difficulties we faced. In many ways our journey would have been far more challenging without our friends—they are our true pillars.

Each health crisis felt like a new tempest, profoundly affecting our family. In the early days, a phone call at work would send a wave of panic through me—instantaneous sweating and a pounding headache. If in a meeting, I would notice whispered conversations or sympathetic gestures—"Sorry, sorry." Everything halted. If I could not exit immediately, emotions from colleagues would often compel me to step out, sometimes leading to extended absences. All the events were leading to a natural termination of my career, regardless of my will. Particularly challenging periods arose when Caesar began to experience more frequent pain and swelling in his hands around 2013 and 2014. Such circumstances would jeopardize most jobs. However, my unique role as the chief developer of a crucial technology for brain recording—part of a prosthetic project funded by the U.S. Defense Department's DARPA—provided some stability. My colleagues recognized the value in my expertise, making it difficult despite my erratic presence, to let me go. Moreover, my job was essential for our livelihood, even though a part of me felt that Caesar would benefit more from my full-time attention. Several times, I have grappled with this dilemma, thinking, "I was not born for this. This is not me." Yet life has its trajectory, often moving forward regardless of our personal struggles and preferences.

As every bump echoed that the situation would become worse, sometimes it truly felt hopeless. We were navigating a massive storm, a situation that seemingly no one had the power to control or predict. Within it, one begins to grasp its dynamics every day. From the outside, observing the devastating impacts and the encompassing sadness, one might only see the surface's disturbances. It is an environment ripe for self-proclaimed experts to step forward with advice on everything—rather theoretically—

much of which they do not truly understand, having never weathered such a storm themselves.

We faced this repeatedly, particularly when receiving comments from some friends: "My friend, things are not clear. You seem lost—what is the next move? The boy is deteriorating." Remarks like these, which a third grader might be able to make (given the whole situation openly exposed), were not proactive nor encouraging. These folks pounced on our vulnerability. Others had suggestions, perhaps well-meaning, but still nudging us to change our course: "Why don't you find a new job and move on; God will handle this..." Such comments, over time, were more demoralizing than supportive, pushing us further down. One way to deal with such comments would be to shut them out, but that is easier said than done, especially when they often come from family members. This led us towards isolation, making us feel like outcasts in our family. Still, they reached my wife, filling her with their so-called wisdom. Between the child's illness and these external inputs, it's hard to say which was more challenging. Thankfully, not all was negative. God stood by us, fortifying my family, providing sustenance, and sending timely support from cherished friends reminiscent of guardian angels. He shielded Caesar from three strokes and me from two strokes and a heart attack, always reinforcing our spirits.

I have always held a deep conviction that we would not falter, but rather we would triumph. My mind has been clear about it since the beginning. I often rallied my family, infusing them with hope and assuring them of our eventual victory. Caesar's smiles, eyes, and words were a constant source of inspiration, a beacon in our struggle. The weight, both seen and unseen, was heavily on him, mostly. Today, having journeyed through our symbolic desert, we can look back knowing that records, both private and public, testify to our resilience. Life continues to evolve, and while our physical bodies change, the ultimate fate of all remains the same.

All the while, we had to learn quickly as we looked around our community of those with sickle cell. Many were doing much worse than us. We must assume that there are some families doing remarkably well, but unfortunately, not all of them have been in a good place. Many lack basic direction and are mistreated. The despair aroused inside me was indescribable by this, which was greatly confirmed in the medical anecdotes and scientific papers. Another factor was that we had to isolate ourselves to keep our minds clear and positive. It becomes impossible to operate with my mind unclear and confused. It was especially difficult for me, as I am fond of being with people. Again, the school system and the teachers were our best friends. For many reasons, a strong private school associated with homeschooling was in our hearts from the beginning, even if our children were born 100 percent healthy. As a result, Caesar (and his sisters) learned the basics at home the old-fashioned way. By the time he was two, he had already learned the alphabet and numbers one to 100. His mother did an astonishing job, especially in these early years; he was virtually a little walking sponge willing to follow any instructions—like a dream come true.

Scant effort was required to convince Caesar's mother that our children should not watch cartoons either in English or Portuguese (the two languages they have known from their birth) but rather in other foreign languages: German, Greek, French, Japanese, Latin, Chinese, Russian, or Hebrew. However, they were more naturally attracted toward some and dropped others, adding new languages. Surprisingly, the bias toward certain languages emerged once they were outside our genealogical roots. This is a dynamic learning process. For instance, they began watching Japanese cartoons alongside those of other languages with the same goal. This approach is enhanced by the presence of friends or a community who speak a given language—it fills a vital hole in the engagement, evoking enthusiasm and joyfulness that should naturally captivate those immersed in learning under this process. Unfortunately, the Japanese language was dropped early on due to a lack of a community around us, while Latin was added. Overall, none of this would prove effective if joy and enthusiasm were absent. In fact, presenting these foreign languages as early as possible to a child's mind is a marvelous gift parents should strive for. Learning foreign languages is an extra advantage in a competitive world, regardless of where a child lives (e.g., native place, languages). The child's best cognitive time would be wasted if they only learned their native language. English is easy to find wherever we go outside our homes. However, this is not the case with Helen whose Portuguese is poor.

Within our home, we speak Portuguese as much as possible— their mother tongue naturally—and we will continue to do so until later when they grow up and gain independence. Furthermore, in time they would speak English better than us—this proved true as they were already proficient by age two. Truly, these other foreign languages represent a significant portion of the world's languages, though the absence of a natural environment in which they are spoken hinders learning. We used YouTube to simulate such an environment.

In tandem, music was the top-priority language to be implemented because of the remarkable way a child's brain soaks up information so easily and quickly, most of which baffles us adults. When we adults eventually grasp something it often sounds broken, especially when considering a foreign language such as Greek, Chinese, or German, which can be quite difficult for an older person—it takes years after one's 20s to master any of those languages without native surroundings. Music and math provide a common cognitive exploration, fostering curiosity and experimentation in an unmatched way. Meanwhile, languages serve as crystallized systems that soothe a child's brain—the core of all cognitive endowments—acting as the best nourishment or "medicine," especially when presented in a creative or rich environment. Being slightly familiar with these basics of educational theories—cognition and brain plasticity—helped to set our educational foundation. Examining the early results, seeing the children develop before our eyes, certainly brought immense joy and pride. However, life changes daily. The body develops, yet the allotted time for us all in this world remains the same forever.

CAESAR'S FIRST STROKE (A LESSON IN RESILIENCE)

When he was two, we enrolled Caesar in various activities, including violin classes using the Suzuki Method twice a week, Kumon twice a week, Greek lessons once a week, and karate twice a week. All of these plans were made within a span of months to take maximum advantage of the predictable healthy period expected. As anticipated, our child excelled in these activities, and it felt like a dream come true for us all. By the time he turned four, he had achieved a lot: he had earned a black belt in karate, began speaking several languages (including Greek, Russian, German, and Chinese), was doing third grade math at Kumon, and began playing concertos. In this video: (https://bit.ly/3naRZd4) we can see him playing Vivaldi in E-minor at the age of four, and about 30 days later, he had his first stroke, which affected his right arm. It is important to highlight that this educational approach is not expected to bloom overnight or produce optimal outcomes in the short term—instead, it is designed for a long-term philosophical-spiritual goal. This will serve these young souls as a key to unlock any door, aiding them regardless of the path they choose to pursue.

Astonishingly, just over a month before the recording of this video, Caesar experienced his first setback: a stroke that paralyzed his arms, especially his bow arm (his right one). Although he recovered after a medical procedure known as an exchange blood transfusion, wherein about 90 percent of his blood was replaced, a notable weakness persisted in his right arm. Hence, the arm regained function but has never been as strong as his left one, and it still isn't today. That is why we frequent the gym and engage in special workouts to strengthen his right arm. However, after his bone marrow transplant, his overall body strength improved significantly. It is evident in all aspects of his improvement, and he often exclaims, "Look what I can do now, but last month I was unable to."

By the time Caesar was transitioning out of his toddler age, there was a palpable sense of achievement among everyone—myself, his mother, teachers, and friends. We had accomplished so much for a child born with a chronic illness, one that was deemed insurmountable by all known literature and medical opinions. To witness such a young child face challenges like strokes is both surreal and nearly impossible to articulate. Each of these events remains an indelible imprint on our minds. Often, I feel like a distant observer, reflecting on what we endured over nearly a decade. The scars from those years serve as living reminders in our minds. Fortunately, not only do our memories stand as a testament, but numerous other accounts also corroborate our journey, which you can further explore in the following pages.

I recall as if it were quite recent that in 2012 when Caesar was merely four years old, he displayed signs of concern. To better contextualize this scenario: I hail from a quaint village, where I spent my formative years on a farm. A few years after my father passed away, my mother chose to prevent our rural property from being annexed by affluent neighboring farms. We were neither impoverished nor affluent, a stark contrast to the environment in which Caesar was introduced to life. My memories are imbued with raw moments of unadorned love and simple living from that time: drinking water directly from a stream, playing in rivers, climbing trees for their sweet bounty, gathering fresh eggs from the hens, and hunting and fishing for sustenance—in some ways I might think it were something out of the movies if not for the fact that I lived it.

Conversely, when I consider my children, particularly Caesar at the tender age of four who had never partaken in these rudimentary experiences of survival—not even sipping water from a stream with his own hands—it fills me with apprehension. Experiencing nature is very useful throughout life, especially when we reach adulthood, and we must be creative to survive. Nature is, above all, the source of everything—the nectar of life. Its characteristics remain the quintessential wellspring, the very essence of existence. With this sentiment, we sought a local farm hotel for a weekend retreat, upon recommendations. The prospect of awakening to a rooster's call and witnessing the milking of cows ignited excitement in everyone. For them, it might have been a novel experience, but for me it was a long-held, almost secret, dream realized. That Friday was meticulously orchestrated; we spent considerable effort to ensure our inaugural wilderness escapade was perfect, despite the destination being a mere 40-minute drive away.

However, I was exhausted from work. By four in the afternoon, the day was already waning. I felt drained, thinking a nap might rejuvenate me. Yet before I could fully immerse myself in rest, my wife's urgent voice struck my sleep. With Caesar by her side, she exclaimed, "Look at Caesar's arms! What's happening?" I jumped, the scene before me resembling a nightmare. Caesar was holding two Lego blocks in his hands. As I hugged him, our gazes met. His eyes were seemingly desolate, dog-like, as if he had fallen off a moving truck. Within a brief period, our tranquil plan deteriorated into disorder. In such circumstances, action needs to be swift yet deliberate. Over time, we would brace ourselves for many such episodes, drawing lessons from this one. In a mixture of concern and confusion, I asked Mamma about the sudden change in Caesar. She mentioned that he was fine all day until she observed him struggling with the Lego pieces. When I asked him to try again, he used his left arm to assist the right. My heart raced, witnessing his ingenious solution to the problem despite his evident confusion. A myriad of thoughts crowded my mind, some influenced by my professional background.

Clearly an urgent hospital visit was warranted, so we went. While we were getting ready to leave the house in minutes, my scientist brain was pondering, working only with what I could see with the naked eye: Caesar showed no signs of pain and seemed alert; *was his brain lacking the essential support of blood—e.g., good cells, energy—to execute the simple action of connecting two Lego pieces? Obviously!* Observing such a thing in your own child is wholly different from reading about it, talking about it, giving your opinion or diagnosis of it, or anything else. If you don't have enough experience, you might sound foolish if you don't show respect.

Terrible! The whole scenario was intense and beyond words. We had never witnessed anything of this nature before. Merely half an hour earlier he had been his usual lively self, behaving normally. Yet, due to the blood disorder with which he was born, internally he was ill. Moreover, I wondered about his calm behavior. Why was he not upset or crying when we were so visibly shaken? Amid the urgency, his mother recalled some unusual instances from earlier in the day, like Caesar briefly losing his balance while taking the stairs. However, she explained, "He seemed perfectly fine, going about as usual, kept playing 100 percent normal with no complaint." He has always been an energetic boy.

Children often experience falls, but in that particular instance it was evident that he did not have sufficient blood in his body, reminiscent of a car running out of fuel and struggling to operate. It is a powerful reminder that such challenges are part of the wider spectrum of children born with sickle cell anemia. One more reason—perhaps the main one—caregivers often fall ill is that they need to be constantly alert, their awareness always at its peak. This, in turn, leads to a life often devoid of rest.

Families with children suffering from sickle cell anemia carry additional stress because at any given moment one might face an unexpected setback, as noted above. Ultimately, as caregivers, if we encounter unrelenting stress it is our responsibility to provide care for our loved ones. But who takes care of us, the caregivers? This is the harsh reality. For instance, we have always been on our toes, hoping to preempt or at least recognize potential health concerns. Regrettably, this episode caught us off guard. From the time he was a child we had taken several measures to increase awareness, believing that we might prevent or detect the most forthcoming health events. Yet we never aimed for an unrealistic control over everything, understanding its impracticality. Regardless of how many events we caught, sadly we missed this one. The paramount lesson: It's impossible to foresee every eventuality. Another lesson: We must be thankful because we were able to maneuver through this messy situation. A difficult question I wrestled with was, "How can I be thankful for unfortunate events?" Before, I didn't quite understand this. Well, after a while, we realized that the word "grace" makes sense only if we are grateful in recognizing that one of us, especially Caesar or us, could die during one of many daunting encounters, finishing his life chapter too early. As we journeyed through, there were no words above to resonate with any of this, yet we could only utter thanks for everything.

While I was examining Caesar and making sure that nothing was missing, no broken or torsional concern for any bone, joint, or muscle in the boy's body, Mamma was checking the bags and we immediately prepared to depart for the hospital. Interestingly, we had been working on this type of preparation together since the beginning. In general, at any medical visit we go with the whole crew. Back then, there were only four. Between the onset of his issue and our leaving for the hospital, it was about 15 minutes or so because we always had emergency plans similar to war preparation. For as difficult as this sounds, in the back of my head I had foreseen that it might come because one of the facets of sickle cell is its unpredictability, though I call it betrayal. In addition, strokes are quite common among those with this anemia, yet nobody is ready for it, much less us.

Furthermore, as parents, especially for our first child, we were still learning the basics, regardless of how witty and astute we thought we were ourselves. Months or years later we looked back wondering, "Well, what if we did this or that together? What if we had chosen another path, this or that? Or closely followed that suggestion?" That being said, a simple question would be posed for the purpose of eventual speculation: Could a normal family who does all this and that and follows all the suggestions precisely, never face any issues with a sickle cell child? Yes or no? Surely, those who were born with chronic health problems naturally possess a high probability of facing such encounters. No matter what, these events would come; more relevant is how to handle them when they do and maintain a tight prevention regime, as we partially discuss herein. Summing up, though words and suggestions are cheap, implementing them requires action—it is akin to carrying our own cross.

From the beginning, as we pointed out before, when we looked around and talked to those in the healthcare field, all that we abundantly witnessed was a lack of health, sorrowful stories, stagnant innovation, hopelessness, bias, all the weight on the weak end of this equation—on us, the patients and families. It generates great distress almost without a break, except for those who had a bone marrow transplant—the only cure for it. Yet there are families that are "happy" with the standard system and what they are doing, but either they are not fully aware of the consequences of their approach, especially the long-term ones, or the child becomes ill quite often. I think the only option that's not trustworthy is to do nothing. Undoubtedly families, caregivers, and patients bear a significant emotional burden. Their concerns are not just about the immediate or midterm future but are deeply rooted in long-term plans—their dreams share a common interest, which is personal. Any flaws must be rectified as soon as possible. Yet the intricacy of even short-term plans can become overwhelming, especially when all decision-making falls solely on the family's shoulders. It is worth noting, however, that a growing global movement is gradually lessening the burden on families. For the record, until that time Caesar never had a simple cold, although he already felt the angst of having his hand swelling. Great lessons were garnered from the sickle cell community—without exception, truly heroes. Sharing this pain, similar to the soldier's feelings on the battlefield, we experience true brotherhood, sharing the little bread we had. You might feel heartbroken by the renewal you see when you visit them or when we occasionally hang out, especially if you get a chance to see the persistent abuse the community has endured. The health system appears to be happy with it. Around $20,000 per visit is being put in the bank. The other parties involved do not have much reason for sorrow or sadness for anything.

In time, we must render justice to countless heroes within the healthcare system—brave nurses and lovely doctors—and very often, they too share frustrations for not being able to pursue more, aspiring for further innovations for the suffering patients. Surely, they are as frustrated as their patients. Throughout these years, we experienced this in various institutions across the board. Our heart goes out to these brave individuals, many of whom we have the honor to call them friends. While on many occasions, some displayed actions that exacerbated problems and were devoid of any empathy, we encountered others who stood at the opposite end of this spectrum. Indeed, these very individuals were completely dedicated, and through their exceptionally bold attitude, my son's life was spared, and thus, his journey is shared with you. We are forever grateful to everyone who helped us.

Undoubtedly, one way or another, they knew that such a miraculous medical procedure would turn Caesar's fate around. Yes, it took ten years of struggle for it to finally happen in 2021, a result of lessons upon lessons—expensive ones—from the beginning. Learning is indeed a costly remedy. The fact of the matter is that we never took these events lightly, and in this case, after hearing this further elaboration from his mother, a glimmer of hope arose that Caesar might have a pinched nerve from his falling. But again, my examination revealed nothing, so we decided to not waste another minute at home with our child and rush to the hospital as soon as possible. In truth, this whole scene was quite fast, as my wife was already preparing the hospital bags. In fact, they were prepared and stored downstairs because those are part of the so-called "emergency items," given the health precautions we had established for our child at home. We must, and always did, maintain preparedness to swiftly proceed to the hospital, thus minimizing delays. In essence, the stress level had been pressing on my family from day one. Thus, from high expectations of having a wonderful weekend at a farm hotel, we found ourselves instead hastening to the emergency care of a hospital. To date, we have never fulfilled the wish to spend time in a farm hotel.

Everyone has seen at least a movie scene resembling part of this incident—a family hurrying to the hospital with a sick child. In our case, only the details would change—it always bears that exact stress. Fortunately we met an attending physician who, after hearing our story, acted swiftly by running a series of tests and scanned images of Caesar's body, mainly the arms and obviously the brain. Everything was normal but within minutes a hematologist intervened. For the first time, we learned the simple and crucial rule: Blood transfusion is the ultimate remedy for such situations. Reaching this time-consuming level which is the key to success—an additional missing piece that we encountered on the third stroke that hit him over a year later. In fact, without much hyperbolizing, it is the only resource the hospital can rely on to restore any compromised function when dealing with this type of stroke, such as lack of enough normal healthy blood cells. Basically, our brain stops working if the optimal amount of healthy blood cells stops within minutes. This happened to our little baby, Caesar, at age four. The hospital performed a special blood transfusion procedure called "exchange" by using a giant machine, during which about 90 percent of his blood was replaced. The boy fell asleep the whole night until around 4:00 in the morning when he woke up asking for water. Before that, we noticed he was moving his right arm and bringing it to his nose. The whole scary event happened Friday night. By Sunday, we were back home with our son, who was back to his normal self and playing with his lovely sister, Maria-Anita, for the entire day. The following day, Monday, he was able to resume his school activities: going to Kumon and having violin lessons. Everything was normal except the teachers' reactions to what had happened. In fact, nobody knew, or were fully aware of, the blood disorder with which Caesar was born and how much "betrayal" and unpredictability it brings. In general, like most afflicted people, we were conscious of the risks of sickle cell anemia and what we are supposed to do, though I was not aware that this debilitating genetic disorder, quite common among the population of African descendants, falls into a category of somewhat unusual illnesses. One of the primary reasons for this is that African Americans, who are sometimes incorrectly referred to as "immigrants" (a prejudicial label), constitute the majority of those affected, significantly contributing to the statistics.

Approximately 100,000 people in the U.S. are impacted by sickle cell anemia, a condition that incurs about $1.7 million per lifetime in each person's expenses[6], with the real cost to each family surpassing millions of dollars. However, this figure might be larger,

---

[6] *"The Cost of Living with Sickle Cell Disease", 2022.* American Society of Hematology: https://bit.ly/4ePNbTx

with discrepancies depending on study methods, as some estimates range from 100,000 to 300,000 individuals in the U.S. alone. The economic burden, especially for family caregivers, is substantially underrated yet significant, with annual costs around $3 million, primarily due to asset losses like houses and cars, particularly with out-of-pocket medical expenses. Notably, sickle cell anemia impacts not only people of African descent but also Latinos, Europeans (mostly from the Mediterranean), and other ethnic groups[7]. According to the United Nations World Health Organization, approximately 5 percent of the world's population carry trait genes for hemoglobin disorders, predominantly sickle-cell disease and thalassemia[8]. Thalassemia, a genetically related blood disorder, is more common in the Mediterranean region.

In summary, sickle cell anemia is the number one genetic illness worldwide, with a higher prevalence in Africa, the Americas, the Caribbean, and India, where in some tribes, 35 percent of the population carries it[9]. The fact of the matter is that it is difficult to fully grasp its societal impact beyond surface-level observations, as the socioeconomic devastation extends far beyond local communities. Consider this modest example: If a company employee, whether a driver, doctor, or plumber, frequently experiences sickle cell crises and becomes unable to work—due to either having sickle cell or being a caregiver, as in my situation—it not only impacts their job but also their family's livelihood,

[7] *"Data & Statistics on Sickle Cell Disease, 2023. Centers for Disease Control"*, CDC: https://bit.ly/4eNtA6w

[8] *"World Health Organization. 2023 Sickle Cell Disease"*. Regional Office for Africa: https://bit.ly/3XRFLZU

[9] *Colah, RB et al., 2025.* "Sickle cell disease in tribal populations in India". IJMR : https://bit.ly/45SEBPH

especially if they are the main provider. This situation could lead to asset liquidation to survive, while the company faces the challenge of losing a valuable employee. In my case, my specialized skills in prosthetics had allowed my team to accommodate my situation to a certain extent. However, many families dealing with sickle cell lack such specialized skills, yet face similar burdens. In these challenging times, hope and patience become vital, turning even small positives into significant victories. Similar to a new breath, even if brief, it is indispensable for catching one's breath. While I am not one to proclaim strong faith, under such circumstances faith becomes crucial, enabling one to see beyond the immediate challenges and envision a better future.

Nothing was more surprising and bothersome than this harsh reality check. The more we read, the more we learn about the disorder, and the more clearly we can see grim prospects associated with it—the older the person gets, the higher the incidences of health complications. While I am not the best religious person in the world, from the start I asked God what did I do wrong to deserve to be put in such a corner; why does a child deserve this, really? My anguish about this subsided somewhat recently, but it always bothered me deeply. It starts with the misleading characterization commonly called *sickle cell disease,* used by the majority—with a few exceptions—of health care providers. Ironically, I earned my PhD in pathophysiology from the University of São Paulo School of Medicine, Brazil, but I never heard about sickle cell lectures or seminars for students there, nor in the U.S. where I have been living since 2003, or at any of the places I have worked: Duke University, Brown University, and Wake Forest

University. However, among the lectures, I still remember learning about the standard criteria distinguishing a disease and a disorder. The first one is a pathological process that healthcare providers can see, touch, and measure, while the second one is characterized by a functional impairment or a disruption to the body's normal function and structure.

Although these terms are often used interchangeably, the differences are subtle but important. A disorder is more associated with a malfunctioning condition that might lead to a specific disease—a possibility of misconditioning. Furthermore, anemia means a lack of red blood, which could evolve into a disease. For example, a person with sickle cell anemia could develop various serious illnesses such as heart disease, kidney or liver disease, etc., due to complications from such anemia. From the beginning, I could not understand the reason for this mischaracterization. Why does the healthcare system confuse these basic concepts that medical students should learn to distinguish around the second or third year? This makes me suspect that the confusion is more than just a matter of terminology; it could be an underlying bias given the fact that the majority of individuals with sickle cell anemia are of African American descent, a community that has historically faced socioeconomic disadvantages. It became glaringly obvious by the approach Caesar received when he was around four months old and a healthcare worker started an awkward conversation saying something like "...Oh, it's sickle cell anemia, it is a black disease, but you have to treat him as if he were normal..." I never imagined I would have to hear that. Throughout these years, with very few exceptions, we have encountered somewhat different versions of this sentiment in nearly all areas of the medical field, but typically well-camouflaged. It is totally unfair to a child, regardless of their race, color, or social status. In contrast, I must also highlight that we have encountered fair and wonderful healthcare professionals in every healthcare institution we have worked with who are totally absent from these prejudices and completely free of such biases. Many have become cherished friends and they hold a special place in our hearts forever, like the NIH fellows!

What happened to Caesar between the first stroke and the second? His recovery from the first stroke was complete, though it was during his violin practice that the first weakening of his right arm was observed. If not for these keen observations, nobody could detect any deficit in his body. The fact that the violin is an instrument that demands special attention—especially in the arms, fingers, right arm, and bow techniques—raised concerns about this matter. Meanwhile, his karate practice and his overall normal activities were undoubtedly compensating for this weakness, as children often have an incredible ability to adapt and overcome uneven terrain, such as physical challenges.

Caesar's Second Stroke

For the three times that Caesar experienced strokes, we were living in our lovely Winston-Salem, NC. We had actually moved to a beautiful house that was closer to my wife's dream home. The house had a large front yard. Our children loved helping with yard work and a simple routine of cutting grass became a fun activity on weekends. One day, after enjoying this fun activity, Caesar was coughing all night. A call to a doctor resulted in an allergy diagnosis. This turned out to be true and only months later did we untangle it with the use of essential oils like lavender—nothing else helped unfortunately. All of the possible medications were administered, but then the second night came and the dry cough still remained unchanged. After the third night, in the morning, I was handing him a cup of hot chocolate, which he loves, but when he tried to take the cup, his right arm (the same one that had weakened before) was no longer functioning. He was experiencing something very similar to what had happened about six months earlier—his right arm was not responding to his brain command, although he was not in pain.

I took him to the hospital immediately. A very similar blood exchange procedure was performed in which about 90 percent of his blood was replaced. This procedure is typical after this type of stroke occurs. The blood contains a high amount of unhealthy cells that not only fail to perform the functions to provide healthy blood cells to the organs and every single cell in the body, but they can also obstruct or at least slow that rate down. Indeed, this is the most effective and only medical intervention available in such situations. Yes, it sounds rough, but when faced with a life-threatening situation, one is willing to do whatever it takes. Once again, after this, Caesar slept for nearly 13 hours and woke up with full function restored to his arm. We honor those doctors for their outstanding job, their vital procedure repeated for the second time. When he had the third stroke, however, we took him to the same hospital. We expected the same service, but he had a horrible fate—the doctors who previously attended him were not there, and we experienced poor treatment. This was a very scary moment in Caesar Sant's life. I was still working for Wake Forest University as a scientist at the same hospital where Caesar's strokes were managed.

Except for the surrounding circumstances, the first and second strokes were very similar in almost everything, including the outcomes. However, after the second stroke, Caesar's right side began to show signs of weakness. A few days after being discharged from the hospital, life returned to normal—he resumed his school activities and family routine. Whenever anything happened to Caesar, it automatically coerced me to leave my job to dedicate myself entirely to him, and the whole crew at work had to go into standby mode.

Nevertheless, we must admit that reflecting on or discussing the past, as I am doing here, serves as an exclamation on the preterit that provided us with bitter lessons—and, to a great extent, everyone eventually walks these lines. To my children, quite often I catch myself in a situation of teaching them with something like this: "You see, you are smarter than I in many ways; for instance, sporadically you correct my English-speaking, which is nice, but guess what: Papa has more experience because the more a person walks in life, being older gives more knowledge. Generally, having to face and encounter a mixture of conditions through which many worked and some not quite as expected; either way, anyone who goes through the accumulation of years has a chance to pursue wisdom."

We must refrain from any attempt to edit the past because the truth must prevail. In other words, over 90 percent of the decisions we made were completely right, supported by science and common sense. Without them, we certainly would be part of the big failure—an ugly statistic of sickle cell lives who unfortunately did not make it through or are hopelessly waiting for something to happen while paying for the healthcare system to just keep them in survival mode. So, those decisions we made were ultimately responsible for our undisputable success. That required an extra dose of courage (and fate, too) that I never possessed, mainly because I was always aware that something certainly would be missing, some mistake would be found later on. At the end of the day, life in many ways resembles endless battles. Sometimes we win, sometimes, not so much. "There is no victory without some loss," a general might say. Overall, as long as the number of victories is higher than the losses, we should be glad to have it. The experiences learned are the factual lessons of this course in life; as for the scars from it, there are many "epistolas" –episodes or parts to come.

For my family, we try to write our own story in the future. Deep down, I can hardly imagine any devoted parents willingly neglecting or postponing their responsibilities to advocate for their children's best interest. Therefore, any healthcare provider should be considered a keen helper and parents should understand that they share the responsibility for their child's well-being, much like a car owner is responsible for maintaining their vehicle. It is essential to recognize that we acquire wisdom through experience, and learning from others can help us avoid mistakes or serious consequences as we walk further. A critical aspect of this journey is finding healthcare professionals whom parents can trust—perhaps the most challenging variable in this whole equation—as they play a significant role in the well-being of our children. Thanks to them (even a few who were not so compassionate), we always encounter decent individuals—very passionate about their jobs—who offer positive words and a hopeful approach in a world where the healthcare system often seems primarily motivated by financial gain—particularly the U.S. healthcare system, very different from other countries like Canada and Germany. The bottom line is that I see all of this as part of the challenging yet rewarding journey—a floating blessing in life.

Every time my son was sick, an overwhelming feeling embraced me, as if I were also on the brink of death. When his condition improved, it was as if my life was given back to me restored, though many scars remain. After this second event, we spun severely; we were profoundly shaken. It is somewhat understandable when adults face hardships; sometimes it seems like a karmic consequence of past actions. But for children, what could be the reason for such suffering? It turns out I had a direct conversation with the Almighty. Was it a reflection of my own past, a way for me to atone through my son's suffering? While I am not perfect, I have led a generally decent law-abiding life, always contributing to my community—something that I always believed in deeply. So, what was the purpose of this torment, God, and how long will it last? My prayers often ended with, "Forgive me, Lord." These prayers gave me some comfort during years of struggle.

I believe we receive messages from God that encourage us with enough hope and patience to find happiness in small things. However, I continued to pray for wisdom. Internally, regrouping happened, which means we always kept moving. "We are alive." You need to face reality because it is your yellow signals lighting up while your head is getting red, saying to you in the midst of brainstorms of looping disappointments, "I cannot believe we won't be able to handle this. I cannot believe there is no medication to mitigate this blood disorder. It is inconceivable there is no doctor working on it and no help other than the hospital's unhelpful prescriptions. I cannot believe that nobody cares. I do not understand that my son's life will be severely impacted, crippled so early." My head started spinning 180 degrees and 24 hours daily, ticking desperately with this elephantine distress.

Moreover, at this point, we were already meeting with families of children with sickle cell, which made these perspectives a reality. It is hard to say what was gloomier as nine out of ten sickle cell families were a pure depiction of what doctors and literature say— a poor life full of suffering and a bankrupted family relying on welfare support with wretchedness everywhere. A few exceptions were those for whom hope and faith were the backbone of courage to keep up in the fight for life. Then, when we looked around and saw our little Caesar still doing something like performing his violin, even in public, smiling, and my family still together, we realized how blessed and rich we were indeed.

From Caesar's early months of life, we sought a thorough physician or hospital that could provide some guidance—at least some hope—for my son. This search, in turn, would indirectly address the growing distress we could see developing. Sadly, it often seems that when we gain an understanding of a specific topic or overcome a small challenge, significant adverse events have already occurred. However, these valuable lessons and critical information have been essential in aiding Caesar's younger sister, Maria-Anita, who was also born with sickle cell anemia, helping her avoid the same fate as her brother. As a result, her condition has remained relatively stable despite spleen sequestration at seven months and a silent stroke a few years ago. She will also need a transplant to be free as her brother is suffering from sickle cell complications in the coming years.

It is crucial to highlight that those born with sickle cell can become ill at any given time, regardless. Above all, seeing a physician (hematologist) frequently is essential to draw blood for analysis of the disorder's actual progression and prognosis. Indeed, finding healthcare professionals to work with in partnership is the number one demanding step to which we put tremendous effort, but it is quite often the most challenging. Although there are no effective drugs to treat sickle cell anemia aside from bone marrow transplants, we have learned many ways to attenuate the disorder's aggressiveness by boosting the person's immunological system and detoxifying the body. However, none would prevent a person from becoming ill altogether.

If a person with sickle cell ignores a regimen of drinking extra water to keep the body well hydrated, other measures taken will not do much good. Indeed, it is one of the best approaches (from the best medical reviews) and a personal practice that we have undertaken from the beginning. For instance, in the past we sometimes noticed Caesar having some mild swelling crises with or without pain in his hands. Upon examining it more in detail, we usually noticed (but not always) that he had not been drinking much fluid in the last few days. Overall, as the unhealthy cells increase the inflammation index in the body, affecting all the organs, the main goal has been to clean and detoxify as much as possible. Ideally this is an attempt to clean the body's cells as much as possible around the clock, which is technically inviable, but every small step helps. This is why we have been working tirelessly to provide the best for our two children's care.

An extensive list of cellular support supplements—non-traditional medicines with which many are acquainted—has been instrumental in Caesar's survival. Such supplements have shielded him from becoming another figure among those with sickle cell who did not survive. Observing the effects of one stroke is unsettling and devastating, particularly when it can lead to lasting impairments. Now imagine the consequences of three such occurrences. It is noteworthy to mention that strokes are prevalent among those with sickle cell, especially during the tender ages of two to five years, accounting for a significant mortality rate within the community[10].

As a father, the gravity of these statistics is nearly unspeakable. Can one truly envision a mother or a father unwilling to do everything within their power to aid their child? Fortunately, we overcame this distressing period despite the number of people wondering whether we would make it through. Despite all the challenges, it was always clear in my mind that we would achieve success, and we persevered through our trials and tribulations. But the price of our journey, though steep, was one we willingly paid.

---

[10] Parikh, T. et al., 2023. "Pediatric *Sickle Cell Disease and Stroke*¨: A Literature Review". Cureus: https://bit.ly/4coOKX1

Actually, we knew it was high, and better, but we were not aware of its magnitude. Truly, it is better to incur a cost in pursuit of our beliefs than to sacrifice for another's convictions. Ultimately, everything comes with a price, whether overt or hidden. Nothing is without cost.

Our meticulously personal list of health supplements is quite detailed. A list providing most of the major supplements' names alongside their purported benefits partially depicts the remedies we had been using in large part. I occasionally refer to this as our "interplay of modulators for homeostasis support"—its cellular impact. We have been blessed to encounter rare healthcare professionals who dared to think differently when everyone else was part of the so-called mainstream. I still remember the first one, Dr. A, a pioneering figure from whom we sought to learn more about how to handle and further help my son in the future. When Caesar was just a few months old and not experiencing any issues yet we were living in Providence, Rhode Island. Among many instructive lessons we learned from him, this one stood out: "If a child does not want, or refuses, to take or eat something, do not force them; it is because the body cannot handle, digest, does not need it (already had excessively), or in general, it is missing some enzyme." It turned out to be true, with exceptions when some habits and other forces are involved in the decision-making.

Addressing this condition demands both creative and sensible alternatives beyond what is normally considered, making this a hot topic for anyone who reads it. There's no joking around here. Thus, experts' help will always be needed. Eventually, controversy has to be expected, since it is a desperate motion of a family taking diligent actions to save their child. Besides, nobody would be willing to take the heat for the parents. Surely, many other families have been taking another approach, which is their duty alone. Yet we counted on a high level of outstanding, lovely healthcare professionals who provided valuable insights through rich exchange to accommodate the unique needs of my two children born with sickle cell. Simply, we would not be here without them.

At the same time, as reiterated throughout the book, none of these methods offer a cure, nor do they possess the endorsement of major drug regulatory bodies such as the USA's Food and Drug Administration. To date, only bone marrow transplants have been shown to cure sickle cell anemia over the past five decades, as mentioned in the sickle cell anemia references. Despite the growing societal empathy for such holistic natural novelties' efforts, they lack a robust scientific foundation. Although this is the case, their fundamental principles are widely acknowledged by academics, the public domain, and a significant portion of the scientific community. Such a methodology is deemed valid by its principles, albeit lacking the formal validation of approval from any particular agency. However, when trouble reaches you, the last thing you need to know is the name of the solution or where it comes from; you only need to have the hardship eliminated—the issue solved. To be candid, numerous challenges accompany the use of alternative medicines, particularly for those without a background in the medical field. From what I understand, the distinction between someone with health science training and someone without it is based on the quality of observation and impartiality we bear during many years of training. However, common sense combined with a passion to address the issue serves both sides. It's imperative to know the right amount, possible side effects, and how each person's body responds because everyone is different. These considerations are crucial and challenging, as they are for any prescribed drug.

Thus, my aim has never been to advocate for our specific method. Yet some may question the wisdom of such an approach implementing those lacking "formal approval," basing their decisions on endorsements rather than mere conjecture and speculation. To this, I would state that in my dual role as a father and scientist, observing my son's distress without an effective treatment, I would embark on any avenue in good faith to diminish his discomfort. The stark alternative of witnessing his torment, with only morphine to offer relief, was both agonizing and unreasonable. Even treatments in the experimental phase, lacking official endorsement, seemed a better option in such dire straits.

Furthermore, debates continue regarding the use of drugs that are not yet approved, especially as the world grapples with emerging pandemics once again, which have never been a new phenomenon. My perspective on this matter is straightforward: Decisions should hinge upon individual circumstances and the extent of suffering. Such determinations should be the prerogative of the family alone, keeping in mind that the true weight of the situation falls squarely upon their shoulders, not the abstract sentiments of spectators, regardless of their social or political-economic status. Ultimately, irrespective of others' opinions or rights to voice their agreement or dissent, it is the individual and their family who bear the consequences of any potential adverse outcomes. For instance, in our experience, every medical oversight we encountered left us to cope alone—nobody ever took any responsibility, even when the mistakes were obviously theirs—just "sorry" for this, for that. Reflecting on a specific one during Caesar's third stroke in 2014, no accountability was assumed by the hospital, leaving our family to grapple with the repercussions. Anything beyond this acknowledgment borders on insincerity.

I am positively convinced that one of the main strengths of our methods, though not promising any cure, is rooted in fundamental science, which boasts millions of peer-reviewed publications. Unfortunately, only a tiny percentage of the findings from these scientific principles are translated into health applications for many reasons that are not relevant to delve into here. Alternatively, anyone willing to invest in learning its further applications—which, once more, I do not advocate—might discover new avenues and perspectives otherwise unavailable. In fact, we met countless families whose health dilemmas were addressed based on an out-of-the-box approach fairly similar to the one we attempted to use— at least mitigations were provided. Massive credit goes to them.

CAESAR'S THIRD STROKE

It occurred on the last day of July 2014. I remember it like yesterday, mainly because it happened on a Saturday, a day when we usually do not do much—it has always been our rest and play day. On the preceding Friday, we had received a punching bag toy for Caesar's amusement. His mother takes great joy in assembling any equipment that arrives at the house. She set it up in the living room but we planned to play with it another day—perhaps Sunday. Here are two other important details from that day: I recollect a vivid image of him walking from the front yard toward the house with his sister, Maria-Anita; at another point he was playing in a large room of our house, sitting inside a cardboard box with his toys.

This episode happened around lunchtime. Then, evening arrived, and the day was over. We went to watch a show via YouTube, a common amusement for us that gave us a relaxing moment to breathe a bit. In a situation like ours, to endure or literally survive, we count on the blessing of moments; we find something that recharges us, otherwise any one of us might simply become overwhelmed. Mamma brought his food for me to help him—he has been eating slowly since he was very little. The last thing we wanted to happen was his body not getting food because the little he eats is better than nothing. A weak body without food would not remain alive long enough to tell the story. As a matter of fact, there are plenty of studies showing that even in a hospital setting or at home, there is a clear difference between those with illnesses who eat versus those who do not. For some reason, at that time I was already in charge of feeding him, not because I wanted to, but out of necessity. Furthermore, the doctor and all of us, especially me, were worried about his low weight—through low food intake, a healthy person can perish; now imagine someone whose health is already significantly compromised! That is why there is a common understanding that when we are ill—especially for chronic conditions such as he had, a child—we must view food as medicine that will aid our body to gain more vital nutrients. Otherwise, if we were to rely solely on medications, the drugs might be effective, but the process becomes much more challenging.

As I was feeding him, suddenly and inexplicably, he started screaming, saying that he had a headache and did not want to eat anymore. Obviously, I stopped. But then he began to cry. At first we thought it was just a brief tantrum similar to those he had previously, like once when he threw himself on the floor for a short period of time, before he turned two years old. However, he had never complained of a headache in the past, and this seemed to persist. As he was not stopping, we took him outside the house for some fresh air, but the pain in his head did not subside. Instead, he kept screaming about his headache. His mother and I began exchanging worried glances because this was different from anything we had seen before. We became extra alert and called his doctor right away. The physician replied, saying, "He needs to be seen as soon as possible. Can you easily take him to the nearest hospital?" Previously, we had switched his care from a hospital 15 minutes away (Wake Forest Baptist Hospital) to another health institution: Chapel Hill University, about 100 miles (160.93 km) away from our house. The doctor's question genuinely gripped us because I was more comfortable taking him to Chapel Hill instead, a place he was receiving more comprehensive support (beyond just regular blood transfusions) and that had earned our trust. In this type of situation, trust is fundamental. The main reason we had transferred his care to Chapel Hill at that time was because they had a hematologist team with more compassion, understanding, and comprehensive support for Caesar's needs—our priority in this matter—as well as better outcomes. Caesar also liked the people there more. But we faced this issue of the trip to Chapel Hill being a three-hour drive, while the one to Wake Forest Hospital taking a much shorter time.

The stress of incidents like this is quite tough. We were on the spot. Deciding in the heat of the moment, though it may sound simple, is challenging. What would you have done in our case? Of course, following the doctor's recommendation must take priority, though my heart was telling me to take him to Chapel Hill because of their more effective, all-encompassing medical strategy. Nevertheless, after a brief moment of reflection between his mother and I, we had to decide whether to take him to location A or B. There was a strong heart instinct within us to take him to Chapel Hill, but at the same time, we held another debate about how he would handle the longer trip compared to the shorter one. We also knew comparing the health care services and approaches of the two groups that we had already experienced—that Caesar may not receive the best care if we chose the closer option—an example that the "easiest" quite often does not bring the best outcome. Despite this, we followed the doctor's recommendation and opted for the closer trip. Regardless of the decision a person makes today, its judgment will be possible only in the future. And there are no decisions without consequences. Therefore, those who are not willing to carry the consequences would be more likely not to be involved with decision-making at all. Consequently, it was only later that day that I came to realize the most significant error of my life had been committed—my child received the most unfavorable treatment imaginable. This choice resulted in Caesar having a genuine (hemorrhagic) stroke due to the disorganized approach that delayed his blood exchange for over 24 hours, done in disarray. This procedure is usually performed by an effective machine, as it was done twice before for him, but it was carried out manually in this case. This not only brings higher stress levels for the health care personnel and patients, but the outcome is more doubtful. I often avoid discussing what happened that day. It is more than delicate—it brings me grief and pain that is difficult to describe. From the bottom of my heart, I do think that health care without compassion is pointless.

Furthermore, it is quite common nowadays to either forget crucial details or retrospectively edit the story, coming up with statements like, "Well, I knew it wouldn't work out that way" or, "I suspected that if I had done this or that, things would have turned out better." Or even worse, when it comes from those who have never faced similar adversities—like a soldier who has never spent time in war but poses special advice about this subject in society without bearing scars from being shot in the battlefield— "No, I would do things completely differently; when we reach the future and check our retrograde facts, everyone will have a sweet crystal ball and a lion's courage." Simply put, it is a temptation I choose not to indulge in. Instead, I'd rather stay in the uncomfortably ignorant zone, if you will, admitting: "I did not know many things by then, as I still do not know presently. Given my limited knowledge, I was certainly confused, and my head was full of doubts." In the end, it is almost like crying over spilt milk. It is over. Similarly, it is worthwhile, in my opinion, to discuss facts intellectually and honestly as an exercise, sharing our experiences with society, and to never stop learning.

When all was said and done, the decision to take him to the nearest medical facility came at a high price. The boy entered the facility walking with minor complaints of pain. A doctor checked him quickly and ordered a scan of his brain called a computed tomography (CT) exam. It was found that a small amount of blood had entered a part of the brain called the lateral ventricle. His immediate suggestion was to acquire a more comprehensive picture via a magnetic resonance imaging (MRI) exam for a more accurate assessment of the brain. This would be logical in normal circumstances; however, it is not acceptable in the context of sickle cell anemia during the type of issue Caesar was experiencing. Had there not been a medical recommendation to conduct an MRI before the blood transfusion, the primary and only option was to perform a blood transfusion where about 90 percent of the person's blood is replaced. Meanwhile, we all held our breath to know what might be happening inside, deep in his brain. The term "confusion" would be the most appropriate description for the situation at hand. The juxtaposition of inexperienced physicians and naive parents are a poor match—both parties should have pushed for a blood transfusion urgently, as it was inevitable. Subsequent steps were overly delayed and handled with clumsiness. When we go back in time to the previous stroke that Caesar suffered less than a year ago, it taught everyone a vital lesson: Blood transfusion is a lifesaving treatment in these circumstances, and therefore it's important to do it right away, in line with all the recommendations by hematologists. There is an undeniable, often understated, well-known struggle when it comes to sickle cell patients—their rights are overlooked or queried to the maximum extent but typically under camouflage. Though I have never weighed much on conspiracy theories, those who are fond of them certainly would find fertile territory in a system akin to this situation.

Every so often, not too sporadically, I find myself questioning why I did not decide to take him to Chapel Hill. We faced too many basic hurdles, all of which were highly predictable and shouldn't have happened in a standard medical practice. Apart from the first odd intervention from the doctor who assisted us when we arrived, all subsequent steps followed in the wrong direction. The primary error was failure to perform a blood exchange using a machine as soon as possible. After 24 hours and all the damage to Caesar's brain, his life was saved by a fortunate shift in the hospital staff rotation where we randomly encountered a doctor who genuinely acted as an angel. We are truly grateful to this physician of Japanese descent—a literal savior—who appeared seemingly from nowhere and brought common sense to what had been a horrific situation that could have ended fatally. They were on the brink of inflicting severe, irreversible damage to his brain through an excessive manual infusion of blood, a technique that was inadequate for large blood delivery. However, the older, magnanimous Japanese doctor managed the chaotic situation without any hassle, almost magically, to prevent further brain damage—incredible! At that moment, the misleading approach that had been causing brain damage since the beginning was stopped, at least temporarily. There was a giant sigh of relief, but it was not over yet.

Caesar was transferred from the ICU to a standard hospital room for further observation and continuous recovery. Then he had another setback due to yet another instance of medical negligence, which undermined some of the progress he was making. His limbs (arms and legs) were weak but somewhat functional; he was responding to the combined physical and occupational therapies (PT/OT). Every day two occupational and a physical therapist would come to work with him—outstanding PT/OT practitioners. Initially, he was unable to walk at all, but after a few days, he was already responding quite well to the therapist's efforts. He was able to brush his teeth on his own with minimal help. With continued professional support, they helped him strive for baby steps in his recovery; he was starting to be able to use both hands, especially the right one, which was a significant achievement.

The intriguing aspect of hope is that if we possess it, it can prompt us further. It somewhat resembles a scene of a completely lost boat sinking in the ocean, but then a piece of driftwood appears on the horizon. Thus, through hope, one begins to visualize this driftwood as a new boat. Relying on your faith keeps your inner fire lit no matter what. It won't succumb, allowing you to swim with determination even in the depths of despair. In such a sense, faith here is quite a practical and sincere approach in our favor. That became the atmosphere in the room—everyone began to be hopeful about the possibility of Caesar's full recovery. You could see it both in his eyes and ours, but before that, it was not quite this way. He was silent. Caesar has always been a child with some unique characteristics—he is always smiling and very often laughs uncontrollably—musically—like his father.

With his sister Maria-Anita, they typically spent most of the day together (mainly because they have been homeschooled from the start), and most of this time, when not studying, they are "oddly" playing like old-fashioned children with few or no electronics around. That is the way in which they have been raised. Now, after that incident, he was in bed with a pained face and almost no sign of life, one would say. Then another angel showed up. "Caesar, you must smile and laugh; otherwise, you won't get better..." said his best companion, Maria-Anita. Thereafter, out of nowhere, little Caesar started doing what he loves to do as if he were not in a hospital. A nurse ran to the room to check what was going on, and she was amazed. As a result, that room became filled with enthusiasm, encouraging our belief that soon we would be out of there.

We were excited to see how well he would do the next day in this scary situation. It is worth mentioning that we usually handle these types of situations as a family—the four of us were together in a room that I would describe as comfortable because we never cared about these aspects. I spent time on a little sofa; his mother—who was about five months pregnant with Helen—and Maria-Anita, rested on that typical large, flexible hospital chair—quite comfortable, too. Our least concern was our comfort rather than Caesar's condition. In fact, we have already learned these basic lessons—sacrifices must be made to arrange close family support, which is fundamental in delicate situations; all of the resources and love must be directed toward aiding recovery.

After a few days slipped away under these intensifying situations, Caesar started complaining of pain in his stomach. Obviously, we immediately suspected what it could be and quickly called for a nurse. Nurses and doctors came, but then he started crying. He was constipated, having gone over a week without any bowel movement. Finally the medication for constipation came, but the more physicians came, the more he cried, which escalated to a terrifying scream. Within hours, everyone had the worst expectations about what might have happened to this little child. To make this sad account short, finally, he had a bowel movement and slept. The next day, *all* the progress in movement that he had been gaining so far was gone. Certainly the uncontrolled and immense stress of crying for almost two hours brought further brain damage, which carried a huge cost to him and all of us. Later on I checked whether there were discrepancies in hospital care for sedentary patients, but in such a situation, it was more a matter of procedure and common sense. In general, at long last, when mistakes occur in this world of hospitals, no matter what, you have to take the "sorry," and that is the end of it—the family is the only one to carry on with all the consequences. All Caesar needed when he was moved from the ICU was simple bowel movement (anti-constipation) medicine. We spent a few more days in that room while we arranged for a transfer to another hospital that had an intensive care unit for post-stroke recovery, the Levine Children's Hospital in Charlotte. They provided another treatment and helped very professionally. In total, we spent around 40 days in hospitals this time. Thereafter, we returned home with our son alive, not able to even sit by himself. But again, without hope, our destiny would have quite certainly descended into the abyss of despair.

Meanwhile, while we were with him in Charlotte for his intensive treatments, the National Geographic company reached out to us, wanting to produce a documentary about Caesar's journey. They spent about six months recording everything, checking all documents with meticulous attention to the utmost detail. This documentary (https://bit.ly/3r1b7Pj) was a game changer in our lives, spreading Caesar's story globally. Several positive events offset the negatives. Among them was a company called BEMER[11], which produces a device that gently and wirelessly stimulates muscles, increasing local circulation and enhancing muscle performance. BEMER therapy brought a sea of change at a crucial time when we were desperately seeking anything to avoid new strokes and help Caesar manage the constant pain he was experiencing. When a family is caring for an ill child, there is no measure too big to help soothe their pain.

Without getting too much into technical detail, BEMER therapy did exactly what we were looking for. The direct effects of the therapy were quantified and documented by his specially scheduled medical visits, daily behavioral observation, and level of physical and mental activity. By an unexplained coincidence, BEMER was holding its national medical conference in San Diego, California in 2015. They invited Caesar to perform for them, which he did, playing Bach's "Air" on the G-string just over a year after that horrible third stroke. That overwhelming ovation gave us all the priceless motivation to move on. In conjunction with all the mainstream medical approaches and our novel ones, all together they aided in the mitigation of any more strokes.

Meeting happy people is more than a blessing, especially those who have undergone similar situations and emerged victorious.

---

[11]Klopp RC, et al., 2013. *"Effects of physical stimulation of spontaneous arteriolar vasomotion in patients of various ages undergoing rehabilitation"*. J Complement Integr Med: https://bit.ly/3zuIf6x also: https://bit.ly/45ObxsT

They are not only experts, like soldiers from fearless battles, but also magnetic figures who inspire us to keep going no matter what. Their stories naturally inspire sympathy and uplift us, speaking directly from experience. The truth is, when you are grappling with an illness, for instance (or similarly with financial or other vicissitudes), this is all that you need: sincere friends, if any are left—real in all the senses that the word might bring, experienced folks opening up their hearts. Alternatively, a purgative (or selective) movement may push away the mostly fake and insincere people, leading to a spiritual, didactic, and synergetic moment for the family. It's when you understand the meaning of this popular phrase: "...better to be alone than in false company..." Around that time, to make matters even harder, I was already without a job.

Close to that time, when we returned home, we learned some sour news. Although we still had what we considered reliable health insurance, they would pay for just 20 sessions of physical therapy in a year. Rushing to give some relief to the child, in just one month Caesar's right to have this valuable service evaporated. Catching up by paying from pocket was quite impossible; just about this time, I had to dig into my last resources to keep going. Then we met a genius physiotherapist, Mr. David Dietz. In the first physical therapy session he taught Caesar how to sit up by himself. It was totally incredible. This comes as a reminder of the old Socratic saying about ignorance—we know nothing.

The simple fact is that Mr. Dietz, a humble healthcare professional working in a meager lodging facility, solved a basic problem that his colleagues 40 days prior were unable to solve. When we are in good shape, healthy, able to eat by ourselves, dress, sit, see, etc., all of these things are just simple activities. We rarely think much of it; we don't pay any attention to these whatsoever. On the contrary, we only begin to value things around us, even the most basic ones, like being able to see, walk, speak, breathe through our nostrils, and go to the bathroom alone, when we have those vital senses threatened. Ideally, we would learn to give higher regard priority and be even more grateful to these core principles of life, not taking those things for granted-at least not too much.

When Caesar began to recover all those "small" things, regaining the lost ground little by little, I was determined to learn from all of these dedicated healthcare professionals how to replicate any helpful therapy at home to speed up his recovery. At the height of this turmoil, his sibling Helen, who is genetically matched to him, was born in December 2014. Helen's stem cells were used for his successful bone marrow transplant in 2021. The chance that we could have lost her and consequently ended up locking Caesar in forever to blood transfusions to keep him alive was real. Throughout this time, he was under what is called "chronic blood transfusion," a medical procedure to give extra blood to the patient because anemia is literally a lack of blood.

It is imperative to understand the basic principle on which life exists—a fine balance must occur. Therefore, what turns out to be too much, too little or out of balance could be bad. Consequently, blood by many means represents life. However, a person having a big volume of it in a given day every month risks overwhelming the body. Though in an emergency accident, for instance, or an abruptly lost organ such as spleen sequestrations, it is undoubtedly lifesaving and ultimately the last resource. Unfortunately for many sickle patients with no other means for help, it is the last remedy to keep a body alive. Even though blood transfusion is considered a relatively safe procedure, it is still susceptible—at very low risk—to contamination. In fact, having it chronically, over time it becomes a toxic product to the body and all the vital organs, especially with iron overloading. However, the degree of aggression varies from individual to individual, depending on how long a person remains under treatment. Yet some individuals are unable to survive without it, or at least find it too challenging to maintain a comfortable level of functioning, as demonstrated by Caesar's case. His metabolism is very fast, similar to an automobile that uses a lot of fuel. Combined with the most aggressive type of sickle cell he had, it puts an ultimate strain on the body. Consequently, his body requires more blood than usual—a realization that came as an afterthought. Nevertheless, due to being long-term under this approach, all his vital organs were already being affected by the blood toxicity (iron overload) to the point that some physicians were already suggesting removing organs such as his spleen and performing surgery in his brain. It is tough to write the words now, even after everything is over. There is no easy way by any means to navigate in this arena, though some physicians believed that by doing this or that, everything would be okay. This is where we learn the meaning of parenting. I never imagined this would be so challenging.

One would say Caesar is very fortunate for having his bone marrow transplant at the National Institutes of Health, NIH. Considering Caesar's health, it is not an overstatement to say that this agency is the best in the world by far. Consider their approach devoid of extra stress—notably, without surgeries, as nearly all the other transplant centers had suggested, it mirrors a narrative straight out of a film—a fictional, magical, alien story, yet it is indeed a terrestrial reality. However, astonishing as it may sound— as it is in the case of Caesar—this, in truth, is what they deliver to the American people and folks from all over the world daily.

Nearly ten years since that last stroke, after I stopped my career as a scientist to be fully dedicated to my son's cause, as well as the whole family enduring indescribable stress to survive, much of the damage has been reversed. Thus far, some damage, particularly to his legs, has not been healed yet. Though Caesar's bone marrow transplant cured him of sickle cell, all of the prior extensive demands caused great damage. Over time, he will overcome all of these challenges. In the end, our survival and Caesar's overcoming and well-being loudly speak for themselves as what can only be described as a true miracle.

VITAMIN SUPPLEMENTATION
A HOLISTIC APPROACH

Sickle cell anemia can lead to a range of health conditions, including severe illness and death. However, there are also mitigation measures available, such as providing a supplement to the body for its fight for life. Meanwhile, though the person may appear in sound health, the underlying illness remains. The main challenge is to be able to repeat whatever means are working. In summary, vitamins serve to provide the body with sustained support against the 24-hour, incessant onslaught of inflammation resulting from the breakdown of compromised cells. This deterioration impacts nearly every function within the body since the system is affected; consequently, the body labors intensively, striving with utmost diligence to counteract such constant debilitation and deficiencies. In the ensuing sections, we shall delve into a select number of examples that elucidate this phenomenon.

Truly, the natural consumption of organic and unprocessed foods took a vital place in our journey from the start. A considerable portion of today's health ailments originate from our dietary choices—somewhat ridiculous—from the food we eat. Thus, for an individual who truly aspires to lead a wholesome life, the focus must be on healthful, unprocessed foods. If a person carries some health preconditions (as Caesar was born with sickle cell anemia), it must be evaluated to figure out the best natural food for them. It may pose a number one demand for tasks ahead.

It has been clear in my mind since the beginning, especially when I read some articles on a rural isolated African community stating that decades ago they found folks with sickle cell but with no symptoms. When a true investigation was pursued, it was found that the reason they had few to no symptoms was due to their pure diet, while those in another community who had a normal diet experienced "normal" complications. Reading those findings influenced my whole thinking about this matter above anything else and brought a simple idea: How about we have a rich natural diet and supplement it as much as possible with all that may be missing? This might sound straightforward, but it's a huge challenge living in modern cities and having a life fashioned by processed foods with many electronics working in opposition to nature and organic living, as we dreamed. The old dilemma is that if you work to solve a big problem, you may reach a minor goal first that will propel the small gains to the next step, and so on until you achieve your set goal. In other words, being humble always pays off.

Yet again, from a biological perspective, a predominant reason many individuals face health issues initially stems from their food intake, a connection often overlooked or entirely missed. Our aim should be to eschew entirely processed foods and sugary beverages, striving wherever possible for organic, raw food sources. This aligns with the fundamental objective of nourishment— feeding the body with vitamins and minerals is essential for life. Adopting this approach can be as perplexing as balancing on a tightrope, from the challenges of modifying long-established habits to the practicalities of locating and affording these food sources, despite having been near such practices historically. Yet this strategy is at the heart of our holistic perspective on health and is undeniably sound.

Following is a quick preview of a large, comprehensive physiology of our approach:

Water: This elixir of well-being is more than relevant in keeping the body hydrated. Ensuring adequate hydration is beneficial not merely for those with sickle cell, but it also fortifies the body's detoxification pathways—a profoundly important function, particularly for people with sickle cell anemia. Additionally, it enhances the health of individual cells and the entire organ system.

Chlorophyll: Analogous to the vital role that blood plays in transporting oxygen and nutrients throughout the human body, chlorophyll is indispensable for plants in the process of photosynthesis where light is transformed into energy. Hence, chlorophyll is sometimes poetically referred to as the "blood of plants." This vibrant green pigment, present in plants and algae, has been valued for its health-promoting attributes for years, particularly owing to its significant alkaline properties. These properties are especially pertinent in combating the acidic, oxidative, and inflammatory environments within cells.

It is notable to mention that the bodily environment of individuals with ailments like sickle cell anemia exhibits certain biochemical similarities to that of cancer patients, particularly in the context of increased acidity—shifting away from the alkaline towards the acidic end of the pH spectrum. Such heightened acidity is often the precursor to a cascade of clinical symptoms and complications that can adversely affect every organ in the body and disrupt physiological processes. Given these challenges, chlorophyll has been employed as a counteractive measure. Through continual refinement (e.g., a daily learning journey) of its application and consistent efforts in understanding its optimal use, chlorophyll has indeed demonstrated its therapeutic potential in our journey for many years.

Vitamin C: Ascorbic acid is possibly the most well-known of all vitamins found in most fruits and vegetables. Observing the expansive roles of this vitamin is truly enlightening. This essential nutrient fortifies white blood cells, a network likened to an army dedicated to safeguarding our health and battling foreign invaders—boosting the immune system's network of cells. Like vigilant soldiers, these cells are entrusted with preserving our bodily integrity. Notably, for those with sickle cell conditions, vitamin C's potent antioxidant properties are paramount for everyone. Yet they are especially critical for those with sickle cell anemia or any condition requiring extra support for the immunological system as these individuals need it in much greater quantities to sustain physiological functions.

This vitamin strengthens the body's defenses and plays a pivotal role in synthesizing collagen—a protein essential for maintaining our skin, cartilage, tendons, ligaments, and blood vessels. Furthermore, collagen is instrumental in wound healing and without sufficient vitamin C, our body's ability to produce and store collagen diminishes. The vast array of studies heralding vitamin C's contributions towards bone health, cardiovascular disease prevention, and myriad other fundamental biological functions is truly remarkable and, fortunately, as instructive as it is supposed to be. Furthermore, emphasizing the indispensability of vitamin C for optimal health is never redundant.

Given the continuous health challenges faced by those with sickle cell disorders, coupled with the immense toll on a body undergoing stress 24 hours without respite, a consistent regimen of this vitamin—alongside other vital nutrients and trace minerals—becomes indispensable to holistic well-being irrespective of one's health status. The need is even more pronounced for those with health complications, albeit with certain exceptions. Vitamin C enhances iron absorption, and for those with an excess of this mineral (iron overload), its intake may be counterproductive[12].

---

[12] *"Vitamin C, Fact Sheet for Health Professionals", 2021. National Institutes of Health*: https://bit.ly/3LarPmh

This was particularly pertinent to Caesar. Due to the regular blood transfusions he received to prevent potential strokes, he was totally averse to foods rich in vitamin C because it boosts iron absorption. This aversion was instinctual—any such food introduced, upon reaching his mouth, would be immediately regurgitated. This is because it risked elevating his iron levels dangerously, mirroring conditions like hemochromatosis, another genetic disorder characterized by iron overload.

Barring these specific circumstances, vitamin C is part of our functional foundation of life. However, because it is water-soluble, our body expels any surplus swiftly through urine, rendering daily replenishment essential. Ideally, one would derive all of these vitamins and trace minerals from natural dietary sources. Yet with the degradation of our soils over recent decades, the nutritional value of our produce has waned—a decline challenging to measure, regardless of the assurances or certifications provided by a product. To expand on this thought, in an ideal world one would think of their sustenance from nutrient-rich soils. This notion kindles reflections on lifestyles from bygone eras, aligning with nature's standards for a nutrient-dense diet[13].

Vitamin D: Called the "sunshine vitamin," this is a fat-soluble vitamin that plays an essential role in various bodily overlapping functions and is seen as an enhanced layer of protection for the body, including but not excluded to aiding bone health, part of the immunological system regulator with muscular system and

---

[13] Giannakourou, CM et al., 2021. *"Effect of Alternative Preservation Steps and Storage on Vitamin C Stability in Fruit and Vegetable Products"*: Critical Review and Kinetic Modelling Approaches. Foods: https://bit.ly/3RUCxRP

reducing inflammation[14, 15]. This provides top protection against respiratory infections (e.g., influenza and even COVID-19[16]) since the virus host organ—the lungs—is one of the places where vitamin D is synthesized. We take giant doses (50,000 IU) and extra water to avoid low oxidation levels and to protect the kidneys. Interestingly, data show that the toxicity of high doses of vitamin D is due to insufficient levels of magnesium, vitamin K, and zinc, which are well covered in our holistic protocol. As expected, vitamin D partially overlaps many roles such as bolstering the immune system, addressing calcium deficiencies common in sickle cell patients, and promoting bone and tooth health by fostering the growth of osteoblasts—new cell formation inside our bones. We must never neglect the solid foundation that vitamin D offers when working in concert with other vitamins (particularly vitamin A, K2, and vitamin C, just to name a few). This is especially pertinent given that a significant portion of illnesses have their roots in some type of inflammation. These vitamins possess the potential to reduce inflammation, thereby underscoring their importance in maintaining health.

Vitamin K2/7: The Menaquinone7 (MK-7), whose vast role goes beyond assisting vitamin D, activates the calcium-binding actions of two proteins—matrix GLA protein and osteocalcin/BGLAP—cracking the calcium packet inside our vascular wall and sending it to the place that is needed—bones and teeth. Many studies depict

---

[14] Kai Yin et al., 2014. *"Full article: Vitamin D and inflammatory diseases".* J Inflamm Res : https://bit.ly/3L8bYor

[15] Wu, Z, et al., 2022. *"The Role of Vitamin D in the Immune System and Inflammatory Bowel".* J Inflamm Res: https://bit.ly/3zBI9tA

[16] Cutolo, M, et al., *"Evidence for a protective role of vitamin D in COVID-19", 2020.* RMD Open: https://bit.ly/4bsbowh

it as an overlapping role of building and maintaining bones that vitamin D performs[17]. Furthermore, vitamin K2/7 potentially helps to prevent heart problems by inhibiting vascular stiffness[18]. The trend of studies rises every day with new findings on vitamin K2's health benefits, and it will soon surpass our current underrated understanding of its benefits; therefore, it will be the popular super supplement in the near future[19].

Zinc: This trace element is essential, signifying that our body cannot naturally synthesize it, yet it is paramount in numerous physiological operations within the human system. It is integral to the proper functioning of our immune system, given its role in regulating enzymes. [20] And the body, healthy or not, cannot operate without the enzymatic system. Astonishingly, over 300 enzymes depend on zinc for their activities, encapsulating the metabolism of proteins, nucleic acids, carbohydrates, and lipids[21]. Delving deeper, zinc is instrumental in shaping the robust bacterial flora of our gut, which in turn orchestrates our defense mechanisms. This relationship augments our immunological readiness, offering heightened protection against infections and stimulating an anti-inflammatory response[22]. The dynamic link between the immune

[17]Zhang, M, et al., 2024. *"Roles of vitamin K-dependent protein in biomineralization" (Review)*. Int J Mol Med: https://bit.ly/4bzOYcu

[18]Yan, Q, et al. 2023. *"The biological responses of vitamin K2: A comprehensive" (Review)*. Food Sci Nutr: https://bit.ly/3L7kpQR

[19] Roohani, N et. al., 2013. *"Zinc and its importance for human health: An integrative review"*. J Res Med Sci : https://bit.ly/3LcssvO

[20] Scarpellini, E, et al., 2022. *"Zinc and gut microbiota in health and gastrointestinal disease under the COVID-19-19 suggestion"*. BioFactors: https://bit.ly/3VINnes

[21]Vallee, BL et al., 1993. *"The biochemical basis of zinc physiology"*. Physiol Review: https://bit.ly/3VPBSSH

[22] Fraker, PJ, et al., 2000. *"The dynamic link between the integrity of the immune system and status"*. The Journal of Nutrition: https://bit.ly/3L7lI7P

system integrity and zinc status has been the subject of thorough scholarly[23] exploration.

Selenium: Selenium represents another essential trace mineral of utmost importance to human health[24]. It plays a critical role in supporting the proper functioning of the thyroid gland, especially in the synthesis of thyroid hormones[25]. The role of selenium in the thyroid gland has a body of literature supporting it[26]. Furthermore, selenium exhibits potent antioxidant properties, making it an invaluable tool, particularly for sickle cell patients. Its ability to combat various aggressors, including certain metals, extends its protective benefits, preventing cellular damage that can lead to chronic diseases such as heart ailments and cancer[27]. Besides boosting the immunological system functions, preventing damage from free radicals, and supporting cognitive function, selenium is **natural brain protection**.

Magnesium: This mineral, with the broad spectrum of healthy, useful discoveries over the last decades, could easily be called the chief mineral since our body cannot work without it. It regulates virtually all of the metabolic processes in our synthesis and two to three at the genetic level[28]. Given that vitamin D regulates the

[23] Prasad, A, et al., 2008. *"Zinc in Human Health: Effect of Zinc on Immune Cells"*. Molecular Medicine: https://bit.ly/45NpxDf

[24] Bachelli, G, et al., 2022. *"The Role of Selenium in Pathologies. An Updated Review"*. Antioxidants (Basel) : https://bit.ly/3VKrZWm

[25] Köhrle J. et al., 2015. *"Selenium and the thyroid"*. Curr Opin Endocrinol Diabetes Obes: https://bit.ly/3ROBlz1

[26] Brigelius-Flohé, R, et al., 2013. "Glutathione peroxidases". Biochim Biophys Acta: https://bit.ly/4crOpTl

[27] Rayman, MP, et al., 2005. *"Selenium in cancer prevention: a review of the evidence and mechanism of action"*. Proc Nutr Soc: https://bit.ly/4bupj4Y

[28] Swaminathan, R, et al., 2003 *"Magnesium Metabolism and its Disorders"* Clin Biochem Review: https://bit.ly/4eNUZ8o

synthesis of roughly 40,000 genes in our body and considering that magnesium is essential for ensuring this regulatory function performs appropriately, there is ample reason to advocate for their more frequent use.

As mentioned before, having sickle cell in many ways resembles the limitations of an older person whose slew of restrictions includes being unable to endure many activities such as walking five kilometers, even though we are talking about a young person functioning this way. Yet, the body's aim is just one: surviving. To accomplish this, it performs all kinds of physiological and biochemical functions to compensate for what is missing. For example, people with sickle cell problems have deficits in growth. Though the publications with valuable findings on using magnesium to mitigate sickle cell crisis[29] shine brightly and sound promising, it is akin to the idea of a remedy that might help you sleep better. However, more studies are needed to make such a statement definitive. It is highly unlikely that a person who seeks to improve their sleeping habits—and takes remedy A or B—will care about any study as long as the remedy is effective.

Honestly, this topic could fill an entire chapter, focusing on alternative remedies combined with raw whole foods taken as medicine. Still, delving too deeply might shift our focus from the central narrative of my son's saga. Nevertheless, acknowledging these alternative solutions is essential as they played a pivotal role in preventing Caesar's health from worsening significantly. Among these, I must highlight this last one—folate, or vitamin B9—and its

---

[29] Than, NN, et al., 2017. *"Magnesium for treating sickle cell disease".* Cochrane *Database* Syst Review: https://bit.ly/4cp9DRV

synergy with vitamin B12, both vital for DNA synthesis and repair, and crucial for red blood cell formation among several other vital roles to sustain the body as healthily as possible. And in his case at that time—not healthy—more crucial than anything while we waited for his bone marrow transplant. Notably, folate-rich foods include leafy greens, legumes, and nuts, while iron sources feature red meat and dark leafy vegetables. The challenge was to effectively incorporate iron-rich foods, particularly balancing those against the backdrop of his elevated iron levels due to regular blood transfusions, necessitating careful dietary management to avoid exacerbating his iron intoxication condition.

Moreover, you will rarely find a physician encouraging the use of magnesium, citing concerns about side effects, albeit those effects were minuscule compared to pharmaceutical drugs and there is no medication without any side effects. It is more straightforward to be honest regarding this topic. Furthermore, it is essential to clarify that even water, if consumed excessively, could have some side effects, just as a sleep-inducing tea could lead to oversleeping and missing the beginning of the next day, causing unexpected issues. As simple as it sounds, nothing comes without risks; it is all about how you weigh the proportions and then decide whether it is worth doing or not. Nevertheless, potential side effects from these holistic approach remedies are negligible compared to the severe side effects and risks of industrialized drugs, some of which can lead to death. Equally important to highlight is that a great effort was made to obtain the best quality of those supplements, given the reality that the market is full of contaminated products, which could equally bring serious health issues. Therefore, obtaining a pure product is key to achieving expected results. This issue is further exacerbated by the lack of healthcare professionals' training in science, which results in less bias towards pharmaceutical drugs and opens up the potential for exploring other treatment methods to benefit the patient. Fortunately, in some countries (like the U.S.), states and individuals still have some leverage to fight for their rights, although this process is often stressful and full of challenges. Indeed, our primary objective is to enhance the immune system's efficacy. Thus, these vitamins and trace minerals (general health supplements) aim for such a specific purpose alone. If we consider only one of those specific vitamins/hormones (vitamin D), it depicts a depth of benefits that can shock anyone unaware of its potent health's goodness. Excessive inflammation can cause a myriad of health issues, including cancer, and is a primary concern for individuals with sickle cell anemia from day one. Over time, this over-accumulation of inflammation can lead to various health complications such as strokes. Those born with this anemia experience exceptionally high inflammation levels due to their genetic predisposition and the toxic environment within their bloodstream. Given this understanding, it is not surprising that I hesitated when a physician prescribed daily antibiotics for my few-month-old child as a preventive measure against infections. Fortunately, I understood the twist in calling it a "baby antibiotic" and other similarly naive and misleading names. Despite certain studies supporting a particular medical study approach, a substantial number of these so-called medical studies are prone to bias and lack of scientific rigor. Regardless of medical or scientific credentials, anyone can recognize the flaws in such studies. Studies that pursue, interpret, or analyze responses to questions driven by interests other than academic, inherently contain biases, rendering them scientifically invalid.

Our exhaustive list of supplements and vitamins, including zinc, vitamin K, colostrum, spirulina, chlorella, chlorophyll (too alkaline for the body), was tailored to fortify the body for prolonged resilience and to provide relief from the ailment's hallmark symptoms, limiting prescribed drugs, whose side effects everyone is familiar with. In contrast, our list of remedies offers virtually zero collateral effects. Thus, compared to prescription drugs, the eventual reactions from our natural approach were minimal. When they happen, they are due to dosing, purification, poor critical analysis, or decision-making. This matter is tricky to use properly because not everyone has the steam to navigate through the biases and remain impartial, especially when such learning takes time. At the same time, we are talking about our own children—our deep assets. In other words, this does not represent an easy road, though it may appear light.

As brought up in the introduction of this book, the splendor of our U.S. Constitution lies in its protection of free speech, granting every individual the freedom to voice their thoughts and opinions. This liberty is perhaps the most precious gift from our nation's founders. Under this banner, we are all entitled to say such things, though we do not intend to induce others to follow our path or jump right into it. We strongly recommend consulting your healthcare professional, doctor, religious leader, family members, and any other authority entitled to your health and well-being before making a final decision. The author, publisher, and seller have no responsibility for any decision you may make from reading this book; therefore, if you do anything upon reading this book, it is your own responsibility. To offer some personal disclosure, my father being a pharmacist and myself a neuroscientist, this gives me an inclination towards "endogenous" industrial pharmacology, which has provided a valuable service, and nobody denies it. On the other hand, however, there is room for those who want to blend a natural approach with industrial pharmacology that is perfectly acceptable, especially considering that the active principles of many drugs come from nature—the primary source of holistic approaches we rely on.

The harsh realities of life eventually teach us all the practical truth of what works best and what does not, or what carries too many side effects and other complications. However, I do not intend to suggest a shortcut to getting things done. Overall, no one is intentionally ignorant; no one has access to all information at any given time. Yet, once one grasps some understanding of this or that, the challenge becomes whether we are able and willing (with the courage and capability) to implement it or not.

Finally, I must say that there are many people and institutions that are entirely against our health approach and the path we chose, though what we did was based on our conscience, knowledge, and belief, which ultimately saved my child's life. It was worth it. We were confronted with the formidable reality of welcoming into the world a child plagued by health challenges that medical experts viewed with a bleak outlook. Having experienced desperation as a father and empathizing with many mothers, I found myself willing to take any opportunity to safeguard my child's life, which is the parents' fundamental responsibility. This sentiment is especially poignant considering that hope rarely reaches dormant minds. An imperative arose to act. In pursuit of this objective, we were blessed with an unwavering determination and resilience the divine bestowed upon us during these challenging circumstances. Caesar's successful bone marrow transplant in 2021 marked the start of a new chapter in his life.

This book is a testament to our journey and the path we pursued. Since the transplant, the once-fragile child has transformed into a teenager with remarkable potential. This is only the beginning of prospecting a new life. His special endowment is comparable to a delicate sapling that requires the utmost care to mature into a fruitful tree. If we had relied solely on traditional medicine, my son might have joined the tragic statistics of those lost to this blood disorder. This sad reality stems from the fact that conventional medicine solely focuses on addressing the problems and symptoms rather than their roots and often overlooks all alternative approaches, many of which are entirely unknown to them, thus ignoring the traditional and fundamental principle of innovation that is essential to tackle complex health issues. Fundamentally, I am discussing medicine's core principles and foundations, universally acknowledged by physicians. Beyond a handful of recent studies, this domain has little novelty, so this entire topic is essential. Indeed, these principles, often labeled as "biological," establish the groundwork for all individuals in this field. This includes medical students and virtually every healthcare professional from the outset of their educational journey. Therefore, this subject is not about controversy, but about purpose. These foundational principles have profoundly influenced our holistic approach.

However, it is essential to note that these innovative solutions do not promise a cure, as we mentioned multiple times. Instead they aim to provide support, offer an additional day of life, alleviating pressure over stress, reducing pain, suffering, and ultimately, making life less miserable and, if possible, closer to "normal." The most fantastic part of alternative medicines is that if success is not enough, the side effects are frequently irrelevant or zero. Additionally, we used a variety of herbal teas, essential oils, cannabinoids (CBD) oils, etc. Above all, this holistic approach, if you will, was designed to suppress the inflammatory and antioxidant effects, therefore avoiding the aggravation of the disorder. We discovered the importance of essential oils more recently—after the second stroke, unfortunately. Suppose one decides to run any retrograde analysis on "what if I knew this or that." It would be a reliable attempt to become insane, since anything could help based upon such endless suppositions. Essential oils, in our case, are a perfect example. If we had known it before, indeed, Caesar's second stroke would have been averted, at least as it was. A few years later, we would learn about another remedy called CBD, which holds powerful anti-inflammatory properties. They proved to be critical in managing my son's unrelenting allergies, which traditional medications had failed to alleviate. Allergies were a significant factor that contributed to his second stroke. We started using CBD around 2017. We learned more recently that these last two ones, the essential oils, for instance, are critical to dealing with my boy's allergy crises. He never suffered from them again, which no traditional drug was able to cease. It was ultimately the primary factor preceding his subsequent stroke.

Fulvic Acid (FA): I deliberately reserved this natural health product for the final discussion in this section, aligning with our sequential discovery of it. As stated earlier, inflammation index is a fundamental root of illness, with sickle cell anemia causing significant accumulation of inflammation over time. Ayurveda, a branch of Indian medicine, has utilized FA for approximately 3,000 years. Given FA's role as a potent modulator within our gut's microbiome, enhancing digestion (a primary focus), it undeniably aids the body's recovery process, necessitating diverse forms of support[30]. This byproduct of humus contains essential elements for those aiming to prevent illness and particularly for addressing diseases like sickle cell anemia, immunological issues, and diabetes, among others. It is critical to understand that FA is not a panacea, yet it undeniably offers support. Scientific evidence underscores that boosting our defense system invariably benefits our health, suggesting a careful interpretation and reading between the lines of scientific literature as a reliable method to discern truth in published research.

Moreover, autoimmune disorders often stem from a variety of causes, some extensively researched and others less so, leading to an imbalance in our defense system and consequent self-destruction, and thus inducing illness. Besides that, enhancing our immune system is arguably one of the most effective strategies for health management. As previously pointed out, alongside numerous natural health aids, FA has been instrumental in my

---

[30] GOENADI, DH, 2021, "*Fulvic acid – a small but powerful natural substance for agricultural and medical applications*". Menara Perkebunan: https://bit.ly/3XOa5El

family's health, significantly benefiting Caesar and his sister, Maria-Anita, who rarely suffer from common ailments such as colds, even without flu vaccinations. Considering Caesar's history of three strokes, one might ponder the outcome if he had not received such comprehensive care. Indeed, this empirical rationale suggests that an enhanced immune system may effectively protect against numerous health issues and support cognitive well-being. Asserting immunity from all illness or colds is not the intent here, as that falls outside this discussion's purview. For instance, my own severe health episodes, including a near-fatal cardiac arrest for about 30 minutes, which was unnoticed by medical professionals until they received the necessary support for a final successful intervention, illustrate the body's resilience when adequately supported. Similarly, a properly supported immune system may lessen the severity of common illnesses, particularly when optimal vitamin D levels are combined with adequate hydration. Interestingly, our incredibly hectic lifestyle nowadays, akin to indentured servitude, barely allows time for basic activities—almost none for dedicated health management of ourselves or our family. Had I not prioritized family well-being over my academic pursuits, dedicating continuous effort to this cause would have been impossible. Courage may not be the term I would use to describe my actions, yet I am profoundly grateful for the strength and guidance my Heavenly Father God provided to help us persevere during these dire times.

Here are some additional contexts about sickle cell anemia. It is essential to understand that sickle cell is hereditary in nature. This means that Caesar inherited the genes for this disease from his parents, though we do not carry the illnesses, just the genes. Sickle cell is not contagious by any means. It is only transmitted through heredity. Parents who are carriers of the sickle cell trait have a genetic marker for the disorder but do not have the disorder themselves because the gene is not "active" in them. Simply put, when both parents are carriers, their offspring have a 25 percent chance of inheriting the disorder in its active form. This is something they may not be aware of before having children.

Every living being is made of cells, including humans and other animals. Our body is composed of approximately 30 trillion cells[31] and an even higher number of bacteria—though we are not referring to our gut microbiome that has much larger cells—which all together perform essential roles for our health. In basic terms, blood cells—red, white, and platelets—are responsible for sustaining life. Red blood cells, the subject of our focus, account for about 80 percent of the total cells of the human body[32]. Their role is to supply all our body cells with oxygen, akin to how gas (or electricity) powers a car. Therefore, these cells' main function is to travel through our blood vessels to distribute oxygen to all parts of our body continuously, 24 hours a day, regardless of the person's state—whether asleep or awake. Furthermore, the red blood cells have a lifespan of about 120 days, after which they are replaced by the same number, essentially to keep us alive. In a healthy person, red blood cells are smooth, round, and bendable, allowing them to flow easily through blood vessels to distribute oxygen throughout

---

[31] Sander, R, et al., 2023. *"The total mass, number, and distribution of immune cells in the human body"*. PNAS: https://bit.ly/3WahxbW

[32] Nemkov T, et al., 2018 *"Red blood cells as an organ? How deep omics characterization of the most abundant cell in the human body highlights other systemic metabolic functions beyond oxygen transport"*. Expert Review of Proteomics: https://bit.ly/4f34jWf

the body.

In contrast, in a person born with sickle cell anemia, a wide range of percentages (10-70 percent), depending on the degree of the patient's sickness and type (phenotype—the degree of the trait and its genetic interaction) of sickle cell, the red blood cells lose their healthy shape and oxygen-carrying capacity, changing to a sickle, classic leaf, or half-moon shape. Physically, those deformed cells cannot roll in or flow normally through the vascular system, and they can easily get stuck in any part of the body, mainly in the joints. Moreover, they share the same network as healthy cells, traveling throughout the body together. The immune system's relentless attempts to get rid of these abnormal cells are likened to the sublimation of dry ice in summer. Consequently, a person with sickle cell anemia may experience a degree of low energy, with less optimal function across all body systems because the body's energy and resources are primarily focused on maintaining fundamental life functions.

This complex compensatory mechanism varies from person to person. For example, siblings Caesar and Maria-Anita, both born with this blood disorder, have displayed significantly different symptoms and health outcomes since birth. This reflects numerous scientific studies, attributing these differences to their distinct genetic phenotypes. For instance, in Caesar's case, the number of conditions such as weight deficits, spleen enlargement, and liver compromises, to name a few issues, are absent in his sister. This is also because all the learning we gained by dealing with Caesar was applied to her—a novelty that must be weighed greatly in the whole equation. So, given these health challenges, it is nothing short of miraculous that an individual with these conditions can survive and live a full life.

The primary biological characteristic of sickle cell anemia lies in the blood cells losing their physiological functions and energy properties. Then those affected blood cells become ineffective, full of inflammatory properties, and useless minuscule sick bodies running throughout the patient. Stiffness is their prominent physiological attribute, besides being sticky, causing them to block blood flow and break down inside the blood vessels, and resulting in pain. In addition, it results in a mixture of a percentage of sick or inflamed cells and healthy ones overlapping the same environment, potentially causing a range of possible health complications and issues, strokes being just one of those. That is the reason excruciating pain is closely related to sickle cell patients once those unhealthy cells become lodged in any place, mainly at joint articulations and in the extremities: hands, fingers, or feet.

Conversely, it is critical to highlight that there is no cure for this anemia, except for a bone marrow transplant, which Caesar underwent in September 2021 with fantastic results. Indeed, as mentioned earlier, we never overlooked the importance of traditional medicine: pediatric care and hematologists. In fact, the last one, due to the specialized nature of the blood disorder, often took precedence over pediatricians. However, I must emphasize that none of the natural approaches we developed cure anything either. Ideally, they should be running in conjunction with traditional medicine, which we really attempted to do. The goal of the natural or holistic approach is merely to support the cellular principles, which aim to mitigate the negative effects of cellular debilitation. Cellular intoxication, the classic sub-product of sickle cell, increases over time due to the severe impact of sickle cell affecting the remaining healthy ones—and it further triggers a range of health issues.

No one could deny complaints by any means, but we must be careful to avoid making it a sort of safeguard for our limitations, therefore, missing natural opportunities to move forward. Alternatively, though I do complain too, I am always aware of it. It is a given with much complaining that, quite often, the problem is real. While many complaints could not brush off or diminish the trouble, opening up with a friend is indeed like a remedy.

By the time of his first stroke at the age of four, Caesar was deeply involved in music, working on *Suzuki Book 4* and learning Vivaldi's concerto in A minor (https://bit.ly/3Np7mLf), following his accomplishments with Brahms' "Hungarian Dance Number 5" and the national anthems of the USA, Greece, and Brazil. This musical engagement, particularly the Vivaldi piece recording after his first stroke and subsequent discharge from the hospital, showcased his resilience and energy, revitalized by the transfused blood. Organizing a pianist to accompany him, we captured these moments in recordings. Yet six months later another stroke occurred, within a year separating the second and third vascular incidents. This pattern led us to further understand the underlying challenges associated with sickle cell anemia, especially the phenotype of Caesar's.

There is an interesting connection between sickle cell anemia and hemoglobin F transition. Sickle cell anemia can be difficult for children when they are young, especially when they are three to six years old. But it can happen at any time because the body's defense system, called hemoglobin F, becomes weaker. This is applicable to any newborn, whether they are healthy or not, though the healthy ones go unnoticed through this automatic process. This transition from hemoglobin F to adult hemoglobin types (HbA and HbA2) [33] exposes children with this illness to health complications such as pain or even strokes. The lower the level of HbF—a protective protein with a higher affinity for oxygen than adult hemoglobin—the more likely children with sickle cell are to need extra help[34]. Interpreting this logically, as children with sickle cell anemia run out of such vital protection (and energy), they are exposed to a wide array of possible health problems because of the aggressiveness of this blood disorder. Your best bet is to work as hard as possible, do what I call "your homework," find a healthcare professional that you trust, and then whatever comes, you have to face like wrestling a bull. In the end, like anything else in life, if we do good "homework," we should expect a much better result than just dreaming and working a little. Perhaps counting on hope to stir our minds is the number one thing to do. Some studies indicate that when a certain crisis occurs it coincides with the decrease in HbF and when the child recovers, this defense adapts. Moreover, this is often misunderstood as a "disorder of aggressiveness" when, in fact, it is a natural biological event that a child is experiencing, losing a natural protector that serves as a significant immunological ally. All that could be done was to mitigate the issues, apart from a

---

[33] Akinsheye, I, et al., 2011. *"Fetal hemoglobin in sickle cell anemia".* Blood: https://bit.ly/3WcrRAA

[34] Morrison, J C, et al., 1976. *"Fluctuation of fetal hemoglobin in sickle-cell anemia".* Am J Obstet Gynecol: https://bit.ly/4cpagLh

bone marrow transplant, which can provide a 100 percent cure. Unfortunately, back then, our understanding of these concepts was somewhat limited.

CATASTROPHE: CAESAR'S FATHER CHOSE TO END HIS OWN LIFE

My child, who entered the Wake Forest Hospital building walking, ended up in a state where even his eyes were not moving and under strong sedatives to block the pain. It was when a new physician came from his shift and gently tapped on my shoulder, saying, "I don't think he will die, but I wouldn't expect anything from him."

From there, I lost my wits. The medical reason behind such a fate was based on the critical, severe clinical scope of the boy: his brain images, with tracer marks across the areas affected by the stroke, covered the whole encephalon. The massive deterioration occurred after our entrance to the hospital, following our initial meeting with the first physicians promptly after we arrived at the hospital reception, with further and serious complications happening during this crucial time there. For instance, two CT scans—one taken immediately after we were admitted to the hospital (within a few hours) and another taken a few days later while he was still receiving emergency care—revealed distinct differences. The first scan showed the brain was still healthy, with blood in one part and blood in another. However, a second scan, taken nearly a few days later, revealed blood not only in one, but also in both lateral ventricles. The crucial, horrifying part is that blood was observed across various upper parts of the brain (cortex), a clear mark of a devastating hemorrhagic stroke that had just occurred. This was a complication entirely new compared to when we entered the hospital.

These complications were mainly due to the first physician's recommendation after seeing the first CT scan—to have a further image evaluation: a magnetic resonance image and angiogram (MRI, MRA) before the blood transfusion. A hematologist did not see him until the next day. This delay halted any further procedures, such as a blood transfusion, that would have greatly mitigated the brain damage. We were trapped in what felt like a no-win situation. Obviously many mistakes were made. Though the hospital had Caesar's records from previous visits, what was supposed to help with his health profiles did not meet his needs. Unfortunately at that point, my brain was so overwhelmed that I was really not able to fight for the best. I sat between a rock and a hard place, obeying that doctor's recommendation of not doing anything before the MRI, which took 24 hours and delayed the blood transfusion—a recommendation that turned out to be contrary to sickle universal common sense. We were all trapped. Surely, on the one hand, obtaining more detailed images for better diagnostics would have been beneficial, but in this case it has proven to be irrelevant. Rather, accessing the major veins in the neck or groin, as had been successfully done twice before on him, would have been the proper recommendation. It is the normal, standard procedure that was supposed to be performed at the beginning when every minute means further risks because it allows the large blood volume to be exchanged from the body quickly and relatively safely, when nearly all of the blood (up to 90 percent) is replaced. Given the fact that most of his blood cells were a mix of completely broken-down cells and those that were not, it was a struggle to keep the vital organs working. The hospital has only one option in such a case and must work on the clock—run a blood transfusion and if done correctly, it works at a high rate—close to 100 percent. That's why they use a very efficient machine to replace up to 90 percent of the patient's blood. Again, sadly, hospital staff missed these life-saving actions at the start, and when they acted, it was too late.

In a hospital, one day feels like one year. If you consider yourself tranquil, such calmness will be tested. Otherwise, you must learn very fast. On the second day, when those specific images were performed, Caesar did not regain consciousness from the anesthesia used during these sophisticated image exams. When we arrived at the hospital, the CT brain images initially indicated pooling in the lateral ventricle only. However, after the subsequent imaging exams (MRI), it showed widespread antagonistic damage from a real stroke (hemorrhagic, blood spread out in the cortex areas) affecting his brain. These were two different images. Therefore, his clinical presentation deteriorated gravely due to a combination of delay and a dysfunctional medical approach. Ironically, the second CT scan showed that the blood that had pooled in his lateral ventricle (the original cause that brought us to the hospital) was decreasing without any intervention. Though almost ten years have passed, I am still overwhelmed and struggle to describe seeing my son under those circumstances. Finally, after that conversation with the doctor about the prognosis for my son, paired with my understanding of those images showing significant brain damage, I was left with no other option but to entertain thoughts of suicide, which I had never, ever contemplated before.

However, my mother had taught me the best of her Christian faith, constantly trying to apply it in practice. My father passed away when I was two, and he was of Jewish ancestry. As a pharmaceutical businessman, he was very witty and practical. My mother learned an ample amount of information from him, combining practical business matters with life lessons learned from his struggle to succeed. Though I lost both my parents when I was still a child, my whole life has been conducted on a core principle— to honor them forever in my behavior throughout my life. In that sense I have been conveying the life principles my parents instilled in me the best I can to my children. Among the numerous blessings that my mother bestowed upon me, she imparted to me the following instruction: "My son, regardless of your location, situation, or the people you encounter, I humbly request that you pledge to *consult God before making any decisions*." She frequently reminded me of this, asking me to swear it. As a result, this simple guiding principle has never failed me. This time, fortunately I remembered it. I have noticed that every time I've followed this wise guidance, good fortune has come my way, whereas when I did not, disaster was looming. In her mind, she was certain about a few things: 1) she was going to depart early from this world; 2) and her children, especially me, would face tremendous challenges to survive. Fascinatingly, everything I have done, whenever I rendered her recommendations, I succeeded; the contrary is true, too. Fortunately, I recalled her advice in that dire moment—which saved my life, allowing me to write this book today, sharing this story with you.

I heard a loud voice in my heart, saying clearly, "Forget about yourself. Stop!" By asking, "God, I don't know how to end my life, help me find a way..." It was repeated as if it were a petition—for each question, one STOP was given—each one stronger than the last. The strongest third one had a follow-up, "Forget about yourself." To me, it was clearly a providential voice saying to resume my life in different ways and not to commit suicide, period. My instinct drove that car straight back to that dark hospital room when I announced to my wife that, "No matter what, and from now on, the ultimate goal of my life will be focused exclusively on the best effort to recover my son—my work as a scientist is over." Though I could get a new job or position, or even return to Brazil to be a professor there, none of these would match the command to "Forget about yourself." Truly, I do remember that I added: "We may become homeless because we'll be a household without the income we always had."

However, I was not aware of the environment that was waiting for me and my family. One thing was echoing in my head—we would be expelled from society, as it was done in the past to lepers, or simply locked up in a sort of dungeon. Every so often, it is worth not knowing what is coming next because, in numerous instances, due to our lack of courage—or a mix of it and a natural fear of the next reality—knowing what lay ahead would make the fight extra hard and barely survivable. As humans such feelings frighten us more than anything else when we have to move without awareness of where we will end up. My situation was similar to a person who underwent major surgery; therefore, the effect of anesthesia was obscuring all current reality. With each passing minute, such reality would become more overwhelming. Looking ahead, only one thing was present: my breath and a new belief in the hope that we would muster enough faith to fight for my child and my family and not perish. In many ways it was somewhat grim but we were already past that point.

Without income to provide the basic needs, there was no logical reason to believe that the Sant family as a whole, not just Caesar, could survive. Luckily, I was still able to access a little of my memory. It reminded me that the human story is full of passages where, to overcome illogical circumstances and battles, we must face the heart and suggest playing for him that concerto, which is available on YouTube, via my phone. The same concerto he was familiar with was played next to his ear—resting on his pillow atop his head— and to our tremendous surprise, those previously weak vital signals started regaining strength, nearly returning to normal. We were alone in the room, but the nurses and physicians had a standard monitor in a control room that displayed the same vital parameters. When they saw these changes, they rushed to our room. Everything was normal; they had assumed an accident had happened or perhaps a choking incident or convulsion, and instead, they found little Caesar now breathing well and all his signals within a far better range, considering his level of sedation. The medical staff did not even notice the music's presence in the room, which was repeated several times a day. Then they started lowering the sedation level. On the third day or so, he was moved upstairs, out of the intensive care unit (ICU), to a typical hospital room for further evaluation and better rest. A clear fundamental milestone was achieved toward recovery—a very long journey ahead of us. From that point onward, it has been a lengthy journey to arrive at our present circumstances.

THE BROADER CONTEXT OF SICKLE CELL ANEMIA

The journey with sickle cell anemia is fraught with medical and emotional challenges, as demonstrated by Caesar's experiences with multiple strokes and the complex care regimen following his bone marrow transplant in 2021. This transformative procedure marked a new beginning, underscoring the necessity for advanced medical interventions and the importance of continual support and care. Nearly two years post-transplant, Caesar's growth into a teenager with remarkable potential signifies the start of a new chapter, highlighting the critical period of transition in hemoglobin production that every child undergoes, with a profound impact on every aspect of this new life.

We now see the payoff of early dreams, which (by their nature) we might never know when they will become a reality. For instance, as life never stops moving on, I was constantly attempting to balance my work commitments at the university with my life at home. My job might have been put at risk if I hadn't been a key player in the university's research group which was under contract with the U.S. Defense Department's DARPA. When my son got sick, an extra challenge emerged from there. The expectation of delivering on schedule put pressure on every group member. Despite needing to take time off from work to care for Caesar, I was genuinely concerned about losing my job when I started losing nights of sleep completely and getting sick—a combination of catastrophes. Not only now, but upon reviewing these memories, I am reminded of how much respect and sincere empathy society as a whole should offer caregivers. This applies to families dealing with sickle cell disease and equally to all those facing illnesses. It is a job that requires real sacrifices—quite often resulting in enduring emotional torture. So, putting family first was a commitment I never imagined would be as demanding as it was. It was an incredibly tough time but we made it. All praise to the Almighty.

PART IV

LIFE BLOOMING

CAESAR'S REMARKABLE BOUNCING BACK

A stroke causes the death of brain cells—neurons. These cells are responsible for every single behavior, thought, and action we undertake, whether conscious or unconscious. The scientific story behind the stroke dates back a millennium, with records from ancient Egyptian and Greek medical texts describing symptoms similar to those of strokes and attributing them to "...an unbalance of bodily fluids or a stroke of paralysis...," and only in the 17th and 18th centuries was the stroke linked to brain damage. It is understandable why brain scientists have been keenly passionate about studying the brain—everything starts from this massive, cognitively complex, physiological, super unmatched computer.

Consequently, any behavior associated with a given part of the brain is compromised in the presence of a stroke. That is why after a stroke occurs, a person loses some skills (walking, use of hands, speech, thinking, etc.) or at least experiences a weakening of them. Still, the brain has billions of cells ready for backup. The issue remains at the same level until those newly replaced cells are as well-trained as the ones that died. If one is young, the amount of advantages to counter the adversities is enormous. For instance, in Caesar's case, those cells were as old as he was at that time, at age four. Conversely, when we are adults, a harsher reality confronts us due to the severity of the condition and the person's age. Nevertheless, there is a variation in outcomes that depends significantly on the individual's willpower to find a way through adversity, and then anything is possible. The new cells must be "trained" as soon as possible to surpass the expected outcome. An early age accumulates numerous advantages in this regard. Besides children being more open, optimistic, fearless, and ready to try things lacking self-scrutiny, there is another intriguing phenomenon that is often mentioned as "...children's brains are similar to sponges..." which holds true because, among many reasons, they possess a powerful physiological phenomenon called growth factor that works in projecting speedy growth.

Nonetheless, as time goes by, this growth factor—upon reaching adulthood—begins to slacken due to inhibitory influences, hampering its potential across the years as aging progresses. For example, in our childhood, everyone has experienced at least some kind of accident involving a cut or even surgery. The younger the child, the faster the recovery. Although the brain is significantly more complex, a similar analogy applies. Given the above, all efforts are devoted to avoiding this tragedy. Still, if it occurs, the best initiative should be taken to counter further damage, avoiding falling into the trap of merely crying over spilt milk. At the same time, much time could be devoted to saving the threatened life. Time is everything and nobody holds more than needed—we just cannot control it, period.

With a person breathing only with the help of instruments, little is possible. It is a doubtful time. Providence had given me a novel idea using a familiar tool with which Caesar already had some experience—to present the first stimulus (one would call a first intervention) to his brain through music. It worked flawlessly. Starting when he opened his eyes, we all witnessed a glimmer of hope and light, with the first smile coming next. It does not matter much what type of input is—his favorite thing could have been a toy with a particular sound, a movie, or a singer. If set accordingly, perhaps a similar result could be expected—at least it is harmless to try. Yet it is essential to highlight a range of other factors—impossible to mention all, mainly because each person and situation is unique—that plays a determinant role here. This method triggers a second class of stimulus, which is not necessarily physical but a neural or simply behavioral one. Our innermost being needs to have a real reason to keep the fire on, to say to ourselves, "I can do this," which translates into a decision to fight, move on, and come back. Fundamentally, many call it one's will or willpower. At a conscious level, you can say, "I will be present at that meeting tomorrow; I will work on this book's paragraph until it is finished..." However, if you are under sedatives, those conscious thought-based decisions have a thoroughly different limited dynamic, though certain decisions can still be made—but now in an unconscious state. A decision-making system operates throughout a life from that unconscious dimension. Nevertheless, we are unaware of it or never thought about this outside the pure mystical world which is in many extensions of our world, full of this unperceived realm, and everyone meets a prospect of this, not only when we are ill. There is little need to believe any of what I am saying at all because everyone has enough experience (or has seen and heard, over time) about it to convince themselves more or less of this nature. Simply, it is often called our spirituality.

I think there is room for me to mention that a few times when my life was nearly over. One specific instance in 2018 when my heart stopped for about 30 minutes, heroic doctors attempted every possible measure unsuccessfully. They started probing my wife on whether I was an organ donor because my body was reaching the point of no return. There was still time to save other lives. Similarly, Caesar's situation showed a commonality to where I was in 2018, except his heart was weakly functioning but still working. Then, an angel spoke through a nurse of Philippine descent, saying: "How about we try once again?" Suddenly, after they had tried everything to resuscitate me through cardiac electrical shock—or electrically assisted cardiac resuscitation—I came back as if nothing had happened. They had to tie me up on that bed to prevent me from running back home. Yes, your thoughts have wide room because it sounded entirely out of the realm of belief; though several years have passed, it still feels as if it was yesterday. Honestly I was forced to believe it. I had a vivid memory of the event upon wrapping up everything. Suddenly my body was out of that inertia and I woke up hearing all the incredible people celebrating. The nurses uttered phrases such as, "Hey, you were dead! Oh my God, I had to jump on you many times, doing my best to bring you back." Others said, "We got you back for the second time and lost you." Some said, "I thought you wouldn't come back anymore." Still others said, "I had a feeling that we could bring you back. Then I suggested trying anew." Even the doctors spoke up, "With over 40 years of working in this field, I never heard anything like this." I owe my life to those "anonymous" superheroes. Furthermore, echoes of those eternal hours being on the other side in heaven, resounding voices of my family still linger to this day. Although stripped of any power, the will to fight was on. This is axiomatic territory fertile to legitimately explore— the faith system, diverse kinds of beliefs, and obviously God. However, the restrictions imposed on me limit deviation in excess; the refrain beyond thoughts and personal beliefs, walling everything in, abstaining on facts, all on the far outside is the exercises' interpretation, which is the reader's duty.

Lastly, one more example can illustrate this subject, which is a spare attempt to depict that confounding situation when Caesar was nearly drowned in this world, even though his eyes were not open. When we reach adult life, our longevity displays all manner of lessons. One of those that we all have seen or heard in testimonials is of a beloved friend who is going to die and we beg them to "Hold on, fight, don't go, we love you…" If those appeals could be heard by the person about to pass away, somehow such a person must find their will, deciding, "Well it is worth coming back, I have an unfinished journey yet. They love me; I am young…" or even more specific in Caesar's case, "I'm still too young to go now." Then the decision to return to life is made. To be honest, I do think this is a territory held by our Supreme Being.

We still have a long way to go, even though we are not in a bind or stuck. Our next step was understanding how insurance works, a challenge we have been grappling with throughout this time. This is an unexpected super headache no family should have to endure in any form. I read many stories about families who faced bankruptcy after a loved one suffered a severe illness. The absence of understanding of how it indeed would manifest sounded unimaginable. One may have faced a challenge during early childhood or endured other kinds of terrible experiences. Yet as undesirable as these experiences may have been, an uplifting event for good or bad was underway for such a person. They will undoubtedly play a crucial role in our lives later—an unwanted, challenging, but valuable teaching in life. However, we don't have the advantage of the kind of training that would prepare us for the fortuitous things that will be brought to us during our journey—we inevitably have to face it without preparation. One could say it was completely unfair because we had no training to handle this and that. I would agree—if I had any idea of what was ahead of us, Jesus! Perhaps it is reasonable that when we encounter those misfortunes, we are certain we will suffer extra, when glances of partial or complete failure loom uninterruptedly threatening like a ghost. It is a foregone conclusion that you will make mistakes. As long as you make them, the results are your only reward, which is totally opposite when someone else fails badly and you have to care about their burden. Under any circumstances, we must be proud and fully blessed to make it through so that we do not let occasional negative results overthrow the shine of our victory, my win, our outcome—the leading headline of our story.

Very often we do not foresee unfolding events, the future obstacles present in the projection of our forward steps. There is no need to know all the details of what I was facing with my family throughout these years—here lies the ignorant presumption. A simple real glimpse of the future—particulars aren't necessary—was enough to make anyone ponder a life reevaluation and quit from the start because everyone is afraid of the yoke of the burden. Nevertheless, there were not only sour events on our journey. Surprisingly, after a few months of all of this (I would say six months or so) the scattered pieces of our lives started to assemble once again magnetically. Life is a mix of pain right at the beginning from birth, which we must overcome with passion to move on. No one can achieve beautiful outcomes without the feeling of our blood boiling to a great extent. Once one crosses these basic burdens (obstacles may sound better), as always, we must find ways to resume and start over. In Caesar's case, it was not unlike anyone else—it felt as though we had to start from scratch. Then, frustrations were our constant companion for anything we were going to do. Maybe the most inglorious of all—he was unable to handle a pencil with his right hand, unable to click an object, inefficient in all of the foreign languages he was learning, incapable of playing a single note on his violin. At the same time, he started to be the cheerful boy he had always been, and it replenished our hearts with the hope that we would overcome everything. Ironically, memories could be the "killer" at this point because all of them were connected to a boy who, at four years old, was doing third grade math, earned a black belt in karate, started playing violin concerto, and had fun with languages like Greek, Russian, Chinese, etc. How to deal with it all? Untangling it all at once would be impossible, but dreams never die in a heart that houses hope and belief as its sustenance. This was the primary source of joy for keeping the family together; we were working as a team to support him, and he was taking care of us with his genuine smile and spiritual soothing of our hearts. Those movements are where I do see God's manifestations. Another reason is hope, which is in many ways more soothing than money. That was the only one thing left for us. It is worthwhile to learn how to make a big deal of it quickly—our number one goal number.

Despite never being the greatest student in school or among my colleagues at work, from early in life to my last position as a scientist at esteemed USA universities, it has been universally recognized that by my colleagues and co-workers I am among the most hardworking individuals. Moreover, I am known for my abundant creativity and unwavering reliability. However, I have never worked so hard as at the start of this new journey with my son. To start with his physical and occupational therapies, the house basement was adapted into a big gym for Caesar.

FOSTERING CAESAR'S HOLISTIC FULL RECOVERY

Finally, once back home, his first experience when he put his feet down was a crisis of unusual crying, loud enough to be heard many miles (kilometers) away. It reached a point where we had to go back to the hospital—an odd feeling considering our trip from the hospital in Charlotte to Winston-Salem, about 100 miles (160.93 km), was normal, relaxed, and full of singing—an environment completely loosened.

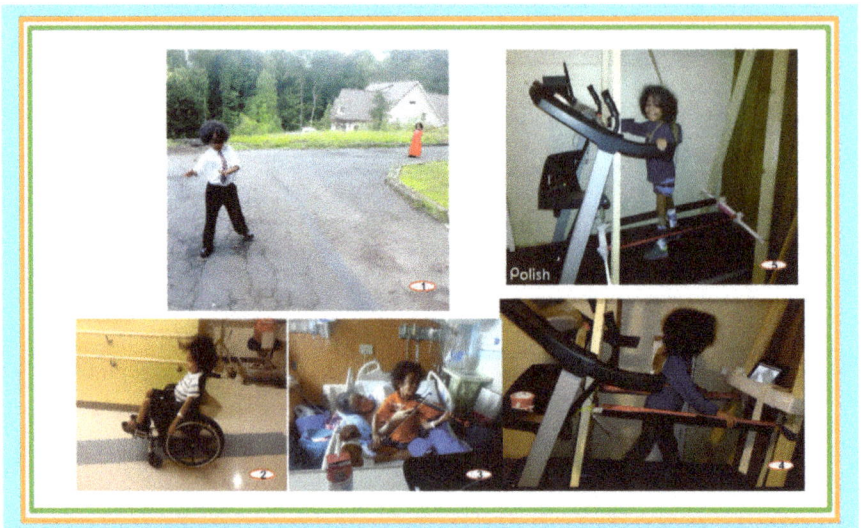

Fig. 2. *Caesar's treadmill stands as a poignant milestone in his journey (4,5). Meticulously crafted, this device was made to support an array of walking exercises from forward strides and reverse movements to lateral ambulation and weight-augmented sessions. Despite its crude arrangement, safety and precision were paramount in its design. Surrounding the treadmill, a wooden framework measuring four by four and two meters tall ensured utmost stability. It resembled a mix of skeletons in a triangle shape. Two vertical cross legs were strategically positioned at both ends of the treadmill. Converging at a 45-degree angle at their top, their broader bases extended over a meter on either side, connected by a sturdy rod. This construction provided Caesar with an augmented sense of safety, further complemented by two hand-support bars. To enhance Caesar's motivation during his sessions, a tablet displaying his favorite cartoons was mounted, serving as both distraction and reward. Six months earlier, a period when Caesar's mobility was quite limited, I sat on a wooden plank set perpendicular to his walking path, enabling me to guide and adjust the motion of his legs (not shown; you are invited to visualize it). As I observed and guided him, it became clear: This treadmill, in its design and purpose, was pivotal in Caesar's progress. The other parts of the figure show him with Mamma lying on his bed as he tried to find some violin notes (3) during his intense recovery period in Charlotte; and sitting in a wheelchair during an intense eight-hour PT/OT session, which is common in stroke situations (3); and the sweet one (1) taken a few months before his last stroke, after we came back from church, featuring his lovely sister, Maria-Anita, in the backyard of our house in Winston-Salem, NC.*

For certain, the dream of returning home and sleeping in his bed was met with the stark reality of a disability, one that neither he nor any of us could have predicted. As challenging as this situation was, he faced it, and we united to confront and surmount it together. While a ray of hope suggested it would be a long journey to overcome, facing it with love and courage could make all the difference. Thus, a new routine commenced, yet we had no idea about the bombs and slew of challenges in front of us. Though the initial step might have seemed daunting, it was essential to take; we must do it. We began by taking him to PT-OT sessions. However, with insurance covering only 20 sessions per year, these quickly depleted. To continue our journey, we took it upon ourselves to set up a private gym out of nothing in our basement. Following this, we dedicated nearly three hours each day to practicing the exercises taught by the physical and occupational therapists (whom we affectionately began to call our "teachers"). Naturally, we also created new exercises using our creativity.

The figure above illustrates a treadmill we acquired through GoFundMe donations. It offered a wide, game-changing opportunity to work with my son. Adapted for varied purposes, it facilitates walking in multiple directions and angles—a truly versatile apparatus. Life seems to be a maze as current happenings sometimes obscure the ties to past ones, hinting at a murky future. Oftentimes, these fragments might seem unrelated or even random—rather, they are all interconnected.

Curiously, during my Ph.D. training at the School of Medicine (though I am not an M.D.) at the University of São Paulo, Brazil, I developed projects focusing on the interplay between brain and behavior. Specifically, my placement at the surgery experimental laboratory while working with electrophysiology and animal behavior in collaboration with the psychology department of the same university, laid the foundational knowledge that aided me in many ways throughout these challenging times working with my son. It was as though this early training which involved crafting multiple experimental protocols from scratch was predetermining a challenge—sometimes I call it the secret preparation in life—to deal with and face, decades later, in a real battle.

This hands-on experience became invaluable when adapting strategies for my son's rehabilitation, with the treadmill serving as an emblematic tool—as if coded with the message, "utilize this device to aid your child." It seems life provides us with the ability to recognize and understand signals that might help us, continuously preparing us for unforeseen challenges. Unfortunately, quite often, one spends a lot of time with complaints through logic and validity, and the opportunities become out of our reach and evaporate.

In 2003 when I moved to the USA, I spent a remarkable time at Duke University. Part of my research there was, to a certain degree, an extension of my earlier work, though under top-level technology. Once again, I was learning new technologies, dedicated to training animals on treadmills under various conditions—initially without any implanted chips and later with them. These chips recorded brain signals, shedding light on the brain's predictive patterns, particularly how muscle movement works (commanded by neural processes) during any walking style. Usually, we do need publications to channel and shape the information for many of our thoughts and strengthen our imagination on any project. From that, regardless of publications, I was training, which would shape our journey later. (Quite like a young soldier during early training, yet not knowing that every single piece of information gathered would help in the future). Indeed, since then, I have found echoes of that work throughout my life, including in my current endeavors. While I was no longer involved with any experimental science working with my son, the essence remains—leveraging knowledge to support my family. These noteworthy parallels compel introspection about our intrinsic roles within our communities and the broader world. Everything seems interconnected in some mysterious way, far beyond our immediate comprehension. Any device might have found its way into our intricate dilemma, perhaps even a bicycle. Which one is quite irrelevant. However, in this unpredictable arena, nobody has the chance to choose. Miraculously, the treadmill served as our guardian angel for arm swing exercises. We could also call it luck. We moved forward with working on this device. We affixed a lightweight belt around Caesar's ankles and attached a robust rubber band to the treadmill's edge. Given his lack of balance, we adapted a canine harness—commonly used to leash dogs—to secure his torso and arms, much like it would on an animal. It provided him the safety to work, though his body would start learning how to counterweight, aiming to restore the basic counterbalance and reflex. The leash trailed behind him, reminiscent of its use on a dog. A wooden rod connected the top two ends of this big wood apparatus around the treadmill, and the leash's tip was tied to this rod. Initially he was hesitant, afraid of falling. Staying behind him, hugging him, and little-by-little loosening up my hug was enough to convince him to start work. This setup provided the pinnacle of safety during his treadmill sessions. Meanwhile, I knelt behind him, guiding and triggering his legs to move in the correct gait and rhythm. Our crying emotions ran high: I knelt in determination while his vocal expressions echoed his feelings—real crying that I will never forget. It is a scene so profound that one might only grasp its intensity by venturing into a deep imaginative exercise. At the same time, you must find motivation. Our key support of this entire environment was motivation, rooted in our hope and willingness to win.

For any situation in life, outcomes depend on your motivation level as the primary source. To keep him engaged on this special challenge for which we had no previous training, a tablet displaying his favorite cartoons—also bought with donations from National Geographic viewers through GoFundMe—was positioned in the direction he was walking. To facilitate the high-knee movement, a board was placed behind him on the treadmill's edges upon which I sat, guiding his legs for the correct motion and performing the above-referred guidance. For backward walking, the tablet was simply repositioned behind him. For side walking, a music stand was set to one side holding the tablet. This way, we could comprehensively train walking in every aspect of his leg movements (360-degree). Depending on the control and ongoing emotional engagements, the treadmill sessions would sometimes go over two hours, though we aimed for at least 30 minutes. Surprisingly, if he engaged with his cartoons, we would set the speed low and let him keep walking while watching his favorite old German, Chinese, or Russian cartoons.

Life's course can be unpredictable—it somewhat runs under the river of God. This is a truth not outlined by any retained memory nor preconceived notion, without any idea where it comes from. Delving deeper, we realized that when faced with unforeseen challenges, events will unfold as they are meant to, regardless of our desires. I encourage you to consider this brief narrative: As we continued our treadmill exercises, Caesar's confidence grew over time. He began to trust not only me, his guide, but also our system. Joy began to replace the desperate crying in both of us. We always worked together, he and I. Later, Maria-Anita started to whisper words like an angel to me, words that wouldn't be easily put in writing. Next, he even began to anticipate our exercise sessions on the treadmill, asking about the time and if we would have news, novelties, or even new cartoons! Facing a unique challenge to maintain motivation in a young child like Caesar, we needed to be very attentive to introducing novelties. Sometimes, it's a slight adjustment in his exercise, making his favorite food, or taking him to a restaurant with his sisters–a family outing they lovingly refer to as "going bye-bye." Other times it was new cartoons or even purchasing his top favorite Chinese cartoons, while carefully avoiding those that might cause excessive laughter during treadmill sessions, as this could lead to incidents. Neglecting any of these aspects could cause complications such as lack of enthusiasm. Once everything is approached correctly, not only does it lead to better outcomes but also to increasing enlightenment. In fact he was a customer of our reward system of collaboration, which meant he could choose his favorite cartoons and watch them for extra time. Given our lack of television and our reward-based viewing for our children, this became a golden opportunity to work more closely with him. The consistent exercises not only improved his physical abilities, but also helped him to retrain his brain. After a stroke, many people face behavioral deficits due to the death of neurons (brain cells) responsible for various functions (any voluntary or involuntary behavior) like walking, seeing, and hearing, to name a few. However, our brains hold a vast reserve of billions of cells prepared to step in during moments of trauma, like a stroke, or to counteract the effects of aging. The primary challenge is that these emergent cells, while new and eager, often require significantly more training than their lost predecessors at times, demanding up to incalculably more effort in teaching an infant. Patience is paramount in this process—indeed, it is the keystone to everything else. Whether we call upon innovation, hope, or faith, none can truly assist without an abundant supply of patience and love. In essence, true patience is a manifestation of profound love—simple yet needed in many moments.

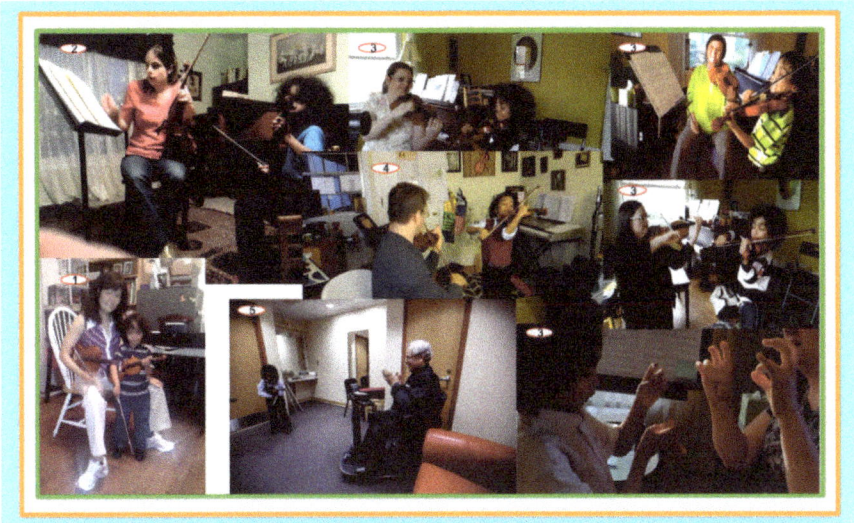

Fig. 3. *From the beginning (1), Caesar worked with his long-term violin teacher and friend, kindly called Teacher Zhou (Hong Mei Zhou), from the age of 2. (2) After 4 years old, he began working with another lovely teacher, Mrs. Amelia, with whom he started a few months before the third stroke. However, after that stroke, he was not even standing up nor holding his violin properly by himself, but he moved on. We found another professional, equally a friend (all teachers, without exception, were/are our friends), but this time a violin teacher and music therapist, Mrs. Sharp, who helped him with the basic (3) exercises, associated the music with each movement of his body and finger coordination, restoring the innermost balance of playing, and then he started gaining some fun as he had before the stroke. (4) Moving forward, he had a wonderful new teacher, this one from Russia, Mr. Lapin, also an exceptional professional and friend. At this point, he was already grasping things faster. When Caesar started feeling stronger, he ended up meeting the icon and most celebrated violinist in the world (5) Mr. Itzhak Perlman, and performed for him "Thais Meditation" by Julius Massenet and "Paganini Boy" in 2016.*

A PHANTOM SUGGESTED NAME FOR THIS BOOK

This book was supposed to be called The Birth of Love. Such a designation encapsulates the purest form of affection and gratitude we could muster—a sincere, heartfelt nod to those who stood by our side. While it remains an insurmountable, even impossible, task to list every individual who has graced us with their support, it is equally inconceivable to envision our triumph without each of our friends and contributors. Whether they played a direct or indirect role in Caesar's journey, they are the true unsung heroes behind the curtain. It might have taken us an eternity to overcome our challenges without them. Yet we eventually made it through a journey that still feels bittersweet, having already lost nearly a decade the child missed of many wondrous moments of youth due to the distress of his illness. In the end victory fills the holes, heals the scars, and repairs the wounds, silencing complaints with joy and enlightenment.

Occasionally I refer to it as a "fight" due to daily tensions. One finds oneself either defending or providing for his family. In Caesar's case, we fully embraced from the outset that our primary objective was to achieve triumph with minimal risk—a bit unrealistic since all the risks were on the table. One must incorporate a personal routine to manage the primary responsibilities—your burden. Friends may offer assistance, but you as the principal overseer (the manager) bears the ultimate responsibility to shoulder this weight, as nobody else is willing to carry your cross. One could hire a set of assistants to cook the best meal, clean your house, drive you and your loved ones, and manage your business, and yet when it comes to our health (yours, mine, our family's), it's not possible for someone else to carry this burden——our shoulders must do it——this is the universal truth whether we love or not. It is harsh, yes, I know it. Still, a celebrated artist once said, "The show must go on." The sense of direction, somehow organizing—every person has their own way of pursuing it—should be preferably determined at the onset. Over time, such a modus operandi or routine can lead to tiredness and occasionally someone must shoulder even more of the load.

To this endpoint, some additional burdens placed upon me by enduring two strokes and a heart attack in 2018, during which my heart ceased beating for roughly 30 minutes, are still unutterable. Despite the substantial medication, my body demanded simply to remain alive and to move forward. We remain resolute in our journey. Otherwise what would have been the purpose of Caesar merely adding to the grim statistics of sickle cell anemia without addressing many times the surrounding systemic issues, as expected, our standpoint and approaches were not understood by the "established" health system? Words fall short of capturing the joyfulness of seeing my son recover—totally priceless. Even if one achieves a high-level of wealth, a lack of good health could result in undeniable meaninglessness to such existence, very often voiced in the end (unfortunately when it occurs in a certain age group, recovery is uncertain) by those unfortunately cornered. And yet one may say you are asking too much. No! Expecting both health and happiness is an excessive demand, resonating as a comic dream! Well we must think and dream about the nature of those things, letting the inward poetry of our hearts speak the truth. Indeed, a life without dreaming is feeble; someone else might cheer us on in this context. Personally, I thought and believed that being healthy was the highest wealth a person could possess, and it must match the need to be happy—the crown of it all—the innermost natural desire we are all born with. Even though not everyone wears a uniform, we all are soldiers in our own right, with missions to uphold principles larger than ourselves. Our purpose is intrinsic to us from birth. It represents our roles deeper than we might initially perceive. Reflecting upon it, the sacrifice decided in the face of overcoming my son's fate would be noble enough, yes—yet who may have the heartened courage to extend such love to others? Obviously, besides being willing to care for your own family and neighbor, it would rise from a noble attitude into a truly supreme hand's blessing—God.

Ruminating on this, I recognize that this sense of mission has chosen me for quite some time, despite the absence of a burning desire for it. When it became apparent that my child's situation was a manifestation of this calling, I felt akin to a character in a suspenseful film, trampled with no escape. Herein, there was an unconditional difference—this was not a cinematic fiction or a dream but our undeniable reality.

Finally, words often fall short when attempting to convey our gratitude for the game-changing figures mentioned throughout this book. Notably among them are National Geographic, the compassionate contributors of GoFundMe, esteemed colleagues, and cherished friends. From Dr. Deadwyler to exceptional individuals like Leo and Debbie, these examples represent only a fraction of the vast support network we have been fortunate to have. Without them, reaching our destination would have been an improbable deed. Perhaps the most fitting tribute would be to honor the service of love they have rendered to us by dedicating our utmost effort to replicate such acts of kindness throughout our lives.

Subsequently, we delved into all available resources to surmount our daunting challenges. First, one comes to a vivid understanding of the true limitations of health insurance; they generally allocate a mere 20 physical therapy sessions per year. Such constraints become glaringly problematic in emergency scenarios that necessitate the aggregation of all available resources for intensive care. The goal here is to minimize the formation of brain scars or, to put it more positively, to optimize the advantages of plasticity— attributes especially pronounced in children. Thus, as aforementioned, our basement transformed into an arena for playful therapy, where we committed ourselves to three to four hours of dedicated labor each day, each session executed as if I were holding my breath.

Fig. 3b. *This figure depicts a simplified representation of our comprehensive holistic approach to working with Caesar in various locations: in our basement and in front of our home in Winston-Salem. It was around 2015-2018 when I had a heart attack. In great extension, it shows our means by working on a new physical & occupational therapy (PT & OT) with him, originally to overcome the lack of health insurance needed. We realized that, after the third stroke, even though at that time the insurance was one of the best in the country, it would provide limited visits per year. On the other hand, Caesar required a daily session of intensive care. So, though I never worked in this field, the situation elicited rolling up our sleeves and digging deep where we instinctively created our holistic health approach. Basically we alternated working in the basement and front yard. At the initiation in the basement, it was more like a disaster—both of us crying while nothing was working well. Then I remembered the fun place where we used to play while my son and I were healthy. All this changed when his lovely sister, three years old at that time, arose from nowhere with an angelic voice and began to advise me. At first glance I naturally rebuked her but she did not take notice of me and kept saying to stop what I was doing wrong, to instead do otherwise. It must have been an angel that directed me to listen to her sweet advice, and since then our holistic therapy of working with Caesar became smooth, fun, and productive. In conclusion, a few months from that day, his progress steadily rose, surprising everyone.*

The following consists of a select compilation of written articles by various journalists, all of whom have chronicled Caesar's journey over time. This curated sample serves to authenticate the events that have unfolded. The material remains minimally edited to retain the emotional resonance inherent in its original composition. As the majority of these articles are accompanied by videos, a hyperlink for copying and pasting into your browser is available to access the corresponding stories. In summary, following Caesar's first stroke, the *Winston-Salem Journal* featured his story on its front page. This material was subsequently picked up by the Associated Press and reproduced in over 30 newspapers across the United States. Thanks to the *Winston-Salem Journal*, Caesar's story was given a foundation from which it soared to greater heights. Below you will find the aforementioned story along with many others that followed. Furthermore, it is fitting to include not only the coverage of Caesar's journey by other media outlets but also noteworthy social media posts, videos, and updates that we have disseminated to keep his supporters informed of ongoing developments. In fact, after the second stroke, we were advised to open an account on GoFundMe. With the loss of my job after his third stroke, donations were our sole source of income

CAESAR'S FIRST PUBLIC VIDEO POSTED ON SOCIAL MEDIA WHEN HE WAS A YEAR OLD (22 MONTHS), CONDUCTING BEETHOVEN'S 5TH SYMPHONY:

(https://bit.ly/3k8Mduj)

The whole thing happened by chance, my wife being asked to record what Caesar was doing. I thought it would be a reasonable idea to share it, especially given the fact that he was not even two years old yet. It seemed quite convincing that he was tuned into the music, its rhythm, and the melody.

Besides playing with musical toys, conducting was something he played with all the time. By listening to the music he would discern the rhythm and in his mind it would appear as though he was directing it. Moreover, he knew the names of well-known musicians like maestros, violinists, and pianists because I watched and listened to them at home. He liked them for some reason. I do not know why—I think it was because they represented the head of a big musical assembly (e.g., maestro). On that day, which was about a year after we moved from East Providence to Winston-Salem, we decided to record him. It was Sunday and I was planning for the following day. Things were going well with my new job at Wake Forest University but the pressure to deliver was high when working under a DARPA contractor—the scientific arm of the U.S. At that point, Caesar was already familiar with the musical environment, so he began to express himself through music before he was even able to speak. When I got home, he would make a sound with his hand up, like "Hmm, hmm," asking me to pick him up and sit him on my lap. He enjoyed listening to my music but not enough for him to sit on my lap and play conducting. Then I downloaded my classical music from iTunes and he just smiled back at me. At first I did not pay much attention because, as usual, I was always busy. But after a while I started observing his movements, which clearly indicated that he was paying attention to the music and having fun. There was some basic understanding of the melody and following the rhythm, with even dynamic changes. Above all, I had never seen a one-year-old so captivated and focused. It was what struck me the most, though it was already a common thing for him to do. But on that particular day, I asked his mother to record him doing exactly that. A week after that, a few friends suggested putting it on YouTube and it turned out to be the first video of him posted on social media. The goal was to reach out to Ellen DeGeneres or Oprah Winfrey, mainly because we knew what would come in the years ahead regarding his expected health deterioration. As he ages, the symptoms of the blood disorder he was born with would start to appear. Although it did not reach any of those shows, our strategy turned out to be right because of the amount of support we received; 90 percent came from our initiative to reach out on social media.

CAESAR'S SECOND PUBLIC VIDEO: CONDUCTING TCHAIKOVSKY'S 1812 OVERTURE AT AGE THREE:

(https://bit.ly/3XLFfZK)

Playing he was a conductor was a kind of exercise Caesar would do after he woke up and had his breakfast. He would go to the CD player system to turn on the music he loved and then start to conduct. This was an everyday routine for Caesar. On that day I was rushing to leave for work and he was literally pushing me to see what he was calling "his work" while I said, "Caesar, I've seen you do it before many times. Please let me go…" I typically had a routine that consisted of taking him in the evening twice a week to Kumon (a math and reading Japanese program), helping him with his daily violin practice, and taking him to his violin lessons. Every single step of the schedule was planned to be carried out smoothly so that both the learning and pleasure would be in balance. As a result, he typically had no annoyance in doing it. Quite the contrary—when a holiday came or for some reason a teacher would not be able to see him, or he fell ill and a certain scheduled lesson was canceled, he never celebrated as many children do but would keep asking why he didn't get to go. I got to the point where I was completely booked—a nonstop back-and-forth between my work and Caesar. But the boy started pushing me even more, insisting that I spare extra time to watch him conducting. "You must see his work, Papa…" I kept saying, "I am running out of time; I'll be late for work. I am sorry…" But under such insistence, of course, I gave up—the boy already knew my number—therefore I recorded him doing his conducting because he not only wanted me to watch, but to record him as well. Immediately as I recorded him, I realized that he could feel the emotion of the music, appearing thrilled and almost as if he was accomplishing something personal. His happiness was evident from the beginning when I said yes until a few minutes after he finished, at which point I had to leave quickly to avoid being late for work. If I did not have to leave, he would have kept going, and then Mamma or his little sister, Maria-Anita (over a year old at that time) would come up, say something and dismiss us. But finally, I was allowed to go to work. Caesar was always a happy boy! Yesterday when I started working on this part of the book and found this material, I streamed the video on the big screen, and we all watched it. He said, "I still remember it, Papa, and I was so little." In fact, he has done it since he was so little. I have a straightforward explanation for this. The same pathway that creates addictions in our brain, which is modulated by a transmitter called dopamine, is greatly involved in mechanisms of learning—both means produce pleasure. The difference between someone being addicted to chocolate and any legal or illegal drug is due more to socioeconomic status, with its resulting health effects. In both cases the brain receives tons of injections of endogenous (produced by the body) dopamine, whose ascendant path from the subcortical regions to the prefrontal cortex is quite analogous. Translating a refined cognitive scientific finding into the subject of our close interest here, the subject of being motivated—even more specifically a one or three-year-old child being motivated—to play as a conductor for about ten minutes. Following the dynamics of music with its rhythm demands the same reward path—it produces happiness. Pleasure makes him intensely happy. (But wouldn't it naturally be the case that in general a happy person is indeed intense?). My original speculation was, "From whom does he get it?" From a genetic standpoint, I didn't think so. I am a simple music lover who doesn't play an instrument, and his mother had not encountered this kind of music before. When this whole thing began, I looked to the environment as the unique source of his love for music.

Caesar's first news appearance in a big journal: "Child Prodigy Fights for Every Note"

Many thanks to the Winston-Salem Journal for publishing Caesar's story for the first time on the Journal's Sunday cover. As a result, the Associated Press picked it up, followed by 20 other outlets nationally. Here is the link to read the whole story and its partial reproduction by journalist Capshaw-Mack: (https://bit.ly/3Sra6Kk).

- As Caesar Sant draws his bow across his small violin, the pinky finger on his right hand quivers slightly. It's the result of a stroke the four-year-old suffered two weeks ago, his second in six months due to sickle cell anemia.

"When he grabs the bow, I can see he's kind of a perfectionist," said his father Lucas Santos. (After becoming an American citizen his last name changed to Sant. All three children were registered as Sant before.) "When he does it well, you see the smile on his face, and I just cry."

Caesar's parents, both Brazil natives, are raising money for a stem cell transplant to cure his sickle cell anemia, which could cost up to $500,000 and might not be covered by insurance.

When Caesar was hospitalized after his recent stroke, doctors said only 20 percent of his blood cells were healthy. Sickle cell anemia causes rigid, sickle-shaped cells that can block blood flow.

Dr. Thomas Russell, a pediatrician at Wake Forest Baptist Medical Center, said sickle cell anemia can be cured by stem cell transplants. The process involves in vitro fertilization and collecting stem cells from the umbilical cord after birth.

Caesar's sister, three-year-old Maria-Anita Sant, also has sickle cell anemia but hasn't had complications. "The ultimate goal is to have her also get treatment," their father said.

Caesar showed an interest in the violin at nine months. "We bought him a toy violin, and he would make the movement like he was playing," his mother said. At two, he began lessons with Hongmei Zhou of the Winston-Salem Symphony. "We are like friends," Zhou said.

Due to his recent stroke, Caesar's lessons have been less frequent, and he is undergoing physical therapy to regain strength in his right hand. Caesar is learning six languages, including Portuguese, and excels in math, earning a spot on the Kumon Math Student Honor Roll.

Caesar's parents say they would be fine if he decided to stop playing violin; they only want him to be happy.

This was not only the first article about Caesar, it was the most profound one about him that happened after he had the second stroke. This game-changing document somehow opened so many doors for all kinds of support; without this help we would very have likely perished. However, the first incident passed unnoticed by the community, except to those close around us: his teachers and friends. It shocked every single person with a special devastating feeling for his violin teacher, our friend Hongmei Zhou, because it paralyzed his right (violin bow hand) motion. I'll never forget when he had that first stroke, as previously mentioned: I put him on my lap, and as he was playing with big Lego pieces, I asked him to assemble two pieces together, but he was unable to do it with his right hand. Instead of sadness, he looked into my eyes and then tried to use his left hand to move his right one to grab the piece of Lego. Then we got access to his diagnosis—the first stroke? We promptly ran to the hospital where they replaced 90 percent of his blood (blood exchange: replacing unhealthy with healthy blood) by using a big machine. Within 24 hours, his hand was back to normal but weak. So, by the second stroke, we did share the incident broadly, including with Father Demetrius of the Orthodox Church, and other fellow members. Most folks either never heard about sickle cell anemia before or thought that this anemia was not as serious as it is. After Caesar's stories came out, awareness about it became a reality to the community, and more broadly as the news traveled to millions.

This additional report, which is also published by the same journal, is a genuine response from local musicians (both teachers and students) with the aim of supporting Caesar. It can be accessed at (https://bit.ly/3EB4wPw).

YOUNG VIOLINISTS PERFORMED WITH AND FOR CAESAR SANT, A 4-YEAR-OLD WITH SICKLE CELL ANEMIA, AT HANES MALL ON JUNE 1, 2013.

"Concert held to benefit 4-year-old violin prodigy":

(https://bit.ly/3EB4wPw)

Another summary journalistic piece about that time on Caesar:

The power of music to inspire was evident as 30 young musicians and their teachers raised awareness for Caesar Sant, a 4-year-old violin prodigy with sickle cell anemia. Midway through their fundraiser, Caesar joined, smiling beneath his black curly hair.

Despite his health challenges, including two strokes, he entertained the crowd at Hanes Mall.

Caesar requires a stem cell transplant costing up to $500,000, with uncertain insurance coverage. After his recent stroke, doctors found only 20 percent of his blood cells were healthy. Sickle cell anemia causes rigid, sickle-shaped cells that block blood flow. Dr. Thomas Russell from Wake Forest Baptist Medical Center mentioned that stem cell transplants could cure the condition.

Caesar's father, Lucas Santos, a scientist, and his mother, a former lawyer, are originally from Brazil. Financial constraints made the surgery appear unaffordable. This prompted support from the community, including Catherine Beeckman Delen and instructors Lauren and Bill Kossler, who organized the fundraiser.

"When you see someone so young with such talent going through such difficulty, it melts your heart to want to help," said Delen. Lucas Santos expressed gratitude, saying the support is "one more step closer to helping Caesar have a normal life."

A fundraising effort on YouTube features Caesar playing the national anthem. Delen hopes the concert will inspire young musicians to give back to their community. The experimental option involves Lucas donating bone marrow cells, with a 67 percent success rate at Johns Hopkins Hospital. The other option is in vitro fertilization, with stem cells collected from a newborn sibling's umbilical cord.

Since the initial article on April 22, the insurance company has shown more willingness to cover the treatment costs. The in vitro treatment is covered by insurance but the family opted for the quicker bone marrow transplant.

"The ultimate goal is to have (Maria-Anita) also get treatment," said Lucas Santos. Caesar showed interest in the violin at nine months, starting lessons at two. He is also learning six languages and holds a black belt in karate. *"Every child is a gift,"* said Lucas Santos. *"Our role as parents is to help them nurture their gifts."*

Journalist Carson Capshaw-Mack contributed to this article.

This above-mentioned news opened many doors of opportunities.

CAESAR'S FIRST TV APPEARANCE NEWS: FOX8 DIGITAL DESK

(https://bit.ly/3SITT3a)

(Apr 27, 2013, | 05:38 PM EDT)

This is another archived article and its information may be outdated.

WINSTON-SALEM, N.C. — A 4-year-old violinist from Winston-Salem born with sickle cell anemia needs a transplant, and his family is trying to raise money.

The Winston-Salem Journal reported that Caesar Sant suffered a stroke two weeks ago, his second in six months.

Caesar's parents are both Brazil natives. His father is a scientist at Wake Forest School of Medicine, and his mother is a stay-at-home mom who was a lawyer in Brazil.

They are trying to raise money for a stem cell transplant in hopes of curing his sickle cell anemia.

The cost of the procedure could run as high as $500,000 and has to be performed at a center that specializes in stem cell transplants. It likely would not be covered by the family's insurance.

Caesar began playing violin at two and has been described by his father as a "perfectionist."

The boy's father, Lucas Sant, said when Caesar was hospitalized after his most recent stroke, doctors said only 20 percent of his blood cells were healthy.

Read the full article: <u>The Winston-Salem Journal</u>. Other local TV stations like the one below followed this.

CAESAR'S SECOND TV APPEARANCE: NBC AFFILIATED WXII 12 NEWS

(https://bit.ly/3SnO7Ut)

Caesar's story was aired on '"WXII12" ——the first time his story was shared on this TV channel. The Winston-Salem Journal also initiated the other branch, making Caesar's story quite popular. Yes, the TV channel WXII12 under Ms. Bleszinski and the TV team opened the doors for many other similar, greater ones. Interestingly, he was so little and adorable that reviewing the material for this book publication made me remember a few extra nice facts about that day. Prior to the interview, the journalist was giving him the basic instructions to keep looking at the big camera. Caesar looked at her and said, "I have to actually look at my violin." It amused everyone present in the room.

CAESAR'S BONE MARROW TRANSPLANT

After all we went through, Caesar's transplant occurred in 2021 at NIH. Although his sister, Helen, was a donor since 2014, many obstacles prevented Caesar's transplant from happening nearly ten years ago when we didn't have a donor. The idea of a parent being the donor using a technique called half match (allogeneic transplant) was considered around 2012. But with every attempt failing, we grasped, learned and understood a little more about practical matters. For example, the number one reason we moved from Winston-Salem, NC, to Memphis, TN in 2019 was the possibility of Caesar having this transplant at St. Jude Hospital. It turned out that we decided to transfer his care to Vanderbilt University, Nashville, since they wanted to pursue surgery in his brain first at St. Jude. With COVID-19 emerging, this attempt became even harder, considering a bone marrow transplant demands a substantial amount of blood for many blood transfusions. The supply of such a product, like many others, turned out to be rare. That said, Caesar's transplant was once again pushed further. Meanwhile, the illness's aggressiveness, the side effects of the medications to keep him alive, and the side effects of a month of blood transfusions started to take a toll on his frail health, posing a real life-threatening risk. Ironically, everything suggested by the hematologist's doctors was implemented; the more we followed their recommendations, the sicker he became. We were cornered in Catch-22 situations: "If you remain, you're the beast's feast; if you flee, you're its prey." We reached a situation of intense pressure, even from close friends and supporters, and the greatest pressure was from ourselves—including from the one who mattered most in the situation—the boy. The most pressure was felt by me, "the driver," who had been working as the exclusive support, and I started to be unwell as an overall result of heinous stress levels. At that particular moment, some fleeting doubt arose, shared by a significant number of individuals in our vicinity, regarding our ability to overcome the state of things. That is why hope is everything. It reorients one's course and ensures the noble cause is pursued.

IN ALL CIRCUMSTANCES, MAINTAIN RESILIENCE

One day, a healthcare professional asked me how we could find so much resilience. As clear as the question sounds, to be able to answer it is far beyond words, and I am totally unaware of how to approach and reply to it. At the same time, it seems in our case that we all started by believing we would win and never stop working toward the direction of victory. Though many setbacks came, we regrouped, fixed the mistakes, and kept collecting the small, random triumphs that ultimately fed us and ensured we'd never give in. Following insights from our minds is the best advice.

In the midst of one more blood transfusion at Vanderbilt Hospital, even though the staff were decent folks, observing my son under this endless situation was akin to a trap that seemed like stagnation. Desperation arose within me, and I felt that clear sensation of dying—depleting the well, one would say. Indeed, it was like a glimpse of death. My blood pressure was at about 230 versus 130 (systolic over diastolic), and under this condition, the threat of stroke loomed; my head was telling me that I was about to have a third stroke, but my heart was saying it would not happen. The worst-case scenario was due to my responsibility to take care of my son, and we were alone in the middle of nowhere, traveling far away from home. Surely, these positive lights were coming from Caesar's eyes of "a dog falling from the truck," whose concomitant smiling banishes all the negative thoughts and brings positive ideas. I just picked up the first one from my heart, saying, "Send a message to NIH, to Dr. John Tisdale." Without hesitation, a short email was sent asking about whether the agency had any update that could be suitable for Caesar's bone marrow transplant. Though we have been in contact directly and indirectly with NIH since he was born, despite their willingness to help, I thought that we knew or could have predicted the answer. Well, the message was sent, and I took my child on the road, driving 200 miles (321.87 km) from Nashville to Memphis. Right at the beginning of our short trip, my head was about to explode, and I was sweating heavily. I pulled the car over to the rest area because this was not the first time. In reality, I knew what was going on—no medicine was capable of knocking down my super high blood pressure. I threw water on my head, prayed with Caesar, and then went back to the road, once again, alone. An interesting detail: Before COVID-19, sometimes the five of us were the whole crew because it helped to dilute the stress, but after the pandemic, the hospital (I think everyone in the world) limited the entrance to just the person who is in need. In our case, because my child is a minor, the caregiver is allowed to accompany him. Back on the road, we arrived home safely, and the child was delivered to his mother. One more duty accomplished, although just partially. Sometimes we'd both have a bath with essential oils in the bathtub; nevertheless, on that day, after checking my email—bingo! An official sign that our trial of suffering was going to end soon. The NIH doctor basically said that they might have some news for us, as he was sending Caesar's information to the nurse in charge of the first steps and transplant screening. We were so happy to see that email.

From that day on, the nurse, Mrs. Nona, was very helpful and asked for basic information and medical records. Within a few days, we got an important email: *"...Caesar is accepted for a bone marrow transplant at NIH..."* This means that the first solid step in the process was a few months away. It was around March 2021, and by May we were flying to Maryland, very close to Washington, DC, where the National Institutes of Health is located within walking distance to the well-planned Children's Inn at NIH. Hotel-like-home or a piece of heaven, not only because it is close to the Clinical Center, but also because EVERYTHING from the staff to the facilities is simply remarkable! Going through a transplant, every single item, like cooking, teas to help with digestion, medicines, and fun moments in a healthy environment, play a giant role for the final results. The truth is, among a number of "rules," so to speak, you have to see this ordeal as going on a big trip to another continent or planet, since after it, everything will change. We learned throughout these long years, way before we were seeking out places for Caesar's transplant, "The pre-transplant and post-transplant are equally relevant for the final outcome as the transplant itself..." Two of those major factors—the location of the transplant and where we would live and spend most of our time—were already well-arranged.

Each step has its particular pace, and the next one went quite smoothly. Caesar and I flew for the preliminary exams that were done in three days, and we returned home dreaming about all these indescribable feelings among all of us. A couple of weeks later, I flew again with Caesar's youngest sister, six-year-old Helen, the donor, to prepare and harvest her stem cells for her brother's transplant procedure. Overall, this step took nearly two weeks, and everything went just as smoothly as the dream came true, with the great contribution of having the Children's Inn within walking distance. In July, we made the second trip with Caesar for further exams, to harvest samples of his marrow and collect his stem cells as part of the transplant's safety protocol. The sample was for further study and simulations related to the donor match. The stem cell collection would be stored for safekeeping in case of the very slim chance that the procedure didn't work. Then the doctor could put it back. The only big deal would be in such a hypothetical case, the patient would revert to where he/she was before, whilst in numerous instances, the body would go slightly back without the need to put those stem cells back. His birthday was literally around the corner, August 1. The transplant team has a custom of asking the transplant patient for an eventual wish besides being free of the illness—Caesar's was to spend his birthday with family in Memphis. Wish granted—on July 25, 2021, we flew back home and scheduled to return on August 15 to undergo the transplant itself. We had a marvelous birthday with his family and friends, and one of those friends cordially offered us a trip to spend a few days with them in Hot Springs, Arkansas.

Fig. 4. *On the left, friends of ours, the Daniel Family, rendered a special invitation that came as if from Providence for us to spend a few days with them at Hot Springs (AR) right after Caesar's 13th birthday. However, at that time he had already started a pre-transplant chemo drug that physicians suggested, which is also used as a medication for sickle cell patients, but always induces huge side effects. It was part of the transplant protocol, so he attempted it again. It brought him a new pain crisis that lasted about a week. The invitation to go to Hot Springs came at just the right time and was very healing for Caesar. The right-side photo was taken during the transplant at NIH. I had to cut his long hair because he was distressed by seeing it falling out little by little, so cutting it all at once solved the issue.*

Meanwhile, a day after his birthday, he woke up complaining of pain in his arms. It is difficult to tell how horrible a life situation is when you have no idea what might happen to your health next. In this particular instance with Caesar, considering that everything was progressing smoothly, and he was content, I often refer to sickle cell as the betraying illness. Caesar was taking a chemotherapy drug called Hydroxyurea, a standard component in almost every transplant center's protocol for sickle cell patients.

Years prior, his hematologists persuaded us to administer this drug to him, and during that period he experienced severe pain crises. However, this drug plays a crucial role for the transplant because it prepares the body for potent chemotherapies. In essence, the body's marrow needs to be minimized as much as possible (or partially depleted), as the marrow is responsible for producing blood. To put it simply, Caesar, like anyone born with sickle cell anemia, has weakened blood—a comparison might be imagining a car running on a gasoline-water mix. As challenging and harsh as it is to grapple with the reality of sickle cell, patients and caregivers inevitably gain knowledge, often referred to as a "graduation," not only about the illness itself but also about the practicalities that can almost predict what comes next. An additional difficulty is that every one of us as human beings has a biological profile that is unique from one to another. Therefore, the approach that family A adopts, yielding reliable results, may not prove to be effective for family B. Similarly, a doctor's recommendation for a specific treatment or drug that did not work well for patient A might show positive results for patient B, considering other variables such as dosage, timing, and whether it is taken on an empty or full stomach. In the end, the more we learn, the more empowered we become in navigating our practicalities for the next day.

In that matter, when Caesar had pain crises, we already knew what came next. It always took about a week to resolve, no matter what. In other words, one week of dealing with pain was on our schedule regardless. When our friends invited us to spend a few days at a nice resort in Hot Springs, we were excited for our first trip to Arkansas. In this case, although the pain would "keep its schedule," at least Caesar had some distractions from its relentlessness.

Finally, we could enjoy a relaxing time that served wisely before the transplant's tough journey. With the positive mindset that everything would work out in the end, we guided ourselves in a positive mode to be available and collaborative with the medical team, considering on the other side we would have honey waiting for us—happiness.

THE TRANSPLANT ITSELF

On August 15 we took our flight to NIH just as the pain crises were over. After a few more exams and the body's preparation phase (chemotherapy sessions and radiation), we were ready to start. Wait, where is the music? Well, on our initial visit to NIH and while passing through the Clinical Center's Hall, Caesar said, "Papa, I would love to perform here at this place for these people. Could you please arrange it for me?" Upon his request, it was arranged. Before starting chemotherapy, he performed a lovely recital that was well-received by the hospital staff.

Fig. 5. *This figure is a combo of the other side of Caesar's saga. During the period of admission for the transplant intensive care, he largely maintained his violin practice, which afforded him the opportunity to engage his mind outside the hospital environment, thereby aiding him in numerous ways. This led to his initial performance at the Clinical Center NIH (Atrium), as previously mentioned (1). Then, once he was discharged, he performed a recital for about 30 minutes at the same place to express his love and extreme gratitude to that special "family" who rescued his life.(2) Six months later in 2022, he performed there again. He committed to doing this every year without any charge as a simple way to just say THANK YOU. Last Thanksgiving another performance was done for the NIH Family when he rendered his first compositions (3) and walked back (4) to the sanctuary Children's Inn at NIH, which is beside the NIH main building where we stayed during recovery time.*

Our preemptive "THANK YOU, NIH" was a token of our confidence in the work that we knew would be outstanding. As mentioned before, it would be ideal if everyone found a way that enabled them to maintain their independence without relying on anyone or anything, holding onto their pure identity, not confused with the flux of interactions, learning from those who sound different, or have opposing viewpoints. It is essential to one's growth. In fact, I strongly believe that when we (anyone) are born, we are given this as a gift. It is a parents' inherent task to encourage this throughout their child's personal journey. For Caesar, this was through music, his violin. Regardless of the situation, music was always beside him to provide some comfort. In such a rough journey, a person must have something enduring to trigger the innermost motor for the present fight and the next day. Caesar is a blessed child, considering his violin always sends out hope and positive energy. During those transplant days, besides being among a lovely medical team, we all were afraid: hearing the reading of protocol formalities implemented for the sake of policies and awareness of potential complications and side effects encountered in this process can intimidate anyone, despite the bright light at the end of the tunnel.

ENGAGING IN RELAXATION AND FUN ACTIVITIES

Relaxing and having fun play a significant role in a child's development. Encouraging even more of that throughout this process was not a big deal since we genuinely believe it's important and have been incorporating it for a long time. However, with the transplant underway, everything was about timing, and my lack of experience with transplants suggested I needed a greater consciousness. Indeed, aside from the violin practices, Caesar and I have the same habit of listening to music a bit loud and often repeating the same song multiple times. In contrast, the ladies in our family do not enjoy the super loud or repetitive music so much. Still, we always found a middle ground. During the transplant, we refrained from turning up the volume, mostly in the mornings. At the Children's Inn, it was kept at a reasonable level until 6:00 p.m.

Fortunately, our neighbors in the adjacent rooms became familiar with our routines—the sound of loud music, violin practices and pieces, and operas featuring the divine Maria Callas. I cooked for Caesar three times a day in the shared kitchen, and our neighbors, now friends, got used to it. In the afternoon, Caesar spent his time relaxing in a massage chair and then walking outside to watch deer go by. As the date of our departure approached and our friends learned about it, there was a sincere mix of sorrow at our leaving and joy for our return home. This added extra hope that they would be the next ones to leave. Virtually everyone expressed these feelings, creating a truly surreal environment that enveloped us all!

Children's Inn is truly a wonderful place, and the staff there are like angels. Caesar aptly described the Inn as follows: "NIH is good, but Children's Inn makes it great." I cannot overstate the significance of the Inn's support in the success of this transplant. This sentiment is shared by virtually all families undergoing treatment at the Inn. They even send gourmet dishes from renowned Washington restaurants (kudos to the generous restaurant owners) to the children and caregivers admitted for treatment at the hospital, thus providing a much-needed culinary delight. Even when we were at the Inn, Caesar wanted to eat the food I made because it was similar to what we cooked at home. He loved the beans and eggs I made, as well as his favorite food, mocotó, which is a famous dish that originates where I was born (Northeastern Brazil). It's rich in minerals, protein, and collagen and is energy-boosting. Since Caesar was a baby, he has eaten it regularly.

The Inn is a fantastic facility—it offers access to all the best movies. Caesar, along with his sister and mom, would choose their favorite Netflix movies to watch together, sharing the screen virtually. Additionally, they used the same approach to select movies from YouTube and watch cartoons in foreign languages, during which I usually went about preparing Caesar's preferred dishes, particularly those that took longer to cook. It is worth highlighting that they spent a great part of the day, usually in the evenings, doing more than watching movies. After a short homeschooling session, we have a Wii Fit Plus game at home whereby sharing the screen remotely, they figured out how to play all types of games (tightrope, skateboard, balance-bubble, cycling) and an infinite number of different related challenges. Usually, his beloved sisters played for him while he cheered for them. Nearly every day they watched a movie together, which seemed quite entertaining. Saturdays were the exception because we, including the ladies, have been watching Mixed Martial Arts (MMA) every weekend for a long time. Caesar is so deeply interested in it that we did not miss a single UFC (Ultimate Fighting Championship) card event, even when he was admitted to the hospital or at the Inn. Sometimes, I was about to forget it when he would remind me, "Papa, the UFC card today is huge, let's watch it..." I would react, "Oops, yes, let's do it." There was only one issue with this: As fans of the sport, we would watch the whole show, but quite often it finished around midnight or so. The next day, we slept until later. Ultimately, the positive aspects outweighed any downsides. Sometimes, during the transplant, when he was still admitted to the hospital or at the Inn, he was homesick and missing his family. Just like the entire country, we were isolated due to COVID-19, but felt double-isolated due to the transplant, just the two of us alone. In contrast, this UFC show injected into us a positive energy, making us shout in joy and completely resetting our mood.

Nobody can live an isolated life. Even so, due to the chaotic COVID-19 situation, it was a matter of survival. This brings to mind two unexpected actors who played a role in helping us in particular and, to a large extent, everyone stranded on the island in one way or another: FedEx and Amazon, by providing necessary items in a timely manner. A single illustration of this is that during the winter, after healing from the transplant, had our clothes and essential oils (a homemade brand over 700 miles away) not been delivered to us on time to prevent infections and sore throat, the outcome of Caesar's story might have been altered. Indeed, post-transplant care is equally relevant to the transplant itself. It is quite common for a transplant center to perform with their best efforts, but if the after-procedure is messed up, then the transplant is jeopardized— a reason we praise those details. Among many friends we owe our gratitude to, a special friend's family from Memphis, the Daniels—Mrs. Lisa, Mr. Hunter, and Mr. Kenny played pivotal roles in coordinating as well as financing the logistics necessary for the timely FedEx delivery of these items to us. Together, their efforts not only helped Caesar to receive his needs promptly at NIH, located 800 miles (1,287.48 km) from home, but also underscored the vital role of FedEx's services, which significantly contributed to Memphis's reputation as a facilitating business global hub continually. This was especially true during the challenges posed by the COVID-19 outbreak.

This period highlighted the company's crucial role in maintaining the flow of goods during our times of crisis. Yet, the boy was still in need of various items for his bath, and as much as it may sound to some like a trivial need, under those conditions any seemingly irrelevant piece can mean a big headache the following day—over a decade of experience working with him has given us great insight into this. Therefore, nothing could match his happiness when he saw Amazon's packages with his needed items. Moreover, although I am reporting our particular case, the challenge of finding our packages in the Inn's mountain of deliveries made it clear that the uninterrupted operations at the Inn, and to a large extent the NIH, were sustained thanks to these two companies.

Sure enough, our schedule was essential for everything. Even Caesar's bath had to be on schedule to avoid confusion about responsibilities. Another benefit of this practicality was that it helped us remember to take our medicine—both he and I.

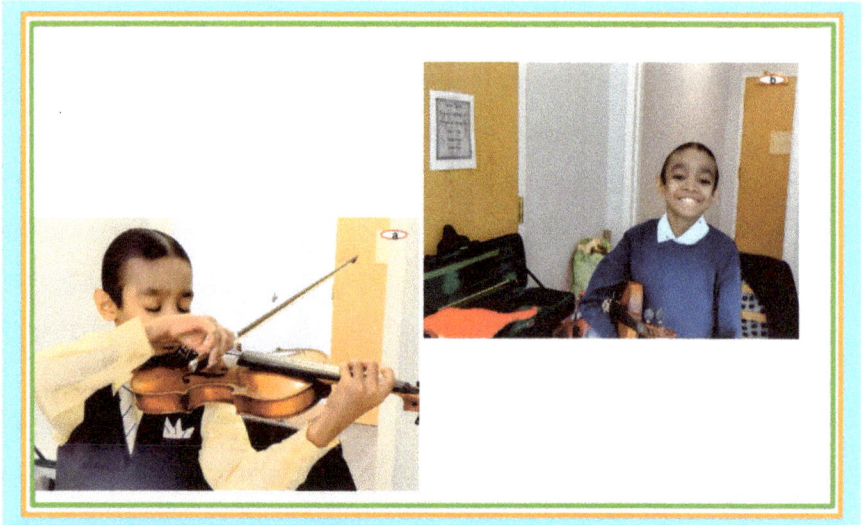

Fig. 6. *During our stay at the Children's Inn, just like in his normal routine at home, he never stopped practicing his violin. Here, (a) before his bone marrow transplant and after it (b), this was a daily action that soothed his mind as well as mine.*

Sunday was the number one priority on our agenda—a matter that was held in high regard. By a profound stroke of Providence, all kinds of spiritual services have begun to flourish in the U.S. and across the world via social media, especially YouTube channels. We had ours: one from Corona, New Jersey, and the other from S. Paulo, Brazil. It served as the highest spiritual support to overcome the battle of the mind. These two vital online programs, at different times of the day, were Christian spiritual services from our "Christian Congregation (CCB)" that we usually watched as a family together, sharing the screen. These online services were not limited to Sundays, as we believe that everything starts from the spiritual level. Even if things were awful, we'd still be miserable, but the "taste" of victory in the mind makes you work harder the next day. Certainly we would win, and it became an obligation to share our testimony forever, as the real Master asked us for just patience.

This is the main reason we didn't feel down, neither isolated nor sad during this difficult yet blessed transplant process. We poured our hearts out, like a lab experiment, by applying God's Law to our cause. Even during our time at the hospital, every day right after the first morning prayer we made our beds and moved away from them, sitting on the sofas—though sometimes Caesar took a nap at my insistence, which he rarely does. Daily, I made sure he was dressed in comfortable sportswear. Ultimately, we kept our minds 100 percent toiling, seeking happiness even during sleep time (as seen in Caesar's dreams of his leisured violin-playing), reminding us that the love we received was far beyond what we thought we deserved.

THE FIRST WEEK OF CHEMOTHERAPY

A drug called busulfan (commercially known as Busulfex or Compact) marked the challenging phase of this protocol, which ironically rings some semblance of welcome relief to the patient. It signals the point of no turning back because the transplant division is underway.

We could never adequately express our gratitude to the NIH Transplant Center (Clinical Center, NIH), Children's Inn at NIH, and everybody involved in this process. As expected, Caesar was a bit frightened at the beginning, but he quickly fell in love with the whole staff involved. Fortunately, the transplant centers excel at acclimating both patients and caregivers. Although that period is undeniably challenging, it also presents an opportunity to begin anew, free from health issues. Thus, our feelings were pure excitement. Back then, we could even envision our current state—Caesar, entirely free from sickle cell and completely healed. No price tag could quantify this. On the first day of admission, another physician came to explain a specific phase pertinent to the ongoing chemotherapy sessions. Because Caesar has always been frightened by this type of talk about risks, problems, side effects, etc., he then told me that he would rather not hear when people came to talk about this. Since we were prepared to do whatever it took, hearing all of the risks would only have caused him to feel anxious about what might or might not happen. Most of those bad things never happened to him, but since this entire procedure operates under a strict protocol regime, the physicians and nurses are required to read all the potential risks and complications to both patients and caregivers.

After explaining these reasons to Dr. John, another remarkable physician, I asked him if he could explain the protocols outside the room. He patiently said yes. You need to be strong at a time like that, considering that at this point, you cannot say, "Oops, all these things are potential problems that could happen. Jesus, I am out." No! You must go on. Surprisingly, a few days later Dr. John became one of Caesar's best friends by playing chess with him, which filled a role in soothing his mind, much like the violin, by keeping it busy with something fun and pleasurable instead of worrying over unpleasant outcomes. Even if those outcomes were to happen, they could not be averted by worrying anyway. Very often, after working hours or during his lunchtime, Dr. John would stop by to play chess with Caesar. When he left because he was a more experienced player, Caesar would "hire" me to reteach him some "old" lessons by attempting to perform better in the next day's match. In reciprocation of Dr. John's kindness, Caesar performed his violin for him. Obviously Caesar was delighted with it and still remembers Dr. John, not only as a physician, but also as a friend who spent time playing with him. Occasionally, we still exchange e-mail messages, through which a heartfelt friendship has blossomed. As the hospital shifts and rotates the medical team on a weekly basis, on the last day of Dr. John's shift, Caesar was a bit worried about missing his friend. I reminded him about how we learned that at NIH there is sort of a "no-contest" competition among the staff of who is nicer! Therefore, he need not worry about it. Guess what? The next physician, Dr. Gonzalez, was just as enjoyable as Dr. John, and once again, Caesar performed a rendition of Bach's Ave-Maria for she and her team, which produced sweet emotions for them.

During that early phase of admission, we had one more kindred meeting with a physiologist, Dr. Lori, who came to catch up with Caesar, preparing and soothing him for what was coming. Primarily, we have been training our children to be formally respectful to everyone, especially with adults, teachers, and authorities—in many ways, healthcare professionals are our teachers, according to what my parents taught me. Taking that into account, at a certain point toward the end of her visit, Dr. Lori asked him what could be done to provide more comfort.

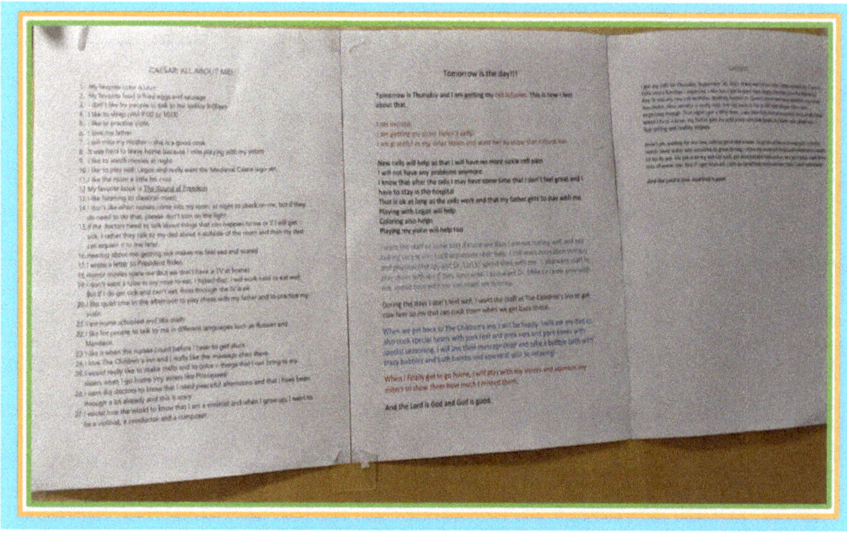

Fig. 7. *This comes from the day of admission of his sort of interview with Dr. Lori, a marvelous NIH healthcare professional who also became our friend. She was getting to know Caesar—his likes, dislikes, and what his expectations were. I must confess that I was disappointed with most of his requests/demands, and I reminded him that we were in a hospital, not at a fancy hotel. Actually, when we work with children, we have the unique opportunity to learn, above all, sincerity, pure love, and a high level of truthfulness. Through these innocent wishes and sincere conversations, I became much happier about these lists; they turned out to be useful in many ways during that time—a lesson etched in my mind forever.*

To our surprise, the child pulled out a list from seemingly nowhere, starting his wishes by enumerating a summary of the following: He does not like being woken up early; no light on his face at night when the nurses come to check his vitals; he would like to practice his violin daily, just as he did at home; he misses his family and homemade food and he wants to eat his favorite food, mocotó (cow's feet, a typical dish that I ate a lot when I was little and fed him since he was two years old), and Papa's beans.

The colossal list and conversation ended with this: "The Lord is

God, and God is Good."

I had to go outside right at the beginning of his wish list, but before and afterward, I had to remind him that we were in a hospital, not at a hotel, so he should be careful. When I returned, the healthcare professional was amazed by his maturity and spirituality. From a simple, unexpected attitude, the entire transplant procedure was largely built around what I like to call the first meeting. Dr. Lori asked if it would be okay to print the interview and put it outside the door of the room.

In the following day or so, while we were working on his homeschooling to keep him busy and out of bed—we received one of his requests from Dr. Lori: his favorite Legos. He was so pleased and amused with his schedule of daily building blocks that he keeps until today.

With that being done, the next team (every week, the hospital was altering the teams) who had just rotated in entered the room and, after greetings, said, "Caesar! I'm glad that we know everything about you…" and, "I just love what I read on the door, especially yours, 'The Lord is God, and God is Good.'" According to many, they had never heard of a very complex medical bone marrow transplant procedure being as smooth as the one Caesar had. It was just perfect, not only in the outcomes, but especially when we compared our experience with most of the transplant centers we had approached previously (except for only one in Minnesota). They had advocated that Caesar would need multiple surgeries to move ahead with his transplant. For example, they recommended removing his spleen and perhaps undergoing brain revascularization. Both advisors proved in practice to be part of the classical medical opinions without serious scientific logic behind them.

Considering the fearfulness a transplant presents to anyone, what Caesar experienced during the procedure was minor given its unquestionable inherent benefits that started emerging nearly immediately after it. You cannot elude the side effects of chemotherapy: loss of hair, headaches, fever on the second day of admission—surprisingly, not on the first day—etc., which are minor compared to previously being sick with sickle cell.

The first day of admission was a long one, but it ended nicely. By the end of the day, when we were seated doing nothing in the dimly lit back room, just cooling down from the day, someone knocked at the door. The entrance brought in someone we had never seen before, whose aura indicated he was a spiritual being. He was Mr. Chapel Mike, a spiritual Jewish counselor for the families undergoing a transplant situation. He asked if we could give him permission to talk, and without hesitation, we answered yes. We chatted for a while, and I asked him if he could help my son with his poor Hebrew skills. A few years prior, Caesar had taken Hebrew lessons from a language institute in Jerusalem; unfortunately, he forgot just about everything (the same for the other languages such as Greek and Chinese), as my family's goal had shifted to chiefly focus on his health and keeping the music active as much as possible. Mr. Mike kindly said yes. Thenceforth, a sincere friendship started among us. He sang the Lord's Prayer in Hebrew, and before leaving he asked if it would be acceptable for him to pray for us. We said yes and asked him if he would mind if we kneeled—as it is the custom we adhere to in our Christian congregation. It was an uplifting meeting from which a new friendship was born. At least once a week, he would come to pray with us and give Caesar a few minutes of short Hebrew lessons. Even this type of service is different at NIH. Regardless of religion, it is all about spirituality, which is beyond measure for us.

SUPPORTING THE BODY AND PREVENTING INFECTION

The core reason I have been serving as my family's health coach is that my background in health, specifically in physiology, gives me the crucial knowledge to collaborate especially with Caesar and his sister Maria-Anita, but also my family in general, beyond just guessing. Though we have managed many critical situations, there were several we were unable to—and this was obviously my fault. Going forward with my son's transplant, the outcomes we are now experiencing were expected to be the best course advised by experts. However, the primary issue with the transplant is infection susceptibility due to the defense system. As with any case under a regimen of chemotherapy and radiotherapy, Caesar's immunological system goes to the limit, enough just to hold onto a given life. It is always good to mention this life-threatening situation due to the body's "current" system, specifically as a result of a genetic inheritance. Therefore, the stem cells that produce the final product that upholds life are failing. As a result, the entire procedure aims to replace the "old" system that produces bad blood with a new one that produces healthy blood cells. The new stem cells will change everything, but a sizable obstacle stands in the way of this procedure happening. This "army" of defensive cells is called our immunological defense system, whose core function is to defend the body from anything, without exception. By attempting to deplete the old system for a new one to take its place, the body is completely exposed to all kinds of infections. Alternatively, the transplant may not work because the process of immunological core cell replacement takes time, during which the body is exposed to various infections: viral, bacterial, and other biological intruders. Consequently, infection is by far the greatest cause of transplant failure.

We prepared ourselves accordingly as follows: Every used item of clothing was removed and while Caesar continued to sleep (a tired body after the bath), I took everything to the laundry. Remarkably, Caesar never left the room during the entire admission period, which lasted about two weeks. The hospital provided all the antiseptics, specifically an antibacterial paper to wrap onto the body after a hot water shower. I used it on his whole body, and mine too. All the bedsheets and pillow covers were replaced by new ones at the end of the day, coinciding with bath time. Shower time was short, no more than ten minutes, bath time was a bit longer because he enjoys hot water baths. Shivering after the bath was a routine noticed during the rough days. One of the side effects of the chemotherapy drug Compact is the dropping of body temperature. The hospital provided hot sheets that mitigated it after the bath—they would be on the bed when we got out. These are a well-thought-out solution—before, I had no idea how to solve the shivering issue without them. The food was not very appealing—it was okay, but Caesar was not very excited to eat much. We made an agreement before that no matter what, he must eat, even if it was just a few spoonfuls of food. We praise the Lord for this, as he collaborated with us naturally and never stopped eating without complaining. This was a bit of a problem when we were completely isolated because I could not go to the Inn and cook something special that he loved. I thought I could bring with me a bottle of special lemon pepper spices we made with Himalayan salt and some light condiments that he loved. He just can't eat without his seasonings. In fact, the Inn brought food every day too. However, he started to remember Mamma's food at home and asked me to go cook what he likes, such as special fried eggs. Can you imagine the complicated dilemma the boy was putting me in?

Fig. 8. From the outset, it has been understood that food should be viewed as a therapeutic agent. During the initial phase of the bone marrow transplant, particularly in Caesar's case, being a diminutive child, it was determined that maximizing his food intake would make the process less challenging. This was perhaps the most important message conveyed by the nutritionist and physicians. Without stretching that, children's cooking apparatus is unique, marvelous! Though we basically do not eat processed food, I never made the effort to arrange anything for him to eat because he always ate everything. Even during admission time, the most challenging period (left top), he never failed to finish his food because we bought a special lemon pepper mixed with other homemade

(secret—haha) seasonings that mixed with everything on top of mashed potatoes. This diet even made him gain weight, which is totally unexpected under this documented circumstance. Usually, the patient loses weight. The bottom part (left) is us at the Inn cooking together the food he loves most. Many of these dishes, he learned from my heritage, stemming from my grandparents' and parents' customs which go back to Brazil, even though he's never been there. The right side is a sample of our happiness together, cooking at the Inn. One might question why we cooked so much food at once. It was not intended for us two alone. We shared it with everyone, from the Inn staff to the medical team. And everyone loved it.

Basically, we placed the same order every day and tweaked it with our little seasoning in our room. For breakfast we had bacon, eggs, special sausage, and pancakes; for lunch we had mashed potatoes, beans, rice, and salmon; for dinner, the same as lunch. Any leftovers Caesar would not eat, I ate. Although the hospital serves meals for caregivers too, in general, I was monitoring my weight, so one banana and one apple was enough for me, with a few exceptions. A mix of mashed potatoes, beans, rice, and salmon seasoned with our super special lemon pepper turned out delicious and always mixes well. It is of great importance—perhaps the most profound among all requirements—that the patient eats, even if they do not desire it. If a patient achieves that, the body will take care of the rest.

Caesar's digestion problem was about to be over. He had reached a point where he was unable to digest almost anything without extra effort—special fibers, digestive enzymes, and special teas—before the transplant. Broadly speaking, we eat to survive, but whatever we eat must be processed and digested to extract the nutrients our body needs to survive. Therefore, we have to support our body because our gut, which handles 80 percent of our defense system, is regulated. Consequently, what we eat and how we digest it are directly related to our health[35]. Breaking it down further, the fundamental reason any living being in general needs a meal, besides the behavioral habit, is merely to obtain the body's primal source of maintenance: vitamins, minerals such as calcium, sodium, magnesium, potassium, carbohydrates, sugars, etc. However, if the digestive system is unable to function such a vital process properly, the body begins "burning" (converting) everything to supply the basic means to keep us alive.

During and after his transplant, especially after great efforts to help his body digest, it began to regulate itself, and its rudimentary functions started to recuperate, leading to stability. The transplant medical community refers to life after transplant as a "new birth," regardless of the person's age. This "new birth" encompasses a full spectrum of changes in every aspect of life. And it is fascinating to have the privilege to observe the process blooming!

Although the special fibers and enzymes were part of his post-meal, the main difference was a super magic tea made of mint, ginger, fennel, and four bags of strong chamomile in one liter of water that was mixed in the evening to be taken during the following day. This was perhaps the wisest decision. It is super simple and practical with zero side effects. Though we had been using it before, after the transplant it became even more a part of our protocol. As a result, he drank a significant amount at night aiming to support digestion, better flush out the breakdown of chemicals and toxins the body was excreting, and obviously

---

[35] Karasov, W et al., 2013 *"Comparative Digestive Physiology"*. Compr Physiology: https://bit.ly/3JAuoNA

maintain fluid balance to enhance homeostasis, an essential autonomic process that helps regulate and counter elevated body temperature (fever), especially during the night in his particular case.

Altogether, these actions helped him to virtually experience no side effects from the transplant. Aside from a fever he had for a few days during the Compact chemo (a drug that induces autophagy by inhibiting the defense system to prevent transplant rejection), overall, there was a total absence of any infections during those days. He was expected to lose weight during the transplant, but by doing the above, Caesar gained some. As a matter of fact, although he is cured, this tea remains—with slight changes—a part of his current daily intake. I hope such a habit will last forever as a proactive basic approach that benefits the body, by nourishing it with essential properties, aiming to improve digestion by keeping the gut nutrient rich in healthy bacteria which is the real host of managed immunological health. As always, it is worth using local sources where we have fresh products with properties better preserved.

Due to the logical link between health and food and the sole source of sustaining the body—our immunological defense system—I feel compelled to write a short paragraph about how our defense/immunological system has become pressing. It is worth bringing forward a useful, empirically supported foundation about our gut's general functionality, a topic that often receives only a glancing touch in medical schools, perhaps because it is associated with a non-prestigious part of our body. Indeed, about 2,500 years ago, Hippocrates, considered the Father of Western Medicine, from

Kos [Κως], an ancient Greek city, coined one of his most famous principles, that "all diseases begin in the gut." Sadly, this is often largely overlooked[36], not just in recent times, but also throughout the centuries, starting roughly with Paracelsus. The last few decades (specifically after the 1930s) have seen a significant decline in its acknowledgment. Reading this mentioned citation reveals one of the foundational ideas that influenced my interest in holistic and alternative natural medicine approaches. These principles are suitable for anyone seeking to mitigate a range of adverse effects from various illnesses. However, for conditions with genetic causes, such as sickle cell anemia—whose underlying root is genetic—only treatments like bone marrow transplants or gene therapy offer a cure.

If we stop and ponder about this assertion and its astounding maxim, everyone will approach it primarily as what to eat and what not to because everything is about our food and DIGESTION. As a result, *all* the diseases we have are the result of the food we consume very regularly. Typically, these are habits commonly passed down from our parents or from the environment we live in. This means that our gut is the ultimate roadblock; our state of health depends on its integral functionality. To achieve that, we have a range between 35 to 100 trillion microbial cells harbored in each of our intestines that literally control everything from basic syntheses of vitamins to complex actions countering intruders and foreign, harmful viruses in our body. The superpower of microscopic life within and upon us (e.g., the microbiota) cannot be

---

[36] King, H. 2020. *"Hippocrates Now: The 'Father of Medicine' in the Internet"* Age Bloomsbury Academic: https://bit.ly/3We8Qy3

overstated. Simply put, they oversee our life completely. Perhaps the most intriguing functions of our gut are related to the control of enzymatic complexes and specific gene proteins that simply either turn them up or on (active), or downgrade them, thereby inhibiting them. Genes induce protein synthesis that is vital for mitochondria, a microscopic cellular structure that acts as our tiny machine responsible for producing energy that truly sustains life. Basically, *all* vital or core biochemistry behavior is altered by our gut[37]. Mitochondria's primary role is to convert our food adenosine triphosphate[38, 39](*ATP*) into which constitutes our body's main energy source.

This conversion is achieved by breaking down simple sugars or using oxygen in a process known as oxidative phosphorylation. Reducing the technical jargon further, some scientific terms must be used for the sake of illustration. Considering the mitochondrial energy generation disorders and the primary energy generation genes that are involved in many metabolic disorders, which could affect individuals of any given age, these are all regulated in our gut by this intestinal river of life, if you will. Yet let's probe it slightly deeper by bringing it closer to our reality. This impacts you directly right now by reading these words and me in another time-temporal space where these occurred. A shared factor is needed for us: ENERGY from our cells. If it were lower, surely our ability to keep our eyes open would be dimmed and absent. All of the above is

[37] Stilling, RM, et al., 2013. "*Microbial genes, brain & behavior – epigenetic regulation of the gut–brain axis. Genes*",   Brain, and Behavior: https://bit.ly/4bq9JaJ

[38] Johnson, A, et al., 2002. "*Molecular Biology of the Cell. 4th edition*". The Cell : https://bit.ly/4ddHXjA

[39] Fagundes R, et al., 2023. "*Beyond butyrate: microbial fiber metabolism supporting colonic epithelial homeostasis*". Trends in Microbiology: https://bit.ly/3UeyyzG

merely stating that the food we eat (our fuel), with its proper digestion in the gut, is directly related to our overall health. It is supposed to be as simple as the elementary arithmetic of 1+1=2. In fact, one of the primary reasons for the surge in illnesses known as environmental diseases is our diet's lack of essential nutrients for our gut microbiota, which comprises tens of trillions of bacterial cells. Fiber, especially dietary fiber (prebiotics), which is indigestible by humans, serves as the primary source of nourishment for the beneficial bacteria in our gut. Consequently, numerous studies, including a notable one by *HelpGuide.org*[40], indicate that nine out of ten Americans fail to consume sufficient fiber, thus highlighting a widespread deficiency. If we do not nourish these bacteria, they will feed on us instead.

In summary, if these bacteria, which significantly bolster our immune system by supplying necessary support to sustain life, are compromised, our health is directly impacted. Our gut microbiota regulates approximately 70-80 percent of our immune system, much of which is located in the gut-associated lymphoid tissue (GALT). Feeding our microbiota allows it to perform optimally, and neglecting this duty can lead to the bacteria backstabbing us. This interaction is closely linked with our brain through the vagus nerve, which forms the gut-brain axis, a vital part of the parasympathetic system that regulates body functions. Failing to adequately nourish this vast community of bacteria can lead to increased incidences of diseases like cancer, heart disease, and diabetes, even among young people. With this in mind, since Caesar was born, we have

---

[40] Fagundes R, et al, 2023. *"Beyond butyrate: microbial fiber metabolism supporting colonic epithelial homeostasis"*. Trends in Microbiology: https://bit.ly/3UeyyzG

avoided processed foods at home at all costs, opting only for whole foods. We started buying old-fashioned wheat called Einkorn Grain, which has a significant concentration of antioxidants such as phenolic acids. Specifically, it contains higher levels of flavonoids and other antioxidant compounds compared to modern wheat varieties. The health profile of this ancient wheat surprises anyone when considering the benefits of eating it. Besides being rich in fiber, vitamins, minerals, and protein, it contains a complete profile of essential amino acids, which are crucial for various bodily functions, including muscle repair and growth. Furthermore, it is also low in gluten, which our bodies can handle without problems.

Perhaps the main reason this rare, old-fashioned "ancient wheat" is healthy is due to its unique primitive profile. It has about 10-20 basic, simple chain amino acids that are highly compatible with our digestion, whereas modern wheat has over 200 due to genetic modifications, which our body doesn't "know" (everything our body doesn't recognize, it considers an intruder and potentially harmful) done around the 1970s. Ultimately, this ancient wheat is rich is antioxidants that can help with chronic inflammation, which is common in sickle cell patients. Indeed, scientific evidence confirms that inflammation is a leading cause of numerous health problems[41,42]. I firmly believe that regardless of a person's health status, consuming whole, unprocessed foods offers immense benefits. Those suffering from illnesses can see immediate improvements, while healthy individuals can bolster their resilience

---

[41] Roma, P, et al., 2023 "Chronic Inflammation". StatPearls Publishing: https://bit.ly/4cws4nC

[42] Hunter, P, 2012. *"Inflammation theory of disease"* EMBO Reports: https://bit.ly/3JxMe43

against future health challenges.

Essentially, what makes a bone marrow transplant really challenging is the fact that drugs must be used to undermine our natural guardrail, which are the core safeguards of the defense system. For this reason, the patient undergoing a bone marrow procedure—a rough process involving chemotherapy and radiation—becomes weak, and the immunological system of such a person will not have enough strength to attack the transplanted donor's cells. Even though these cells bear some compatibility profiles, they have many other biological features that are not, which are considered intruders, foreigners, and dangerous. Therefore, the immunological system must do its duty to expel them, even kill them if its strength is unimpaired. Once again, the main reason those drugs exist is to make a person weak (his defense/immunological system) during the transplant. Correspondingly, in Caesar's case, the energy reduction is expected to be low because his defense system is temporarily decreased to avoid rejection of the ministering angel's healthy donor cell when they are deposited into him. On the other side of this equation, if a body is unable to hold itself together, it could cause death.

Balancing this sort of engram is a real challenge. Therefore, it is imperative to establish a delicate equilibrium. Besides maintaining a positive mindset, it is crucial to ensure the ability to eat and digest, even a little, as anything is better than nothing (since anyone in this condition cannot handle much food at all, anyway). This ability is an essential requirement intrinsically linked to a favorable transplant outcome. Herein is a common piece of wise advice that virtually everyone in a hospital says: "If you eat, everything will work faster and better, versus not eating..." My task was to meditate upon the above with Caesar through this challenging period. Thus, the mindset: Even without hunger and no enthusiasm to eat, the person's mind must be resolved to consume food. The food at the transplant center is lifesaving, with the National Institutes of Health scoring ten plus points for tailoring patients' meals. It's not the same as what we normally eat at home, but it's still better than hospital food. My last words on this subject would be that a person in these conditions must grasp this crude truth: Regardless of who you are or where you come from, your life's next page depends on finding a way to internalize it by taking action.

A critical aspect to further explore is the question of dietary intake. Given Caesar's young age, our primary focus was on the quality of his food, particularly what he needed to avoid. We were vigilant about potential allergic reactions and sought foods that could provide the most energy—essential for sustaining his body effectively. Food is not merely about quantity—the emphasis on quality is equally crucial. In the same vein and in the context of nutrition, a brand new incident may entice our curiosity. This occurred at the beginning of 2010 when he was barely two years old. I had to travel to Brazil to renew my special H-type visa, as I was not yet a U.S. citizen, and my wife was expecting Maria-Anita. During this time, Caesar was teething, which made him reluctant to eat anything, not even the special dishes he typically loved. Under "normal" circumstances, a child born with sickle cell could experience crises at any time; not eating would only increase the likelihood of such crises occurring. As I was working on my research with monkeys at that time, we had a reliable number of new plastic syringes boxed for feeding the animals under specific conditions of sickness. I brought home two of those new sterilized syringes, about 200 mL each, and we blended everything he enjoyed eating, thus making a kind of vitamin mix. He started being fed as if he were a small calf on a farm where the mother was absent. We were so pleased with the solution to this puzzle that it made me travel in peace, certain that my child would not fall into sickle cell crisis (he had not yet experienced any illness at that time; this began to occur after he turned four years old). Moreover, he gained a little weight due to an excess of his usual intake, and we supplemented it with appropriate supplements to enhance his energy levels.

Furthermore, from the beginning I always asked myself: Why do physicians ignore the food benefit principles hailed by Dr. Hippocrates who acknowledged the importance of the gut's healing potential or at least its ability to mitigate virtually any ongoing illnesses? Maybe because it comes from a source too old. It makes no sense whatsoever. Certainly, there is nothing more troubling to me than this particular fact—namely, pure ignorance, in any case! In fact, our intestinal microorganisms our gut—is in many respects the central hub of our survival and wellness[43]. Truly, it bears a striking resemblance to our brain in many aspects—it carries a responsibility that could arguably be ranked as the most crucial for our body. For instance, our brain, along with all other organs, requires the proper function of our gut to work optimally and to ensure survival. It acts as the main control center of our health and, in broader terms, our life. When we are healthy, our gut microbes

---

[43] Yu, D, et al., 2021. *"Implications of Gut Microbiota in Complex Human Diseases"*. Int J Mol: https://bit.ly/46av7jj

function as they should, representing our body's homeostasis and harmonious balance, which is also influenced by our environment, specifically our diet. This is supposed to be the number one mantra that should be taught to any medical school student[44], as Dr. Hippocrates stated since ancient times.

Unfortunately, our society is in a disturbing trend to virtually turn down almost all the well-cemented knowledge proven in the past. Despite having all the conveniently advanced technology, our society is becoming sicker than we were in the past. For example, let's take a serious look at the hard block diseases; when we take a single look at the numbers of heart attacks, cancers, and diabetes, they're at a thousand per case, regardless of where they're found in the world. It is incredibly astounding when one compares this data each decade retrospectively. However, when a person falls ill, the gut's role becomes even more vital by triggering the core function of our immunological system, simply to keep life on at all costs. It is designed to work harder, prioritizing some organs such as the brain, by putting forth extra effort to combat whatever ailment we might be facing. This diligent work is incredibly important and, in many instances, ends up prolonging a person's life as much as possible when a proper approach is taken.

Ideally, all our efforts should be focused on nurturing the flora of our intestinal cells, which are part of our gastrointestinal (GI) tract. Approximately 60 tons of food pass through it over a lifetime, emphasizing the need for the most natural food possible. Yet, the microbiota (the collective bacterial cells in our gut) undergoes

---

[44] Weeks, F, 2012. *"Make yourself better :a practical guide to restoring your body's wellbeing through ancient medicine"*. Book: https://bit.ly/4bvPk3V

changes from birth, whether through natural delivery or C-section, and is affected by antibiotics and other medications a person takes from infancy. The mother's diet during pregnancy also affects the child's microbiota. Thus, it becomes imperative for us to consider how, with the significant amount of food passing through our gastrointestinal (GI) system over time, a strong relationship exists between the harmony of our diet and its ability to modulate our GI system. This interaction can predict whether or not a healthy individual might be able to face health issues. Conversely, for those already with weak health conditions, poor dietary choices (e.g., processed foods, beverages, sugar-laden foods) can exacerbate their chronic health condition. For someone like Caesar, born with sickle cell anemia, the focus of family health efforts must be dieting harmonizing with the gut's cellular microorganisms, regardless of any regimen chosen. This approach played a crucial role in Caesar's journey, often being the deciding factor between maintaining health and succumbing to disease. A significant behavior change mitigates potential harm from certain foods and protects the gut's flora to the greatest extent. Furthermore, we limit the use of antibiotics to only genuine cases of bacterial infection by avoiding prophylactic use. This is vital because about 80 percent of these bacterial cells are beneficial "good" bacteria, essential for our health. Interestingly, the total number of these gut microorganisms is estimated at 100 trillion, far exceeding the number of human cells by approximately ten times. The amount of human genetic material with the microbiome contains over 100 times more genetic content. Regrettably, most drugs and antibiotics[45] can be

---

[45] Modi, SR, et al., 2014. *"Antibiotics and the gut microbiota. The Journal of Clinical Investigation""*: https://bit.ly/3XNjNaw

potentially harmful to these "good" bacteria. When we fall sick, the immediate and logical response is to regularly resort to whatever medications are available without considering their potential impact on our gut bacteria. While it's instinctive to follow professional healthcare advice for any illness, we must also consider approaches to restore our gut flora cells as swiftly and completely as possible. In conclusion, our diet plays a crucial role in our overall health. Remember that our diet means fuel for our body to provide energy and maintain its constant temperature[46, 47]. It is true that our modern lifestyle makes it virtually impossible to resist all the temptations and navigate toward a holistic health initiative. Consequently, it becomes even more paramount to avoid harmful foods that lack nutritional support, such as processed foods, as well as those particularly with high fructose corn syrup and sugar. Choosing what to avoid eating is just as important, if not more so, when it comes to gut microorganism health. Hence, to support this immense army of roughly 38 trillion special bacterial cells in our body[48], it is imperative to safeguard them by consciously selecting a diet suitable for this assembly of forces.

Our diet plays a pivotal role in every aspect of our body, from regulating and protecting our brain to influencing the on/off expression of genes, except in cases like sickle cell anemia where the gene trait is inherited from the parents. The control of metabolism and the regulation of protein synthesis form a cascade that ultimately determines our daily energy levels, primarily

---

[46] Vukovic, R, 2020. "*Food to fuel your body and mind*". Wellbeing: https://bit.ly/4bvZ4va
[47] Bloom, A, 1982, "*Diet and the Supply of Energy*". Book: https://bit.ly/3xBMahj
[48] Sender, R, et al., 2016. "*Revised Estimates for the Number of Human and Bacteria Cells in the body*". PLOS BIOLOGY: https://bit.ly/3RX1s79

through ATP production. This is in addition to the 24-hour task of eliminating toxins, viruses, harmful agents, and poisonous substances to safeguard life. Furthermore, it is important to recognize that although adaptation has occurred over millions of years, this entire mantra has been fundamental to overall well-being since the dawn of life, and it is, in essence, freely accessible. We must think beyond conventional wisdom, perhaps even making sacrifices, to properly nourish our gut's microbiota—because its ongoing adaptation is crucial for sustaining life, regardless of the environment.

After a successful bone marrow transplant, my son became free from the anemia that had afflicted him. Considering our journey, I believe it's perfectly appropriate to impart one key lesson to everyone that rings true—a genuine concern for our gut—which in turn underscored a tremendous success regardless of a person's improvement. Whether someone has any health issues or not, the desire to attain optimal health is the most legitimate and universal goal anyone desires to achieve. Nonetheless, it is imperative to reiterate that none of these measures have the potential to cure sickle cell anemia at all, as its root cause is genetic. However, they may mitigate its impact on one's life. Again, this book is not intended to be used as an advocate for any health purpose. Rather, always consult your primary healthcare first, before trying out any of these ventures as a universal rule. In fact, I do not recommend using any of the excerpts mentioned within it at all. The sole purpose of this book is to recount the story of my son Caesar Sant, a gifted child born with sickle cell anemia, whose determination and perseverance can be a source of inspiration for anyone, especially those hopelessly facing similar challenges when hope is waning. Many of the resources and inspiration we found came from other successful families' stories, though most of them had different ongoing illnesses. Now it is our turn to pass this torch on. Caesar, along with his family, spent over ten years enduring his battles with three strokes, but we never gave up the dream of him being 100 percent cured—no surrendering, no negotiations. We had many proposals about halfway options throughout this time. We never accepted any version apart from being completely healed. Yes, it is a tough pill to swallow—and again, we cannot recommend this to anyone, as it was held close to our hearts as a personal family decision. The emotion and precise details, some anecdotes, others scientific, and many that still haunt my family and me, were all part of the tumultuous rollercoaster of emotions that have been indelibly etched in my heart. It would be impossible to discuss this matter without mentioning it.

INFUSION DAY = THE NEW BIRTHDAY

It was a cheerful day for Caesar and everyone. It still brings me goosebumps throughout my body. The dream became a reality culminating in a joyous conclusion. Occasionally, a dream comes true in a way that sticks with us forever, like on this particular day. Everyone was eagerly awaiting the infusion day, which symbolized a rebirth for those who had endured long-term suffering. Setting lofty goals seems worthwhile, a sentiment applicable to transplants and any endeavor. Reaching such a milestone feels almost surreal, marking the end of all pain, scars, and burdens. Regardless of our collective wishes—yours, mine, hers, his—these merely motivate our struggling journey toward the ultimate goal. I want to tell you that it's better to focus on what we're doing, learn from our mistakes, and celebrate our successes every day. Without these intermittent successes, we wouldn't be able to discuss this significant achievement. Those previous triumphs sustained our alertness, resilience, and determination, but this one was the greatest triumph of all.

The procedure started with the nurse hanging a bag containing several billion of cells collected from his sister, higher than normal—the more cells that are harvested and accessible, the greater the likelihood of faster engraftment where the cells begin to function and a higher chance for the transplant to be effective. In a matter of a few hours, all cells harvested (i.e., T-cells or T immune lymphocytes) from his sister, Helen, were in his body. Interestingly, Helen called them "my magic cells for my brother." The sight of this world through the eyes of a five-year-old girl made everyone weep; it still gives me goosebumps like it was yesterday. And as Helen said, it worked like magic.

An unheralded surprise was that those cells bore a natural smell quite unique like the essence of life! I have never seen anything like it. Another exceptional nurse at NIH came to run the stem cell infusion and brought plenty of cut lemons to buffer the cells' powerful smell, which was completely irrelevant to Caesar and me. We were unconcerned about that odor; actually, it smelled lovely.

At night, after the transplant itself, he had a fever. We knew this was normal, considering how weak the body faces stronger new cells, which are to be housed inside the bone to produce new healthy blood cells. From that point on, his platelet count—tiny, colorless blood cells (2–4 µm in diameter) produced in the bone marrow, primarily responsible for clotting and preventing bleeding—began to drop significantly. This decline was expected, as the platelets originated from an old marrow that had been intentionally damaged by radiation and chemotherapy. This treatment was necessary because the marrow had been producing malfunctioning blood cells, which were the root cause of his illness. Thus, the system must make a U-turn. While the old marrow cells weaken, the new marrow cells start to produce new platelets, which takes time—weeks or so.

Meanwhile, Caesar started having platelet infusions every other day, as these types of cells have a lifespan of around seven to ten days in humans. Still, the physicians are well-trained to know the exact amount per kilogram the body can receive without having issues. This is the main reason the patient's blood is collected for analysis on a daily basis. Translating it better, among many universal laws in biology, a master teaches us that a negative effect could occur in the body if you have too little or too much of something. After a few weeks, the number of platelets became more stable, which meant that the new cells started working as expected and needed fewer infusions. Initially, Caesar was scheduled to spend about one month, but he was discharged just a little shy of two weeks after his arrival. We then moved back to the Children's Inn at NIH, with our return visits depending on the weekly platelet count for platelet infusion. This continued until the count was no longer considered to be at risk. Subsequently, visits were reduced to once a month, as platelet recovery is typically one of the last parameters to normalize. This schedule was in line with the protocol, which mandates a 100-day stay after the transplant (T-cells infusion) to ensure close proximity to the hospital for critical observation.

As far as I can tell, drawing from the insights of nurses and physicians, who have been working in this field for a long time, Caesar broke all records in every aspect of the transplant. This includes recovery with no infections, fast engraftment where the new cells started functioning effectively, and no need for any medical intervention beyond what was scheduled in the protocol for periodic reviews. Astonishingly, he had no infections or even skin rash after the transplant. We returned earlier than everyone expected to the Children's Inn at the end of September to complete the rest of the requirements laid out by the study protocol steps. Between the NIH Clinical Center and the Inn are long stairs leading downward from the hospital. We have taken this short route (about five minutes walking) back and forth many times. Now, for the first time, he took those stairs, requiring much less assistance from me than ever before. He glanced at me and said, "Papa, I am already feeling stronger, and today is the first day we left the hospital after over two weeks of being there!" We embraced each other at the bottom of those sweet steps and prayed, thanking God for putting his life in such good hands. This whole bunch of NIH people are like heavenly beings.

Caesar has a long-term custom of pampering himself with a comfortingly hot bubble bath, complete with essential oils. Beyond the cozy comfort, this routine's therapeutic purpose helped save his life. When he was in a sickle cell pain crisis, regardless of the types of medications he was prescribed, this kind of hot bath was the only source that dissipated the pain. It even brought some smiles, considering the entertainment created in the bathtub by he and his two sisters, sometimes the whole family together. They often set up a movie to watch from there. Looking back, this is a familiar environment that he genuinely enjoys. Back at the Inn, a place dedicated to accommodating the needs of children and their caregivers, Caesar especially missed the Inn's special bath with plenty of bubbles, essential oils, and some toys. This bath was more comforting to him than anything else—the best day!

Not very often does life present us with a warlike moment in its paradoxical reality. While a few may like war, most people detest it. We hear all kinds of genuine reports stating that all opinions about the war are extinguished when a person arrives at a hot battle frontline. The goal from now on is to survive and deliver victory. If you've never maneuvered an out-of-the-way gun type, you must learn to use it to defend your partner, who is also defending you. When the shots hit you, who knows? A controversial story of Hernán Cortés' speech upon entering Tenochtitlán (August 13, 1521) may help even in the case of tragedy. The goal is to fall into a protective position so your comrade can use your body as a shield. I offer my prior apologies to the descendants of the Spanish community (especially those of Mexican descent, including the orgullosos guerreros aztecas—the Aztec warriors), in case my reference to this controversial story might cause any offense. I acknowledge that the story is completely disdainful. Any injustice is repugnant. If there is one figure to honor, it is the brave Aztec warriors and their descendants—remembering some "old" stories. The purpose of this citation is solely to illustrate the profound commitment of those who may face death, dying in corroboration with the cause of the battle. Additionally, it was mentioned due to a lack of a better example currently coming to mind exemplifying the above points. In this sense, the similarity to a caregiver is striking. I love my family above all, but I would do anything to never be in that position. However, after a while, a providential sense of pragmatism takes over our worries and concerns, boiling it all down to one objective: survival. From there, life takes its course, as always.

THE POST-TRANSPLANT CARE

(Discharge date: October 4th, 2021 – Transition from hospital to the Inn)

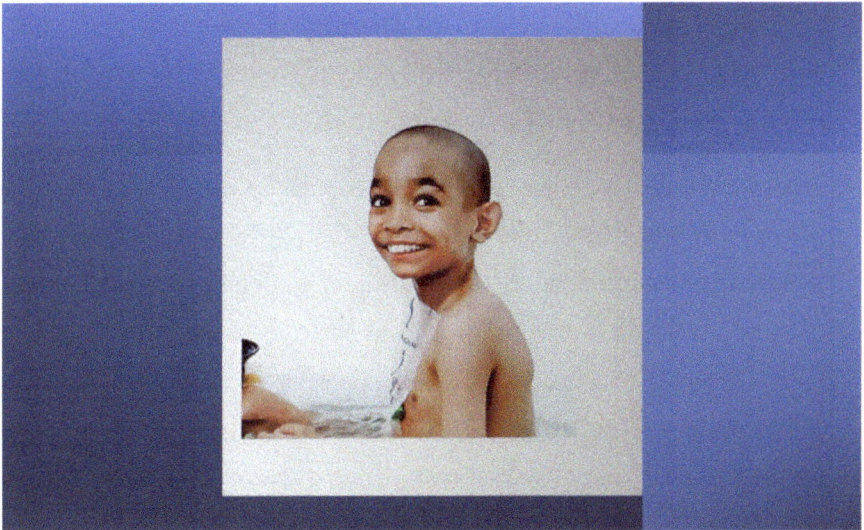

Fig. 9. *Taking his prized bubble bath and essential oils at the Children's Inn was a dream come true. Throughout his admission, one missing element he mentioned daily was his bath, adding, "Papa, when will we be going to the Children's Inn? I can't wait to take my bath..." The unique challenge was a tube hanging in his chest, which was surgically implanted in his jugular, the primary artery vein in his neck, right before the transplant.*

This tube, not meant to be soaked in water, was a crucial lifeline through which essentials such as blood, platelets, serum (transfusions, later reduced), and medicines were administered. This was because the chemo/radiation had significantly depleted his body's ability to produce them. The new stem cells infused were still in the early stages of generating his new blood and healthy cells—his new life.

Like a magic trick, a transformed individual comes to life! It's quite surreal! In September 2021, while staying at the Inn, each day of Caesar's life blossomed like a new chapter in a book waiting to be read. Above all, I had to prepare his specialized warm bath. There was a slight obstacle: a surgical tube implanted in his jugular, the primary artery vein in his neck, through which essentials such as blood, platelets, serum, and medicines were administered into his body. He was still receiving platelet infusions twice a week (later reduced to once and so on), so the tube hanging on his chest presented a concern as water was not supposed to reach the level where this tube was surgically implanted.

Similar to protecting a recently discharged patient, special extra care was needed to shield that area effectively. The situation was nerve-wracking because, on one hand, he wanted to fully submerge his head in the bath, but on the other hand, if he did so, the risk of infection was substantial. Thankfully, he was a compliant child, and his discipline proved beneficial. To summarize, that initial bath was extraordinarily memorable. Undoubtedly, it was the most joyous moment of our lives. Just one issue arose—how to coax him out of the bath. He was not only reluctant to leave the tub, but also persistent in requesting me to join him as was our custom at home. Usually an additional 30-minute grace time was granted to him before I gently persuaded him out. Then it was my turn (finally, a gracious relief) alone in the bath, where essential oils turned the warm water into something that seemed like a magical potion.

"Roll up your sleeves." I grew up hearing this phrase, which signifies there's no time to rest and never to stop digging until the task is complete. Furthermore, when I was a kid, I read another profound phrase in a German philosophy book: "What doesn't kill us makes us stronger." These sayings hold some truth we barely understand about life. Thus, Caesar's never-ending wish list for me was extensive. We will come back to this theme later, but before that, there's one incident that nearly jeopardized his transplant. Apart from the bath, we're a popcorn-loving family. We consume it consistently and there are certain occasions where it is considered mandatory, like during or right after this bath. Occasionally, as an additional treat, we set a music stand beside the bathtub and a tablet on it as he watches his cartoons and films. At home, he was often joined by the girls or even sometimes the whole family— quite hilarious, loving, and adorable scenes. Nonetheless, we always aimed to eat organic and natural food as much as possible, and we habitually made popcorn from raw grain corn, heated in a pan with oil and a sprinkle of salt at the end. The heart of this issue lies in the necessity to constantly improvise for survival. Nobody has everything perfect, especially when you are under medical care. We are fortunate to have more than the basics and virtually the best.

Eventually, we ended up with a type of popcorn I had never seen before. I popped a small pack in the microwave, and it was ready in minutes as a complete snack. Like a famished teen lion, the boy was eating it while talking to his mother and his beloved sisters, Maria-

Anita and Helen, via video call since they were in Memphis, Tennessee. Unbeknownst to me, the three children had figured out a way to watch the same movie together. So, after a wonderful bath he was feeling super happy with a full belly, relaxing, chatting with his family, and watching fun movies. Then it was time for a peaceful sleep. However, in just over an hour, Caesar began to complain about his upset stomach, followed by vomiting. He expelled everything he had eaten, especially the popcorn. During both the pre-transplant phase and the recovery, we were trained to intervene appropriately by taking the proper steps when such a situation arises. The primary step was to reach the medical team overseeing his care. We had a kit for typical cases of upset stomach and similar issues, which had never needed to be used. Still, upon analyzing the material (only the popcorn) and its smell, before taking any action, he requested his special tea, which I knew might help with this issue. There was little to do once his body naturally expelled the offending substance. It was primarily about keeping his body hydrated and soothing his stomach. Once done, in the morning we walked to the Clinic Center for a proper evaluation. He threw up again when he took the standard transplant medication. It is not uncommon to experience stomach discomfort when this happens. We returned later to the Inn, and I prepared a simple meal of rice and chicken breast, sprinkling some fenugreek powder on it. The issue was fully resolved the same day. The remaining popcorn was discarded as it was clearly not fit to eat, especially by a recovering post-transplant patient. It was perhaps the most regrettable mistake I made. Fortunately, it was bypassed without further consequences.

SPECIAL BEANS AND COOKING MOCOTÓ AT THE INN

It may seem that since the job was done and the transplant successfully completed, that we could simply go home with a fairy tale ending. But no! Patience is truly the key to success, and once again, it was something we had to exercise. As mentioned earlier, it was September, and we were required to stay at the Children's Inn, just a five-minute walk from the Clinical Center. The transplant protocol requires 100 days of being near the transplant center after the procedure. Therefore, we had to stay at the Inn until December 2021. We set a routine to avoid falling into the overthinking trap during these two months. Although we were focused on this period, our minds were filled with home scenes and the desire to return soon.

First, we went to see the transplant team every two days. This interval extended to one week in October, followed by two and three weeks until December when we triumphantly returned home. Despite feeling tired during that recovery time, it was just the beginning. Now it was time to put his taste buds to the test by cooking my special brown beans. Given the circumstances, it's important to provide some context. Besides being in a transplant center, we were amid the harsh time of the COVID-19 pandemic, which was no joke. I was determined to make these beans, but the question was, how could we obtain all the ingredients? The problem was that we didn't have much room to handle this on our own. The Inn was always ready to provide the necessities, but the beans were special—not your everyday type. Therefore, the ingredients were not readily available in the typical American marketplaces.

Through the brotherhood of our Christian Congregation, I connected with Brother Antony, whose daily commute conveniently passed near our Inn. He kindly agreed to purchase all the ingredients we needed from a small Portuguese retail store. His efforts went above and beyond, bringing us dried meat, yucca flour, special sausages, mocotó, and even hot pepper—things unfamiliar to most Americans but integral to the traditional Brazilian diet I grew up with.

Cooking has a therapeutic power that has benefits both for the cook and the eater. For me, already starting to feel unwell, and for the NIH staff helping me but whose work was bound by protocols. Eating this type of homemade food made Caesar feel stronger and happier. Fortunately, I am incapable of cooking small portions because I feel utterly unsatisfied if the pan is not large enough. Thus, the Inn's large pans came in handy, one for Caesar and me and another to share with our new friends, particularly the medical team, staff, and other caregivers.

When all is said and done, life teaches us that the only way to feel true happiness is by making others happy. Sharing delicious, nutritious, healthy food is one way, but there are many others, such as giving someone an opportunity or helping others. In our case, most of those we shared this food with had never tasted anything so flavorful and packed with ginger, garlic, cinnamon, onions, rosemary, cilantro, nutmeg, and approximately 100 other different spices from my culinary secret. How did we manage this? Transplants are a well-scheduled process in which families are fully informed. The main phase of the transplant takes around 100 days, and it's usually spent far from home, which is something to keep in mind. In our case, it was over 700 miles away.

So, one of the first things we packed was a huge pot of seasonings to be shipped to the Children's Inn at NIH, where we spent most of our time. With these ingredients, all kinds of cooking was possible, including mocotó (cow feet), which is especially beneficial for someone in recovery due to its nutritional content. Eating mocotó provides collagen, a protein that supports joint health, skin elasticity, and connective tissues—exactly what a recovering body needs. It also contains minerals such as calcium and phosphorus, essential for bone strength and development. Additionally, mocotó can provide gelatin, which may support digestive health and aid in the absorption of nutrients. As a result, Caesar's bone density quickly returned to normal, and his overall health improved rapidly because we consider food as medicine. Nevertheless, none of this would have been possible without being in a place with all the necessary resources and arrangements, like the Children's Inn.

Still, every single day I had to deal with this question, "Papa, when can we go home? I am feeling good. Shall we ask the team [the transplant medical team] about this question?" My answer was, as you can already assume, how it should be, "Sir," (he does not like it when I call him that because it means it's serious), "you should know better than me that your day to go home is already well-scheduled, and we must follow what they have decided. So please avoid mentioning it too much because it upsets me." Though his request is completely understandable, it would not be helpful if the caregiver entirely dismissed it, treating it as an 'invitation' instead. Undeniably, this presents another tough situation for the caregiver to manage.

A kind nod of acknowledgment, then back to business—focusing on something that brings us joy—because our minds can easily fall into confusion in a tense environment. I said, "Caesar, when the dust settles, we must reset our lives. Since music is what you do best, let's get back to practice." A month earlier when he was still admitted to the hospital, even during chemotherapy and radiation, we had a violin practice schedule which worked sweetly. If I am not mistaken, I cannot recall a single day he did not practice his violin throughout his bone marrow transplant. Typically, it worked as a balm, alleviating the anxiety of being in a hospital. That was an extra reason why I set the schedule—when we are in a hospital setting without any other options than being stuck there, regardless of the purpose, we can easily feel annoyed, allowing our mind to dwell on abstraction that will not help the cause. Thus, the "medicine" for this would be occupying ourselves with something we enjoy, even if doing so would alter somewhat the other schedule. Still, in the grand scheme of things, if what you are doing brings a drop of happiness, it is a million times worth it to just lie down or spend time fixated on a screen watching something enjoyable.

Obviously, each family's or person's reality is individually different. In our case, we have music to dwell on, but someone else may have computer coding, drawing, Legos, chess games, sports activities, or even reading books—though this latter one has somehow become "too old-fashioned" for many to pursue nowadays. The fact of the matter is that we ran the same schedule whether at the hospital or at the Inn. Though at the hospital, the environment set out some natural limitations. Incremental praise to the NIH Family because even on this subject, they were able to adjust for all their patients, including Caesar. He had his own daily schedule throughout the treatment, except when the medical team arrived, which was always at the same time, around 10:00 a.m. I allowed him to stay up until 8:00 p.m., and around 7:00 a.m. I would wake him up. I always counted at least eight hours of sleep because we have a long-time funny habit of going to bed late.

Another challenge is proper coordination. When Caesar awoke, his breakfast was waiting for him. I had already diligently washed any remaining extra clothing from the previous day, usually doing so when he fell asleep, except for those used overnight. And I would double-check on his special tea—the miracle ingredient, if you will, that played a giant role in his well-being to avoid any upset stomach complications. He drank one liter of this unique tea during the day, plus apple juice during his meals; at night he was drinking only water—our home routine.

Regardless of the situation, virtually every single family has some sort of health issue. In our case, we are so blessed to have music as a counterbalance to it. Music for us has been working as a perfect balance, which provided Caesar and us with all kinds of soothing. Simply put, it is impossible to imagine his world without it. From the most challenging moments of his life, the transplant was far less difficult than his past because when a person has spent time in blazes, even days of sunshine without shadows are nothing. Of course, he faced tough times during the transplant, experiencing fevers and intense shivering, like a green stick trembling on some nights. Still, it was all part of an unavoidable process that we were fully aware of, anticipating what would come next. It was a short period of suffering with a 90 percent chance of being forever free from the blood disorder that nearly claimed his life several times. In the end, we view the entire transplant process as a true blessing.

CAESAR'S MUSIC SAVES HIS LIFE IN COUNTLESS WAYS

Honestly, I cannot see Caesar triumphing over all the challenges that confront him without his violin. His music becomes his savior, weaving an intricate tapestry of solace, inspiration, and triumph, guiding him through boundless paths. From the start, it was understood that nobody is interested in hearing sorrows unless you present some enchanting mode, motto, or smile as a natural behavioral trade-off. To be honest, a person needs to give something in return for the other to help or join in—I call it an unblemished passion that everyone shares. The main reason we help each other as humans is in helping, we feel better, regardless of the inner stirring of who received it. Herein lies the context where the music was introduced into my family through my son. Further input from the same context conveys a spiritual perspective similar to the reasons parents invest in their children—aiming for them to carry on the family brand beyond whatever fortunes they possess. In the case of professors, by feeding their students' minds they intend to, subconsciously, promote their name, perhaps forever, through their pupils' future success. The innermost appeal behind why a person receives certain support is because **nothing comes free** at all. Only music translates it all in the simplest manner, which by all accounts, goes along with the task of making people spontaneously happy and even cry via a simple song. In this regard, when Caesar played heartwarming tunes—Bach's "Ave-Maria" and Beethoven's "Ode to Joy"—in Las Vegas (MGM Grand) over two years after the third stroke, the striking part forever etched in my head was observing around 3,000 adults cheering and weeping like infants. This served as a big additional relief to me because my old thought was that I was the only person to cry, but it vanished altogether. Music can do all this. As I have mentioned before, Providence always provides ways to counter life's challenges. I am unable to conjecture much based on what-ifs because it is virtually impossible to imagine our lives without Caesar's music. Completely infeasible!

This brings us back to the beginning when he started getting sick, and we had no other way to shake things up after his first stroke—a real shock to everyone. People saw him as remarkable, full of potential to ace special tests of IQ, etc. He was performing far above everything at four years old in every subject he was in. Though we always spoke to everyone about his illness, especially to the teachers, I doubt anyone realized how serious it could turn out to be. But after the first stroke, nobody had the same thought anymore.

Acknowledgments go to the first journal, *The Winston-Salem Journal*, for writing a lengthy journalistic piece with Caesar on its weekend cover featuring his violin and links of him playing (https://bit.ly/3Sra6Kk). This event brought an unprecedented game-changer of epic proportions. Astonishing! At first we had a hard time finding a copy due to the overwhelming demand of people rushing to buy it unprecedentedly. This was just the first one, but the *Associated Press* reproduced it throughout the U.S.

And then the boy's story went out to everyone from an obscure small-town case—our lovely Winston-Salem—apparently without many expectations.

At the same time, the transplant was on our radar, but with no donor or financial resources available, the hope to keep pushing never left us. It was in 2013, we re-contacted the NIH, yet at that time they still lacked suitable protocols for him. We had no choice but to place our faith in the hope that by keeping up the hard work, the violin would bring a positive outcome. In such a situation, you do not have much to lose and doing nothing will likely seal the hope out. Among the number of ideas we received, one was to record a CD of him playing some short classic tunes, hymns, and national anthems. At that time, he was already playing well the U.S., Brazilian, and Greek anthems. Thus, we thought it would generate enough revenue for his transplant. The fundamental issue for a situation, when an illness like this affects a family, exists by the simple fact that your health must come first. Anything you aim to do requires a monumental effort once you are physically, emotionally, and economically exhausted. Despite that, the show must go on, as the famous saying goes. We worked on this project and recorded it years later, but we were unable to finish it because as we ventured on, his condition worsened, thus intensifying the challenge. Above all, we kept doing our best efforts and his musical abilities continued to grow as we waited for his transplant, hopeful that we would make it. Understandably, we had to drop most of the extracurricular subjects, with the violin remaining the chief. Surprisingly or perhaps not, the third stroke symbolized a profound resurgence of vitality if you grasp the nuance. Just weeks after this event, Mrs. Katherine, a journalist from National Geographic in Washington, D.C., reached out to us. Until that moment, we had no prior knowledge of her existence, nor had we been in contact, despite her parents residing in Winston-Salem—the same city in which we were living at the time. She had been moved by Caesar's inspiring story and was eager to create an extensive international documentary about it. However, they were not yet aware of his third stroke. When I informed her about it, she offered sympathy and sorrow, and she was obviously even more enthusiastic to put his story out. From that standpoint, Caesar's story gained international recognition. Despite being stuck in a situation with limited prospects and little progress, but never lacking the enthusiasm to work, we started receiving support from a network of people we had never met. It spread across the globe, bringing significant but impressively substantial gains. We give massive credit to *National Geographic*, not just for the phenomenal job, but also for further linking our already existing GoFundMe to the documentary. Indeed, our heart goes out to this crowdfunding company because it allows us to receive donations from all over. If we could nominate the three key players in Caesar's journey, it would be **Winston-Salem Journal**, **National Geographic**, and **GoFundMe**. Caesar's violin complements them in a perfect trio, and we are forever grateful to them. Consequently, an account associated with the previous one provided the necessary funds to assist with the fundamental necessities. To a certain extent, it has been beneficial until the present moment, when we generate some news or post updates on the account as a family without income nor health insurance. Now I must pose this fundamental question: Can you perceive the vital role music has played for us from the beginning?

Propelling forward with a major leap, finally after nearly one decade, Caesar was admitted to the NIH for his bone marrow transplant—the first visit lasting several days. They arranged for us to stay at the Children's Inn, where nearly all the patients stay. As a custom, wherever he ventured, his violin faithfully accompanied him, becoming an inseparable part of his endeavors. On one of those evenings, he gave the first of a total of seven performances, playing Bach's "Double" from Partita #1 for the Inn staff, to express his deepest personal gratitude—simply saying "thank you!" That performance led to another one over a month later at the NIH Atrium during the so-called pre-transplant phase, which served the same purpose: to show his gratitude to those fantastic nurses and doctors.

To our surprise, with an extraordinary date coming up— Thanksgiving—arrangements were made for him to perform once more at the NIH Atrium. This was a slightly better-organized event where the agency's director, Dr. Francis Collins, would join in a trio format playing his guitar, with Dr. Robert Masi on the piano. Selected tunes were rehearsed, and a lovely event was staged to say thanks to the National Institutes of Health. This was a proof test for whether and how well Caesar's transplant was working. Caesar performed his violin for about an hour, standing up, smiling from the beginning to the end, with a strength he never had before; his bone marrow transplant had been performed merely over a month earlier.

Due to a myriad of coincidences, the national TV channel CBS was present and recorded the entire program. In the official program, he closed it by saying, "Thank You, NIH" in several languages: Greek, Hebrew, Chinese, German, French, Spanish, and Portuguese. Meanwhile, the future schedule was going through everyone's heads. After we were given the discharge to go home, already formally scheduled for December, six months later he had to come back for an utterly critical first post-transplant review. Depending on the date and his condition, we have to return within the subsequent intervals of six months with an eventual extension to a year. Then, every year, Caesar has to go to NIH for a short date review, more for his sake because the entire process is part of a study-run based on a serious scientific protocol.

One might wonder: Can you imagine the value of data points from someone who had a bone marrow transplant 20, 30, or even 90 years ago? The insights gained over such a vast interval would be invaluable to scientific research. This represents the intrinsic scientific timeline every researcher aspires to observe. How would the collection of these data points, year after year, align with his health trajectory? Remarkably, scientists have similar data and understand that transplanted cells follow natural biological patterns, much like those in individuals who have not undergone a transplant. However, there is not much data on a person with Caesar's background of events that happened before the procedure: an enlarged spleen (splenomegaly), three strokes, liver and kidney compromised, followed by a considerable list of other ailments. These data points are crucial for advancing future studies. When the slope of these data points changes, the rate at which it returns to normal raises a billion-dollar question that dedicated scientists work tirelessly to answer, seeking deeper insights for society. In other words, once the data is thoroughly analyzed, the scope and insights gained from the protocol can be lifesaving for future generations. To date, Caesar's results have shown tremendous promise in every measurable aspect.

Practice holds the key to any activity anyone may pursue at the end of the story. Irrespective of the field, practice casts the same meaning: It is the universal path to mastery in any subject. On the other hand, it's natural to lose enthusiasm for practice, especially after long periods without a regular teacher. This feeling is common among children and even professionals. Recognizing this shift in energy, I instinctively suggested, "Let's reorganize our practice schedule. It would be unwise to neglect it, my friend. Why not start the day with violin practice, placing it at the top of your schedule?" This routine became our daily practice during the transplant period, starting every day right after breakfast. This schedule evolved beyond mere violin practice—it served as a psychological tool to redirect our thoughts and maintain focus. Creativity is indeed crucial for avoiding the monotony of repetitive practice. We somewhat followed Mr. Arnold Schwarzenegger's blueprint for "shocking the muscles" in various ways. If I recall correctly from his book or YouTube gym videos, after spending some time in the gym (or, in our case, at the hospital), our muscles begin to memorize every single routine we perform. This familiarity leads to a sense of apathy. Every task, every movement—from muscle A to E— becomes so "memorized" that it feels like attending the same repetitive meeting day after day. At that point, what's the purpose of attending the same meeting tomorrow? Unsurprisingly, a lack of enthusiasm is expected, potentially hindering the program's goals.

We counteract this by inverting the muscle training order, shocking them, and making the next move unpredictable—perhaps starting with muscle C instead of A, and proceeding randomly. One could call it an intuitive approach to maintaining freshness in training—inverted inner gait enthusiasm. This creates a sense of novelty with a fresh incentive to work. Ironically, spending time in the hospital often gives rise to a different kind of ailment, a mix of anxiety and sadness, which could evolve into apathy—by exacerbating the situation and leading to a dangerous mindset of "it doesn't matter." This struggle prevents patients from improving their health to escape the confines of the hospital. Innovation and intense spirituality can bolster the mind, supporting collaboration with healthcare personnel, medication adherence, and proactivity in the uncertain hospital environment, as events can change at any given time, affecting outcomes. Cultivating hope and positivity isn't just about the mind acting on its own. We must incorporate additional small components (some already mentioned above) that may seem unimportant to some. Without them, our outlook could potentially deteriorate.

Despite popular belief, it is true that our moods fluctuate based on our violin practice. If we were a baseball, football, or basketball family, would it convey the same meaning? No! The argument I present here is clear-cut and leaves little room for debate: From a humble street performer (klezmer) and MMA fighters to Olympic athletes, each experiences a surge in enthusiasm when their mood is elevated. This shift in mindset isn't exclusive to victory alone, it also stems from a simple yet effective practice session, often conducted in solitude. Such practice can alter one's mood for the day and, in some cases, leave a lasting impact on their mindset. This shift is especially powerful when we witness and follow along with their practice journey. Then, why not do a simple practice in the morning to have a fun day? But what if the practice does not meet expectations? It's the flip side, of course. My job as a general helper has been simple and easy to understand since the beginning: Guiding Caesar on the fundamentals and practices, ensuring he reaches his études lessons with proper warm-ups, avoiding the urge to skip the "not exciting part," and doing the finger, elbow, and shoulder exercises—a sort of yoga before touching the violin bow. Even after that, it's crucial to start by playing open strings as a beginning, which is a healthy routine that everyone in this field, from beginners to superstars, follows. This is the hard part of practice, especially for a young fellow—they want to spend as little time as possible on this part and jump straight to the top pieces. Additionally, I help him understand the lessons and make things simple, but not too simple, to avoid the common aphorism that the simpler things are, the harder they become.

I have learned from various teachers (through books and masterclasses) how to effectively assist in Caesar's violin practice to prevent disappointments. Working with our own children, regardless of the subject, is entirely different from teaching someone else's children. It's inherently a significant challenge, but when the subject is music—specifically the violin—this challenge escalates to an entirely new level. You are perceived primarily as a parent, and whatever you try to do is seen merely as a helping hand...it's rough. That said, teaching one's own children, particularly in violin, is always formidable. Yet we often find ways to discover joy almost daily. Despite periods when he went months without seeing a violin teacher, his learning still progressed through consistent practice, especially as he developed a mindset for composing, which became a fun yet serious hobby. In truth, everything we do carries a sense of commitment. As a child, he often wanted to skip the suggested routines, but he ultimately adhered to about 80 percent of the recommendations—a commendable effort overall. The key lies in the creativity we bring to the process. It's straightforward: We must find ways to maintain enthusiasm and create as much excitement as possible in the learning journey. In Caesar's case, practicing his violin during his transplant was more of a psychological game to keep his mind away from the stress of being in a hospital bed or even at the Inn, where he felt awesome. An extra responsibility automatically assigned to me was to mitigate the immeasurable amount of stress, so we had to use every resource available to make it work. To give extra insight, I was particularly thrilled by two observations: his smile, especially during the morning—sometimes even before his prayer right after waking up—and his dreams. A reasonably predictable day could be deduced from these. I understand the roots of some wild dreams, but not completely once they touch a distant past reality.

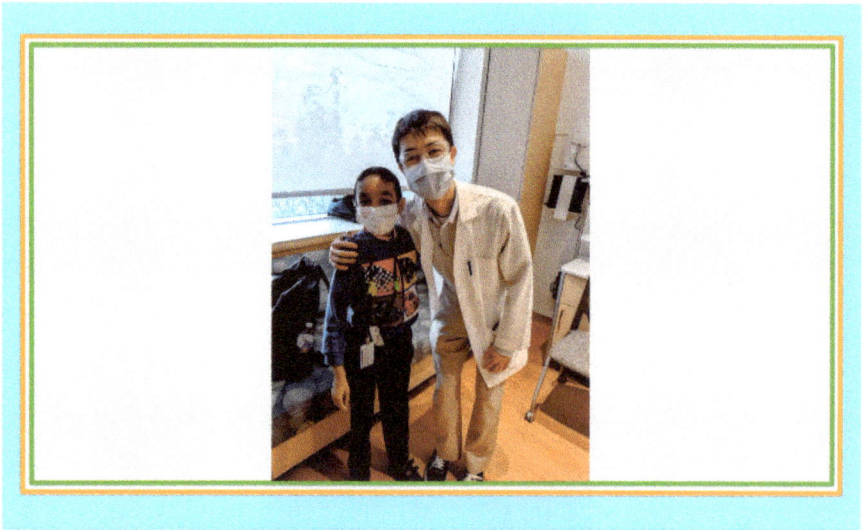

Fig. 10. *The lead physician for Caesar's bone marrow transplant, Dr. Hsieh, at the routine review six months after his successful procedure. Indeed, there is no doubt (not only from Caesar's positive results) that Dr. Michael Hsieh is the best hematologist transplant physician in the world.*

If properly analyzed together, they can provide final measures for his innermost state (which is not prone to worrying), perspective for the day, and happiness. Every so often, Caesar would begin his day by sharing his dreams of meeting Mr. Itzhak Perlman again and playing Bach's Sonatas & Partitas for him. He imagined performing not just for Mr. Perlman but also for his (and our) cherished artists like Mr. Heifetz, Mr. Elman, Mr. Oistrakh, Mrs. Ginette Neveu, Mr. Vengerov, Mrs. Hahn, and many others. Without dismissing his dreams, I would inquire more about the specifics of his dreams, hoping to discern any patterns from the nights before; not really, but logical reverberations were totally expected given the fact that he never stopped listening to those iconic artists' recordings. I must confess that by breaking this down, I truly learned that the old saying "the true artist never dies" rings true since their legacy remains forever, especially musicians with remarkable recording like Mr. Heifetz, Mr. Oistrakh and Mr. Elman. It compels me to ponder what it will be like a few thousand years from now! Furthermore, by examining a bit more closely, I concluded that there is some "sense" from his environment because those are some of the top violin players he has been listening to since he was a baby. Now, attempt to imitate them, as we all do until we amalgama our own way (style). On the flip side of it, he never verbalized any nightmares or bad thoughts during this time of the transplant. This led me to conclude our approach was satisfactory, exactly matching our goal——to keep his mind calm, away from worries about his medical procedure, leaving that job for the best healthcare professionals—the result of which is now shared with you.

During the very core of the transplant process, which is the admission phase, tight rules dictated that leaving the hospital was not an option at all——no exception until discharge day. In addition to his daily violin practices, Caesar would often fill his room with the harmonious sounds of his music for the staff; the remarkable assembly of nurses and doctors who attended to him was nothing short of transformative. The music had an almost magical language, allowing raw emotions to be unfurled, thawed from the cold clinical confines of the hospital environment, and causing them to spill tears from their eyes. I had never read or imagined anything so surreal and beautiful as that.

The change in atmosphere was palpable and so profound and natural that the sterile hospital room was transformed into a vibrant concert room for an ephemeral moment. One could see the room's walls vibrate. In that space, love was the dominant language, effortlessly transcending the barriers of speech and communication. Caesar's worries vanquished completely at the end, leaving only his smile and lucid speaking. This extraordinary transformation was far beyond any scholarly explanation, beyond what can be comprehended by the human mind. In my humble perception, it felt like a divine orchestration, a manifestation of what I interpret as God being in control.

This goes much further, considering the journey to finding the best place on this planet for my son's bone marrow transplant was arduous. We had a plethora of options, each reputed in its own right, and yet we ended up in a place that exceeded all our expectations and was unparalleled in its excellence. I always reminded Caesar that "making friends in the hospital is not joyful at all as it means one moves into trouble and becomes ill; however, once there, we must find blessed ways to make friendship our healing grace." Indeed, there is not much logical explanation for this outcome. On our journey, we visited countless places and engaged in discussions with hundreds of physicians, all while Caesar's condition was gradually deteriorating. We had to hold on to a reservoir of patience that seemed almost inexhaustible.

The credit for our resilience, I firmly believe, goes to Caesar's indomitable spirit that remained unbroken, uplifting us all. His unabashed, heartfelt smiles nurtured his family's spirit and touched everyone we had the fortune to interact with during this trying period. While I do not identify myself as a deeply religious man, my faith in God is my lifeline, a beacon that keeps me afloat amidst the chaos. If this unwavering belief of being guided and supported was not under the control of the Holy Spirit, I confess that we would be completely lost. Fortunately such a situation never arose, and it leaves me with no basis to fathom what else this experience could be referred to as. Blending sweat with hope results in winning.

By no means were all the intellectual activities isolated to music alone during Caesar's transplant. That would not make sense. However, it was as it has always been, the real motivational power for he and I, overshadowing everyone under a divine reality that blessed us abundantly. Someone would say, "music is our divine cane." A rethinking: I refuse to ponder Caesar's life without music. Certainly, a survival mode would be present, yet equally, none of those shiny outcomes could have been achieved.

From the bottom of my heart, regardless of everything, all the credit is supposed to be primarily attributed to this. That kept his mind busy with something outside of the transplant itself. Letting the medical professionals perform their job is marvelous to anyone. Moreover, this is likely why such procedures, including other similar medical interventions, carry significant risks, including death. From my own experiences, being in a hospital is marked by constant agony and heightened anxiety. Therefore, our hormone responses (e.g., cortisol) soar through the roof. As a result, sometimes even a tiny procedure eventually turns out to be an adverse outcome. This is not always the case, but our inner issues manifest under these environmental and physiological conditions, and we must counteract them to achieve better results. However, handling such an environmental situation is the boldest task. Luckily, Caesar had some tools on his side (e.g., his violin) that were marvelously soothing. In fact, with slight changes, we carried on the same education holistic concept we have been training under for a long time. We changed the intensity form for obvious reasons. Thus far, everything is fine. However, it would be too isolating and not productive at all, which could be detrimental in several aspects if we counter with music alone for the preceding purpose. In practical terms, besides the music training, we have used various approaches that go from reading special books, trying to learn a little more of an intricate language (e.g., Hebrew), regaining some math skills, chess, Wii, game-sports, meditation, watching movies, Netflix, Legos, social interaction, etc. Through one of his local physical therapists, Mrs. Janet from Le Bonheur Children's Hospital, we learned about Wii games. It fascinated us from the beginning, although we had never heard about it before—my family is not a big fan of certain types of games, typically ones with violence, and we do not even have TV. However, we ended up purchasing a Wii which became the main hobby for my family's living room time together. The Three Kids, as they sometimes call themselves (Caesar, Maria-Anita, and Helen), enjoy inviting any close friends visiting us to play it; most of them, like us, have never heard about it. Nevertheless, everyone loves it and, quite often, our living room turns into the most exciting, entertaining, enjoyable space with everyone roaring with laughter very loudly. Its playfulness does not irritate our lovely neighbors because our house is, to some extent, isolated.

YouTube has sounded more appealing to my family since the beginning, mainly because they can have a chance to choose their favorite cartoon with the opportunity to grasp ancient mother languages such as Greek, Hebrew, and Chinese, of which otherwise, they had not many opportunities to learn. All the same, they are part of our broader society, even for the ones lacking awareness of it. Here is more justification for advocating an open mind to grasp novel income opportunities: until now, we had never heard about the Wii, which plays a great role in a very emotionally demanding situation, as we would expect. Faithfully retrospective to that, yes, when we were asked whether we would have any objection about games (many, yes), she agreed to discuss it following a demonstration by showing us how it works. After observing Caesar trying it on and playing balance games (e.g., tight rope, balance double, ski jump, skateboard, golf, ping-pong just to name a few) instantaneously captured my heart. Encouraged motor skills and cognitive enhancements for my family and—I think—for anyone. Immediately, I called it not a game in the sense we conceived it nowadays with kids screaming and copious violence. No! As predicted, we became Wii fans and purchased a set of other games to boost variety. Virtually, they nicely integrated countless games into visual animation that my children enjoy playing with. To our surprise, NIH and Children's Inn have a Wii, and staff came to Caesar's room to play with him the same games he usually has at his home. It was one of those countless echoes we experienced during his bone marrow transplant. He was so happy with it, Jesus! Shall we call it another game changer? At the end of the day, happiness is fully priceless. Finally, I started to grasp a bit of this aging axiom, saying that "everything has a reason."

Maria-Anita, Caesar's best friend, unlocked many progresses of the Wii's game, such as the "obstacle course," which is wonderful for her health since it resembles sweating in a gym. By working on these games for several hours a day, the body presents similar complaints as if we were going to the gym, full of physical exercises with rhythm. Interestingly, Maria-Anita was born with the same blood disorder that nearly killed her beloved brother with strokes. In this way, all the knowledge she gained from working with Caesar was translated into her best support. Consequently, though she had a stroke a few years ago, her health has been considered steady. Even so, soon we will have to pursue a transplant for her as well since this type of disorder tends to progress over time as the patient gets older.

Nevertheless, music is our flagship and a holistic comprehensive reality that we have been blessed to pursue from the beginning. Incredibly powerful and attractive, it exercises force in all directions starting with angle arrangements of all sweet things and affable people gravitating to us. Since it is impossible to number them all, please forgive me for the ones not mentioned. We are attempting to highlight the substantial overall content and balance upon fine lines of not being lengthy or overextending—a reason this book was trimmed from 1,000 pages.

It is inconceivable to imagine us here, with me writing this story, if at the beginning we had not envisioned the benefit of Caesar's music education. Moreover, without it, he would not have had the global engagement of people coming to help him. This message is suitable and may be feasible for you and someone you may have an acquaintance with a similar location. Furthermore, it can be envisioned that a similar outcome could be achieved for a child's gift (or lack thereof) in any other activity, particularly with the parents (or a relative, a teacher) taking the lead and thereby incurring the cost of courage to sacrifice for the cause. In the end, every child is born gifted, period. An elaboration will be given in the following paragraphs.

Still, none of this would come in handy without the practice of humility. We must empty ourselves to receive natural incoming. The more humble you are, the more you may progress. A little would be enough to make you happy. Feeding none is a perfect, perishable invitation because the act of giving comes from the law of love—Life. Hence, it is crucial to formulate your will from the initial stage. Indeed, you, me, and everyone would love to have a hundred times more than what we achieved yesterday. Nonetheless, lacking the basic rules of humility, our gain for the next day would be renounced to zero or even below it. We must be extra careful in making decisions in this limbo field of mind. In conclusion, it is imperative that we approach this matter with solemnity and meticulousness. Furthermore, it retains a thrilling analogy to our spirituality.

"Ok, let's go home!" Oh finally, the anticipated good news of going home earlier than we expected. We would no longer have to spend Christmastime at the Children's Inn. Caesar's post-transplant responses had been thrilling, and he would no longer need any more blood products such as platelets (the last parameter coming to work with my son) for nearly two months. With all the numbers going up beautifully, the medical team anticipated our returning home one week earlier. Caesar's full discharge to go home was set for December 23 of 2021, but on December 14 we were at home with my son fully healed. If this is not a tale of success and wish fulfillment, I honestly don't know what else it could be.

I truly believe that every child is born naturally gifted, ready to fulfill a remarkable role on this planet, almost without exception. There is vast evidence that supports such a statement based on the biological bulk of human beings—our human genes making us all similar—we are all the same species, after all. You may dispute this, saying, "Ah, how about a child born blind?" I would say to you that despite lacking sight, as saddening as it surely sounds, physiology teaches us that the other special senses, such as hearing, touch, smell, and taste, are on homeostasis response (the steady internal balance that keeps us alive) to work as a slight balance compensation by mimicking the lost function of sight. Truly, this compensatory system (e.g., final adjusting for invisible things, function) holds true for any other missing element encountered with another part taking the lead. I broke my foot soon after moving to the U.S. in 2003, and in my mind, there was no relying on my broken foot. Unconsciously I placed more weight on the unbroken one. This is a minor example, but it can be extended to someone who has a broken leg or arm. Going beyond someone born without sight, a similar analogy suggests which sensory weight would be shifted, beginning even before birth in case the issue originated around the conception stage. On this subject, you can expect that such a person's other fundamental senses would be much more heightened than any "normal" person born with regular sight. Moreover, the inherent genius may arise from what was naturally expected to be one more sorrowful life wandering around.

Thomas Wiggins, a prodigious pianist born blind in Georgia (May 25, 1849 – June 14, 1908), stood tall among esteemed contemporaries such as Franz Liszt and Arthur Rubinstein. While Mr. Wiggins' name may not have reached your ears until now, his story is nothing short of astonishing. He blossomed into a piano prodigy as a mere toddler and later exhibited his talents as a composer.

Just today, August 5, 2023, while taking a pause from my work and scrolling through our social media feed, I stumbled upon the intriguing post about Mr. Wiggins' life. A post titled "From slave to virtuoso. The incredible journey of Blind Tom, becoming the 19th Century's highest-paid Pianist at the age of 10," by Newsmoi caught my eye, matching exactly with a topic that I was working on today. The fact that he was born blind but went on to achieve such remarkable heights where all of his other senses converged to support and enhance his life is a human's resilient power well-supported by physiology. Peering further into the fascinating tale of Mr. Wiggins, I also learned of his inconceivable memory. The pianist was reportedly able to accurately recall and reproduce a speech delivered by U.S. senator and presidential candidate Stephen Douglas a year after it was uttered. Not only did he remember the words, but he could also mimic the timbre and vicissitudes of Mr. Douglas's voice enchantingly. Given such a remarkable story, there is no room for twisting it based on race or religion. Indeed, we are fortunate to glean insights into what can occur to any family, irrespective of time frame, family surname, city, country, or socioeconomic status. When it comes to events in life, like the birth of a child with a particular illness, we all find ourselves in similar situations. Anyone could drink the same water, which brings a similar sensation. From that to moving on, the primary difference lies in our attitudes and the courage summoned to champion the cause of such a child. Naturally, a wealthy family has a high potential to draw upon more resources and potentially overcome obstacles earlier. However, history is full of examples that are not always this case. Once again, a fervent heart brimming with enthusiasm, a fusion of optimism and faith, along with a dash of sweat and perseverance is crucial.

Faith. If I were to choose a single attribute, it would be faith, for it is not only the bedrock but also the very substance of the hope we yearn for. I find faith to be practical as it encompasses envisioning and empowerment. It allows us to envisage triumphant outcomes, like leaving a hospital entirely healed, against numerous dissenting voices and potential side effects, untouched by any negative repercussions. It's like visualizing a perfect day, a vivid daydream, albeit the tangible, physical aspects we have yet to materialize.

This conceptualization applies to various scenarios: someone bettering their health, turning around a failing business, or mending personal relationships. These outcomes can all be nurtured by faith. I perceive faith not as a purely subjective concept but as an active endeavor. Pursued wholeheartedly, it can lead to any achievement, highlighting its undeniable practicality: If I do this, I may achieve that, with the "when" being the real mystery. Still, when we receive and achieve our goal and get our final desire, it always comes at the right time. It sounds like a person needs to go through something, and passing through tests directly correlates to the readiness for the next chapter in life with a higher level to play out. Might all of this serve as a secret purpose in life?

One facet that mystifies people is faith's timelessness: You possess it, but its fruition lacks a known timeline. If we experiment without faith, what would we stand to lose? What would be the expected outcome? Yes, upon the advent of any event, we naturally anticipate its effects, though the timeline for these outcomes remains unknown. In such instances, only hope and faith can prevail; without them, patience and the drive to work even harder may falter, leaving the mind vulnerable to despair. In this context, faith becomes not just our innermost virtue but a practical tool if one seeks it. This is why faith is more than just belief in the unseen; it's a cultivated understanding, nurtured by the heart even before tangible signs appear—having the onset taste of a victory before our physiological sight perceives it. Yes, to some it may sound a little unusual, but it is part of faith's spiritual nature. Nothing is wrong with embracing it. Upon reflection, I've learned that the absence of faith often leads to constant worrying about what-ifs, negative thinking, and depressive ruminations on unwanted outcomes. I am not suggesting that one shouldn't be concerned about their problems, whatever they may be. Everyone has their struggles; some are more formidable than others, but all are unique to the individual. Typically, a pessimistic mindset can be the principal barrier to triumph.

We carried several books for the transplant, from *Plato's Dialogues of Socrates* to the Bible. One might say, "Wow, thoroughly different approaches—rational thought and faith." However, these are not antagonistic; they occupy their own spheres. To have faith, one must master one's inner thoughts, which in turn graces the heart. This organ is pivotal, but its function depends on our mental state. If my thoughts are misplaced, lost, or tortured, my heart will struggle to function properly. Without the pillars of faith, we would be blind to our minds, barely grasping the present. Despite the potential cost of solitude, my faith needs nurturing and my future needs envisioning. Books such as those we read daily can help in this endeavor, and as I explained their content to Caesar, I found myself learning from his angelic heart. Hospitals are places that demand discipline if health conditions allow it. Lives hang in the balance and are subject to a myriad of decisions. Adherence to medication is one such critical decision requiring strict discipline. Therefore, physical alertness and proper communication with the medical staff are crucial to prevent fatal errors.

As mentioned earlier, we established Caesar's routine for his transplant long before we even knew the name of the transplant center. It was essentially an extension of our home routine: We woke up, prayed, changed clothes, moved away from the bed (as advised), and sat on a sofa or chair. A nurse would arrive around 7 a.m. for daily blood draws and Caesar would have breakfast. We spent time homeschooling, reading, and doing violin practice. Occasionally, Caesar would copy music or simply listen to it. He'd play with his Legos, then interact with the doctors who showed up between 10 and 11 in the morning. After lunch, he would nap or engage in activities like playing Wii, a sports entertainment sort of game. In the afternoon, he video-chatted with his sisters and Mamma in Memphis. After dinner, we would bathe, watch a movie or cartoon, and then go to bed early. We only watched UFC on Saturdays because we like fighting mixed martial arts (MMA). We ended the day by discussing the day's events, acknowledging our blessings, reading the Bible, and praying. Ultimately, I genuinely believe that this attitude of resilience shaped Caesar's miraculous outcome. A pessimistic mind yields nothing fruitful. Hope, indeed, is everything.

We are in August 2023. Caesar has recently celebrated his 15th birthday and is in radiant health, having triumphed over a decade-long health battle. This monumental victory is shared with everyone who lent their support and aided him and our family. Our gratitude is boundless, and mere words feel insufficient. Simply saying "thank you" would hardly capture the depth of our feelings. However, Caesar's walking continues to be a challenge, and progress is slow. There are two primary reasons. Firstly, our therapeutic efforts aren't as rigorous as they were before his transplant. Secondly, despite multiple clarifications from the medical team, Caesar harbored an unconscious hope that his leg issues would magically disappear post-transplant. This was a misconception; such miracles aren't the nature of his condition. Even though he's never voiced it, I can feel the weight of his disappointment, especially when he recalls the karate lessons he can no longer participate in.

Physiologically he may be 15, but a growth hormone deficiency has stunted his physical development. He bears a closer resemblance to a ten-year-old. Yet there are silver linings. From a biological standpoint, the human body will always prioritize overall survival overgrowth when faced with illness. The ravages of sickle cell anemia on Caesar were profound. Now, with hormone replacement therapy underway, his doctors are optimistic that he will catch up with growth in the coming years. His endocrinologist in particular, is buoyed by the progress he's seen. Considering the age of Helen, the stem cell donor whose cells were harvested when she was five (she's currently nine), and adding the time since the transplant, Caesar's cellular age roughly translates to eight years. While this may seem like a mere footnote against the backdrop of his overall recovery, the lingering effects of past strokes on his legs present hurdles that need dedicated physiotherapy and time.

Our journey would not have been possible without the unwavering support of the NIH Family and Children's Inn during the treatment, as we have already mentioned several times. The trajectory of Caesar's recovery, with its ups and downs, reminds me of the unpredictable nature of sowing seeds, each phase bringing its own challenges. One lesson stood out—the undeniable value of patience. Truthfully, life is unpredictable and filled with an array of twists and turns. The adage "everything happens for a reason" often surfaces, leading to introspective questions: Are we atoning for past actions, or is there a larger reason or design at play? For many, such thoughts were our constant companions and had boggled my mind for a while.

In the face of adversity, pressing is vital. At times, life's troubles can feel as relentless as being hunted. Surrender, however, is not an option. In 2014, witnessing my son's agony, I was engulfed by such despair that I contemplated ending my own life. But a maternal precept echoed in my heart: "Always ask God first." Ironically, I turned to the divine, asking for an end. A powerful sensation coursed through me in that vulnerable moment, banishing those bleak thoughts. It was a turning point. I forsook my career as a scientist to focus entirely on Caesar and our family. In a twist of fate, a month later, *National Geographic* approached us with a proposal for a documentary on Caesar. This, coupled with other blessings, fortified our family's spirit. Neither my time nor Caesar's had come to an end. After nearly a decade-long struggle, the sweet taste of victory came as I witnessed my son receive his bone marrow treatment at one of the world's premier institutions under the esteemed hematologist Dr. Hsieh. With Caesar now fully cured, we have the blessed privilege and honor of sharing my son's journey with you.

Finally, we recorded Caesar's composition of his first violin concerto in the aftermath of his profound journey. These pieces emerged unexpectedly as a graceful call of gratitude for his renewed health and an additional incentive for readers to delve into his story. We hope that this book delights you as much as it has us. At 14, Caesar composed his violin concerto in D minor, which concludes in D major. This piece, spanning four movements, is aptly titled *Caesar's Four Seasons*. The movements are as follows: 1st – "Aurorae" (Spring); 2nd – "Vida" (Summer); 3rd – "Health" (Autumn/Fall); and 4th – "Love" (Winter). To honor this book accordingly, he wrote two new pieces, which he then transcribed to sound like sonatas. They are mostly inspired by fragments of his concerto, which he called Sonatina Aurorae and Sonatadagium. A reason for his album "The Gates" is to pay special tribute to all his lovely supporters, including you, the reader. It contains those two pieces and other showcase works from Bach (among other composers), which were properly recorded and are available for you to download by scanning the QR code on the book's last page.

On his 15th birthday, Caesar premiered the first movement, "Aurorae", to an intimate gathering of family and friends. He has yet to complete the piano part of these movements. He is now exploring the potential of developing a full orchestral version with the help of his violin teacher. If everything goes as hoped, he aspires to join a prestigious music conservatory in 2025, with the Curtis Institute of Music in Philadelphia being a top choice.

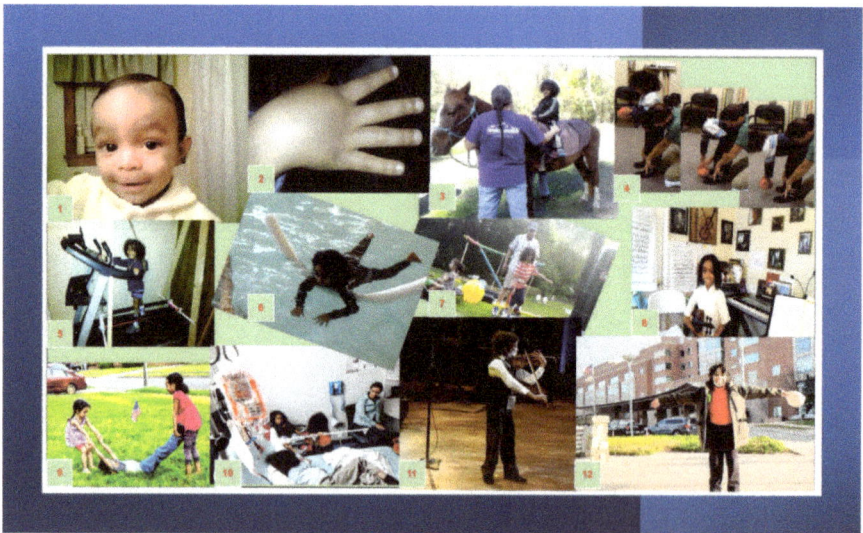

Fig. 11. *Here are some remarkable events: from his early life as a baby (1) to when he started getting sick, including a photo of his hands super swollen around 4 years old (2), after the stroke; having horse therapy with the diligent Mrs. Debbie (3), working with the therapeutic genius Mr. David (4), Caesar on the special treadmill in our home basement (5), undergoing water therapy with the marvelous water therapist Mrs. Dixon (6); enjoying the outdoors with the whole family (7), with Helen being just over one year old, Caesar in his violin practice room (8), and playing with his best friends — his two sisters, Maria-Anita and Helen — in the front yard (9) of our home in Memphis/TN; his last blood transfusion at Vanderbilt Hospital, Nashville, in 2021 (10); performing at the Kennedy Center, Washington, D.C., six months after his successful bone marrow transplant (11); and finally, the triumphant open arms (12) in front of the NIH Clinical Center, the place where his medical procedure took place, two years after the event.*

Once again, our hats go off to Dr. Michael Hsieh, MD, head of the sickle cell transplant program that Caesar underwent, who represents all the healthcare professionals in charge of Caesar's transplant care. Nobody can deny that Dr. Hsieh is the world's leading transplant hematologist. Meanwhile, Dr. John Tisdale, the NIH chief scientific program director who oversees the innovative approaches for sickle cell research in the U.S. and, to a certain extent, globally, is also worthy of praise. In truth, I've come to call them the NIH Family since they work incredibly well as a team, like a close-knit family, endeavoring to bring the best from their services. That being said, it is almost pointless to mention all the names when a few sample names are enough to represent the entire team. Furthermore, I believe it is appropriate to conclude the text with Caesar's favorite phrase: "NIH is good, but Children's Inn makes it great."

Fig. 12. *My family, the Sant Family, has reached a turning point. For instance, our Thanksgiving in 2023 was the best. The left figure captures that, whereas the right one shows Caesar when he was still sick in 2019 before going to our Temple. He never stopped*

smiling, even if one of us wore a moody face. Caesar's smile always acted as a sweet balm.

The photo below comes from the occasion when Caesar was invited to showcase his music skills at the U.S. Senate in October 2023. Besides performing Bach's music, he debuted his compositions that were appreciated beyond expectations by the audience.

Fig.13. *This figure of Caesar performing J.S. Bach and debuting his own compositions at the U.S. Senate represents the highest unexpected dream, especially for a person who survived three strokes. Mingling dream + belief + hard work is indeed the path for triumph.*

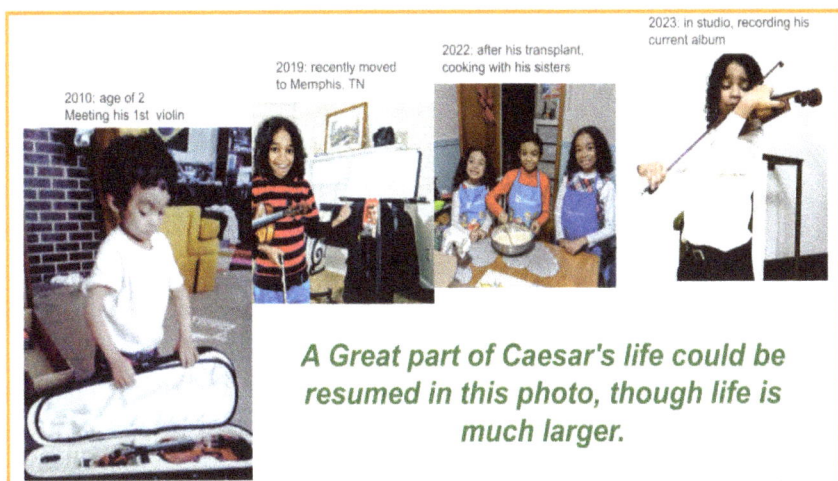

Fig. 14. *This figure greatly represents parts of Caesar's life. From left to right: his first encounter with a violin, followed by a photo of him after his violin practice when we moved to Memphis, TN, in 2019. Next, a scene of him having fun (making some cookies) with his sisters after his successful bone marrow transplant in 2022. And the last one, Caesar in a studio recording his current album.*

After this figure, I feel as though a sort of epilogue could be used to wrap up this saga. Surely, I am a man with a strong belief that among the few fundamental duties of parenting, the greatest task is working for our children: protecting, guiding, and educating them. Three crucial and irreplaceable ally words are incorporated: **patience, faith, and wisdom**. This might sound a little redundant because these three words are interdependent. With that, onward action can take place. If I were to conclude here, the secret would have been thoroughly reviewed.

Nevertheless, there is a compelling feeling to add a few more words to emphasize this section. Thus, any plan, regardless of the circumstances, if it is implemented accordingly, has a real chance to cement the future of new adults. Therefore, the degree of opportunities that the world will open for such people is remarkable. It is impossible to think of anything more thrilling and resilient than children. This thinking held me in meditation for about 20 years before having my children. In summary, it is quite normal for any mother or father to be imbued with such a mindset starting from early teenage years, hence the thought of having bright offspring is quite a common denominator among these potential parents—the real dream of having special families. However, the outline of life will bring, as with Caesar's, the real issue that virtually nobody can avert it, but rather must be faced head-on. Certainly, it is challenging to imagine who, if given the choice to foresee the future, would not move to the other side of the ocean. The unambiguous reality is that this particular burden can befall any family, irrespective of their place in society, their level of prayer, or their social and economic status.

At the beginning, incomprehensible in our shared agony, I learned and shared with my wife that almost every family must deal with some type of difficult illness. Learning from families navigating this difficult process served as a real lesson for me. Though I'm not the most faithful person in the world, I never doubted that we would prevail. However, when my health began to decline, it demanded even more effort from me not only to safeguard my son's health and well-being from deteriorating or worse, but also to prevent our entire family from disintegrating and losing hope. I was engulfed by a mountain of stress, which led to my two strokes and heart attack. Even though this conundrum is over, its memory still haunts me with sorrow. At such a low point, I felt utterly alone as everyone looked at us in disbelief, offering not a single word of encouragement. Ultimately, it was at that low level that our faith sustained us, reminding me that even in the darkest moments, God was with us, guiding our path. Therefore, the only option left for us was victory!

Thank you for reading. We appreciate it.

Scanning the QR code allows you to download Caesar's music album—The Gates. **Caesar7Sant** is the password to access the album that is part of this book.

9 798330 551774